SUCH A PRETTY GIRL

SUCH A PRETTY GIRL

*A Story of Struggle,
Empowerment,
and Disability Pride*

Nadina LaSpina

New Village Press • New York

Published in the United States by
New Village Press
bookorders@newvillagepress.net
www.newvillagepress.org
New Village Press is a public-benefit, nonprofit publisher
Distributed by New York University Press

Paperback ISBN: 978-1-61332-099-0
Hardcover ISBN: 978-1-61332-103-4
EBook ISBN: 978-1-61332-104-1
EBook Institutional ISBN: 978-1-61332-105-8

Publication Date: July 2019
First Edition

Library of Congress Cataloging-in-Publication Data
Available online at http://catalog.loc.gov

Front cover and frontispiece photo of the author at age 4 or 5, courtesy of the author.
Back cover photo: Nadina LaSpina being arrested at the Occupy Wall Street action, New York City, November 17, 2011. Photo credit: Stephanie Keith. Courtesy of Stephanie Keith.
Interior photos are courtesy of the author except where indicated.
Cover design: Lynne Elizabeth
Interior design and composition: Jordan Wannemacher

This book is dedicated to my parents,
Giovanni and Maria LaSpina,
and to my husband,
Daniel Robert,
in memoriam

Those with power can afford
To tell their story
Or not.
Those without power
Risk everything to tell their story
And must.

—FROM THE POEM "TELLING," BY LAURA HERSHEY,
POET AND DISABILITY RIGHTS ACTIVIST

In this memoir, aesthetic and emotional truth is given precedence over factual truth. To protect privacy, the names and characteristics of some people and places are changed, and, in some cases, two or more individuals are made into one. Some events in my personal life are compressed and their sequence altered to improve the flow of the narrative. Dialogue is recreated. The disability language changes according to the usage of the times. I use "cripple" in some instances for its shock value. I regret if anyone is offended. In no way do I intend to speak for all people with all different types of disabilities.

CONTENTS

❀

SUCH A PRETTY GIRL

PART I

Che Peccato: What a Shame

1

RIPOSTO

❋

When I was four or five I wanted to be ugly, and got very angry when people said I was pretty.

"I'm ugly, *brutta*, say that I'm ugly."

But no one listened to me.

"*Che bella bambina,* what a pretty little girl," they all said. And inevitably, they added, "*Che peccato!* What a shame!"

There was such sorrow in their voices, such an anguished look on their faces... I didn't want my being pretty to make people sad. Better to be ugly, I thought.

I especially didn't want my being pretty to make my mother sad. As soon as she heard those words, even if she had been laughing a minute before, my mother's eyes filled with tears and her face turned into a mask of agony. At those times, my mother looked just like the *Addolorata*.

The *Addolorata*, the "sorrowful woman," was the name of a statue in the church across the street from where we lived, in the little town of Riposto, in Sicily. It was a statue of Mary holding the dead Christ, a Sicilian version of Michelangelo's Pietà. The mother dressed in gold-embroidered purple silk, grief carved deeply into her painted face, on her lap her dead son, red-stained slender limbs draped in lifeless abandonment.

People seemed as mournful when they looked at my mother holding me as they were when looking at the *Addolorata* holding her dead son. Sometimes I thought my mother and the *Addolorata* were one and the same. They even had the same name: Maria.

I have early memories of being on my mother's lap as she sat outside with the town women while my father was at work. We sat in the afternoon sun in the winter months, and in the summer we sat in the shade.

My mother told the women the story of when I was born. The midwife, *mammana* in Sicilian, was impressed that such a slight woman as my mother could give birth to such a big baby as me. She left my mother bleeding on the bed, with my grandmother tending to her for a few minutes, and rushed with me in her arms to the bakery around the corner to weigh me on the bread scale. Not even washed yet, crying loudly because my lungs were so vigorous, wrapped only in a sheet, for it was very warm on the afternoon of May 16, 1948. Over four kilos I weighed, almost nine pounds.

And I was growing so healthy and strong, my mother told the women, already talking, at sixteen months, and walking on my own, and I was never sick, never a fever until… until that fateful night when *Crudele Poliomielite,* Cruel Poliomyelitis, invaded our happy home and stole me from my family.

I imagined *Crudele Poliomielite* as an ugly monster with a weird name, who actually appeared out of the darkness to grab me and steal me away. But how could I've been stolen when I was still there in my mother's arms? Could it be what got stolen was the healthy baby she'd given birth to? And what was left was a changeling, me? It took a while before I understood she was talking about my getting sick. Only then could I get over the secret fear that I might not be my parents' real daughter.

My father's name was Giovanni. He was always at work. He built houses—that was his *mestiere,* his trade. He was a master builder, *mastru.* Young men worked for him and he taught them how to mix cement and build walls with bricks.

Even when he was home, my father worked, fixing anything that needed fixing, covering up cracks with plaster, changing the color of the walls to make our house more beautiful.

I adored my father. To me, he was the smartest, strongest, most handsome man in the world. I loved it when my father picked me up and carried me in his work clothes all smeared with cement. My mother complained about my getting dirty. But I liked it. And as my father held me, I felt the muscles in his chest and arms.

"Muscles as hard as his heart is soft," my mother said.

I liked the way my father smelled—of cement, sweat, and cigarette smoke. I wrapped my arms tightly around his neck and clung to him. My father kissed me and called me *gioia,* joy.

Sometimes my father carried me on his shoulders. I laughed and grabbed on to his head to keep my balance.

"I'm falling, *Papà!*"

My father laughed, too, and, his strong arms raised, wrapped his hands around my waist. His hands were so big, they almost entirely encircled me.

"*Non aver paura, gioia!* Don't be afraid!"

But I wasn't afraid. I felt I was on top of the world. He moved his shoulders up and down in a rhythmic motion, mimicking the galloping of a horse.

"Where does my princess want to go? Your wish is my command!"

I laughed and laughed.

Whenever my mother told the town women the story of my getting polio, they looked up from their knitting and sewing and murmured "*Che peccato!*" I leaned against my mother's chest, hiding my face in the folds of her lace-trimmed blouse, and smelled the lavender she rubbed on herself when she washed.

Wasn't her story proof that my mother was blameless? She had made me big and healthy and strong. What happened to me was not her fault. But those words, "*Che peccato,*" were not just an expression of regret and sympathy; they carried the connotation of guilt. *Peccato* means "sin" in Italian. What sin could my mother have committed to deserve such punishment? And if not my mother's, then whose sin was it that caused me to be the way I was, *ciunca,* crippled?

Or was it my fate to be a cripple? Fate, destiny. *Destino.* That word was used incessantly in Riposto. Everything happened because of destiny. Everyone had his or her destiny. All Sicilians knew they could not escape their destinies.

"*Che destino!*" the women muttered after my mother finished telling her story, trying with that word to exonerate her and comfort her. "*Che croce!* What a cross you have to bear," they said, quickly moving their right hand down from their head to their chest and then from shoulder to shoulder, making the sign of the cross.

I understood I was the cross, though I didn't quite understand how or why. Was it that my mother had to carry me, since I couldn't walk, like Christ carried the cross in the pictures around the church? Was I such a burden for her? Was I growing that heavy?

My mother rarely complained. She was resigned to her destiny. She knew she had to atone for the sin of having a crippled daughter. She accepted her suffering like a good Sicilian woman. After all, in Sicily all women suffered. They believed a woman's destiny was to suffer, to atone for the sin of being a woman.

Sometimes, as I sat on my mother's lap, the women talked about their sufferings: the curse of menstruation, the toil and the ravages to the body of pregnancy and childbirth, the exhaustion of raising children, the rigors of poverty... And many of them suffered their husbands—their brutishness, maybe even their beatings.

My father never beat my mother. He always hugged and kissed her. And he worked hard all the time so we could have all we needed. But because of me, my mother's suffering was greater than that of all the other women. Carrying the cross of a crippled child, my mother was the epitome of suffering womanhood. She was indeed the living *Addolorata*.

I was glad when my mother finally took leave of the women and got up from the rush-seat wooden chair someone had brought out for her. Since she had to carry me, my mother couldn't bring her own chair out of our house. I hoped none of the women would decide to hug me. But usually at least one of them did.

"*Pietà!*" the woman whispered, almost to herself, taking me from my mother's arms to hold me tight against her ample bosom.

"*Che peccato, che destino, che croce,*" all the women continued to murmur as my mother walked away with me in her arms.

We went past the *pensionati*, retired men, middle-aged or older, who didn't have to work and sat smoking cigarettes and cigars, far enough from the women so they couldn't be heard, as they talked of important matters like the Mafia, the weather, and the government. They didn't comment, those men, but just looked at my mother and me as we passed by, and clucked their tongues and shook their heads.

Then my mother carried me into our house, through the first room and the second room—that's how our rooms were named—all the way to the kitchen, where my grandmother was cooking.

"What are you making today, Nonna?"

We all lived in that house, which always smelled of tomato sauce, my maternal grandparents, my parents, and I.

The house was on a street named Via Libertà. Liberty, freedom. How I wanted to be out on that street! But usually, my mother sat me behind the glass panels of our front door, and I looked out at Via Libertà, watched people go by, watched the neighborhood children play.

Until I was three, maybe even four, my mother pushed me in my baby carriage. Almost every day, all through the warm months, she took me to the beach. She'd been told by the doctor in Catania, the nearest big city, that she should bury me in the sand and let me get very hot, then put me in the water to shock my nervous system and cure me of polio.

Or maybe the advice came from the wise old women, who knew how to mix potions and were called witches.

I loved the sea but didn't like being buried in the sand. Other children, playing nearby, kicked sand into my eyes. Sometimes, I had to beg my mother to take me into the water, because I got so hot that I thought I'd shrivel and turn to ashes like the coals we burned in the middle of winter in the *conca,* a large iron basin or cauldron.

Finally my mother realized the hot sand treatments were useless. By then, I'd grown too big for the cradlelike baby carriage. I felt embarrassed when the other children pointed their fingers at me and laughed. But though I was glad to be rid of the carriage, I missed our trips to the beach. Now that there was no alternative to being carried, I didn't get out as much or go as far.

My mother usually didn't carry me any farther than down the block—to join the women knitting and sewing. But she carried me to our sun-drenched courtyard, where I sat with the geraniums in the pots; and sometimes up the steps to our roof terrace, from which we could see the sea. Every day she carried me around our house and to the bathroom whenever I had to go.

"I have to make *pipi, Mamma.*"

As I got bigger, at times she moaned, "Oh please, not again. My back is killing me. Can't you hold it?"

If my grandmother heard her, she reproached her: "Don't yell at the poor little girl, *povira picciridda!*" though my mother was not yelling. My grandmother couldn't carry me, for she wasn't strong enough. She was a very slight woman, always dressed in black, with her hair tightly pulled back in a knot.

My grandfather was tall and handsome, with well-groomed white hair and a mustache, and he did carry me. If I asked sweetly, he carried me outside on Via Libertà, if only up and down the block. My grandfather was not *pensionato.* He didn't sit with the men to talk about the government. He despised their idleness. Though he was even older than my grandmother, he sold fruit from a cart he pushed around the town's streets. What he didn't sell, he brought home for us to eat. Because I loved cherries, when they were in season, he made sure he saved some for me before selling them all.

I wished my father didn't have to work, so he could carry me more often. He was so strong, he carried me up Corso Italia, which everybody called "*u stratuni*," the big street, all the way to the next town, Giarre, where my other grandmother and my aunt lived—my father's mother and sister. My paternal grandfather had died during the war, so I never knew him.

My other grandmother was short and chubby, with a round face that was always smiling. My aunt was even slimmer than my mother, wore an apron, and baked cakes and cookies. My favorite cookies were called *piparelle* and were crunchy and a bit spicy.

"If you eat too much, your father won't be able to carry you back home; you'll get too heavy," my aunt said.

"I can never be too heavy for my *papà*!" I laughed.

Though he was a kind and gentle man, my father got angry at times. But his anger was not directed toward any of us. He got angry at what he called *ingiustizia*. He hated those guilty of injustice, the politicians and the mafiosi, who he said were one and the same, the fascists and the idle rich. Sometimes he headed down to the town square, yelling for people to follow him, to protest against injustice. My father also hated ignorance. Whenever he heard anyone saying "*Che peccato, che croce*" while he was carrying me, he muttered, "*Ignoranti!*"

Rather than accepting destiny, my father always spoke of fighting injustice.

While I ate cookies, he sat with his mother and his sister, talking fast and smoking. When my grandmother called my being *ciunca* God's will, *volontà divina*, my father said it was *ingiustizia divina*.

My grandmother crossed herself. "*Bestemmia*, blasphemy!"

After I turned five, my mother carried me every morning across the street to the convent in back of the Church of the Addolorata, where the nuns ran their elementary school. At the door, she handed me over to a nun, who carried me into the classroom and put me in my seat, right in the front row.

At first, the nuns were scary in their long black habits, but I got used to them. They smelled of incense and flowers. In the afternoon, they carried me around the convent. I was passed from one nun's arms to another's. They carried me into the church, bending one knee and telling me to cross myself as they passed the altar with the tall crucifix; to the vestry, where baby Jesus, a beautiful doll, slept in a basket covered in lace; and out to the garden, where the palm trees were so high that, no matter how far back I tilted my head, I couldn't see the tops, and the sparrows flew in circles and sang.

I loved those little birds that always sounded so happy. They woke me up every morning with their singing.

Sister Teresina, the youngest and my favorite, even carried me into the huge kitchen, where they had the biggest pots and pans I'd ever seen. Sister Prisca, the oldest, stirred the minestrone in a blackened iron pot with a giant wooden spoon.

But sometimes, while they carried me, some of the nuns started holding me tighter and tighter against their chests, kissed my head, and whispered, "*Pietà, pietà!*" That scared me. I felt I was suffocating. Out of fear, I'd start weeping. Thinking they were comforting me, the nuns held me even tighter and rocked me like a baby—which I hated.

Every Sunday, my mother carried me into the church. My father never went with us. Before Mass started, she knelt with me in her arms in front of the *Addolorata* and lit a candle. I couldn't stand to look at the *Addolorata*'s face, which was the same as my mother's, so beautiful but so sad. I kissed my mother, trying to make her smile, but she never smiled in church. I wrapped my arm around her neck, bent my head down, pressing my forehead against her shoulder, and kept my eyes shut. But though I couldn't see anything, I was painfully aware of the gaze of the whole congregation.

The nuns did their best to instill in me a sense of guilt and shame, and to teach me to embrace my own destiny of suffering.

"Offer your suffering to the Lord!" they always said to me. I couldn't understand. What would the Lord possibly want to do with my suffering? One day, when Sister Angelica started her "Offer your suffering" routine, I rebelled.

"But I want to be happy!"

She started stroking me and kissing me.

"Oh, my poor darling, how could you be happy? *Pietà!* You can never be happy!"

I got furious. "I can so be happy!" I yelled, hitting the nun's chest with my small fists as I struggled to free myself from her ominous embrace.

But how could I expect to be happy when I didn't know what awaited me? How much longer could I be carried? What would happen to me when I grew up? What would my destiny be?

In Riposto, every girl learned at an early age that "a woman's destiny" was to get married and have children. Unless, of course, she was too ugly to find a man who would marry her. Then, she could become a nun or, horror of horrors, end up a *zitella,* an old maid.

At an early age, I learned that getting married and having children was not my destiny. The message came across quite clear, though never loud; it came in hushed tones and sighs. Since I was not like other girls, I couldn't grow up to be like other women.

The other girls, who came to our house to play with me once in a while, didn't bother using hushed tones. They played with my dolls, dressing and undressing them. They unbuttoned their own shirts and held the dolls' heads against their pink nipples, like they had seen nursing women do. I tried to do the same.

"No," one of the older girls objected. "My mother says you shouldn't play with dolls. You should give us your dolls because we need to practice. You're never going to get married and have children. You're crippled, *ciunca*."

The others chimed in. How could I argue against them?

If I were ugly, I could at least become a nun or an old maid. I didn't understand why the other girls thought being a nun or an old maid was so horrible. The nuns seemed content enough to teach us children, do their chores, and pray. I didn't think the nuns were ugly, at least not all of them. They all spoke of Christ as their husband. I didn't understand how that could be. But I figured, even if I were ugly, Christ wouldn't want me as a wife. He already had all those nuns. He didn't need another wife—especially not a crippled one.

The only old maid I knew, a distant cousin of my mother's, seemed rather nice and not at all ugly. But whenever she came over, it was to ask for money.

"Why doesn't she have any money?" I asked my mother.

"Because she has no husband" was always the answer.

If I couldn't have a husband and children, like other women, what could I do? I couldn't go around asking relatives for money, since I couldn't walk. I didn't know any women who worked outside of their homes. I had heard some women cleaned rich people's houses. I knew I'd never be able to do that. My mother, who was an expert with needle and thread, told me women could earn money as seamstresses. She tried to teach me to sew, but I hated it. I pricked my finger with the needle and got blood on the cloth.

When I was in third grade, a young woman came to work as a teacher at the convent. I was surprised because I thought only nuns could be teachers. She had long hair, which she wore in a ponytail. I fell in love with her and decided I would not let my mother cut my hair anymore, and I would be a teacher. My heart was broken when she didn't come back the next year. I heard the nuns say she had gotten married. So I let my mother cut my hair short again, and I called myself stupid for thinking I could be a teacher when I couldn't walk.

In school I was a model student, the nuns' pride and joy. The other children resented me. "My mother says the nuns give you good grades because you're a cripple," they sneered. Or: "My mother says you study because you can't do anything else."

My progress in school seemed to make my father happy. Other girls' fathers didn't care how their daughters did in school. With their sons, it was a different story. Was my father glad I could use my brain, since my body was no good?

I was constantly trying to figure out what my father had in mind for me. He seemed to be making plans. But what were they?

My father had been taking me to doctors and hospitals since I was quite small. We had been to Catania, Messina, Rome, and Bologna. Rome and Bologna were far. It took many hours for the train to get there, crossing the straight on a ferry and going through many dark tunnels.

In Rome, my parents and I stayed with cousins who lived there. A few times, my father carried me to the Trevi Fountain so I could throw in a coin. I liked being in Rome, though I was always nervous knowing that, without a doubt, I would be taken to a doctor.

Doctors scared me, because they always hurt me. One doctor in Messina gave me shock treatments to regenerate the nerves in my spine. The shocks went through my body like a thousand snakes on fire, burning and biting me inside, making me shake all over and pee on the treatment table. I was already big enough to feel embarrassed about peeing. After we got home, for weeks my mother squeezed aloe leaves on the blisters that formed on my back.

In Rome, the doctors made braces for me, but I never learned to walk with them. My mother put them on me, lacing them, starting at my feet and going all the way up my thighs. Then, holding me under my arms, she stood me up. I learned to keep my balance by holding tightly on to my mother's hand.

"Look how tall you are!" she exclaimed, but I didn't care.

"They hurt my legs, *Mamma*."

When I got those braces, my mother, in order to hide them, made me a pair of pants. I must have been the only little girl in Sicily who wore pants. The other children laughed at me, but I rather liked wearing pants. The best thing about the braces was that when she took them off, my mother always massaged my legs. The doctor in Catania told her massage was the best therapy. I loved to feel my mother's cool hands moving up and down my thighs and shins. Then she tickled my feet and made me laugh.

The braces made me too heavy for my mother. She put them on me less and less frequently, and when I grew out of them, I didn't get new ones. But even when I stopped using the braces, she had me wear pants.

"This way, people can't see your legs."

My mother's words forced me to pay closer attention to my legs. I noticed they weren't growing as fast as the rest of my body. They seemed smaller and thinner than the legs of other girls my age. In place of calf muscles, I had only soft flesh. My mother thought it best to keep my legs hidden, because she was ashamed of them. So I learned to be ashamed of them, too.

If I had to choose between going to doctors or being taken by one of my grandmothers and my aunts to healers and witches, I'd choose the witches. Oh, they scared me, but it was an exciting kind of scared. All they did was say funny words, rub my legs with weird-smelling herbs, or have me drink something bitter. They didn't hurt me like the doctors did.

I never thought they could make me walk, but I secretly wished they would teach me how to fly. Some people swore they'd seen the witches flying in a circle, holding on to one another's hands in the dark of night! My grandmother said that wasn't true. But I liked picturing the circle of flying witches. What a great game it seemed. Even better than *giro-tondo,* ring around the rosie, which all the girls loved and the boys snubbed. Once in a while, I played *girotondo.* My mother sat me in a chair in the middle of the circle and I sang along, watching the other girls go around me.

Whether I was taken to doctors or witches, it was clear to me that I

was no good the way I was, *ciunca*. I needed to be fixed. I wished my
father could fix me himself, like he fixed everything else. The people
who loved me—my parents, my grandparents, all my relatives—none
of them wanted me to be the way I was. Only the nuns thought I should
accept my destiny and offer my suffering to the Lord. But they agreed
such a destiny was a cruel one.

My father worked hard and saved money so he could take me to the
best hospitals and the best doctors. Every time we went to a new doctor,
his hope was renewed, only to turn into disappointment afterward.

"Italian doctors are too ignorant," he told me when we came home
from yet another trip to Rome. "They don't do research. They'll never
find a cure."

Then my father smiled his big bright smile to show me he was not
defeated. A new plan had been germinating in his mind. We would leave
this backward town and this country where injustice and ignorance
ruled. We would go to America.

In America, doctors were different. They were brilliant, and they
were always doing research with money that was collected on television.
"In America," my father told me, "every house has a television set, and
when they show children like you, people send money to find a cure."

The American doctors, my father was sure, could accomplish what
ignorant people in Riposto would call miracles. There was even a president in America who had been cured of polio.

"In America, *guarisci,* you'll be cured," my father promised. "In
America, *cammini,* you'll walk."

I always believed everything my father said. I wasn't sure how far
America was, or how we'd get there. But if that's where my father
wanted to take me, that's where I'd go.

As the years passed, I started to worry, because sometimes my father's
plans didn't work out—the money he expected to get for building a
house never came, or the mafiosi put their dirty hands in his business

and caused him all kinds of trouble. What if we never made it to America? What if I never got cured?

As I got bigger and heavier, my mother had difficulty carrying me,
and she complained about her back hurting. Sometimes an uncle or an
older cousin carried me. Once in a while a big neighborhood boy offered
to carry me. At first, I was happy, especially when he took me on the
main street. But then I started not liking it. He squeezed me too tight
and tickled me in places where I didn't want to be touched.

I didn't mention it to my mother, because I didn't want her to get
sad. I wanted her to laugh. She always laughed when my father was
home. And when she outran my grandmother and got her pick of the
fruit my grandfather brought. But sometimes she also laughed when it
was just the two of us. She laughed when the neighbor's cat carried her
kittens one by one by the scruff of their necks to our house, and laughed,
rather than getting angry, when I knocked over the ink bottle on the
table while doing my homework. She struggled to carry me up the steps
to the roof terrace, complaining about my being heavy and her aching
back; then once we made it all the way up, she pretended to drop me,
laid me down on the cement floor, and lay beside me, both of us laughing
wildly. At those times, my mother didn't look like the *Addolorata*. She
called me *gioia*. I kissed her flushed face, and wondered how I could be
both her cross and her joy.

I knew my mother worried about what would become of me as I
grew up. Sometimes she said, "I should have given you a sister who could
help take care of you."

"Oh, yes, I want a sister! Can you give me a sister, please?" And I
imagined that sister, how she would play with me all the time. But then
my mother got sad and said it was too late; she couldn't raise another
child when she had to take care of me.

I heard there were disabled people living in the town, but I never saw
them. The women talked about a man who had fallen off a scaffold
while working in Catania on a tall building, and was left paralyzed. A
good-looking man he was; God should have taken him, *poviru ciuncu,*

the women said. His unmarried sister sacrificed her youth to take care of him.

My grandmother talked about a friend of hers who took care of her husband, who'd had a stroke and couldn't walk anymore. Her daughter helped out when she could. I understood crippled grown-ups had to have wives, sisters, or daughters to take care of them, and had to stay home all the time because they were too heavy to be carried.

I didn't know any disabled children. I often asked my mother if there were others like me. Ever since I could remember, my mother had always told me that, yes, there was a girl just like me who lived in another town. Maybe she made her up, so I wouldn't feel I was the only crippled girl in the world. I thought of that girl as a lost sister. I fantasized that I would one day find her, and we would talk and laugh together, and hug, and play *girotondo*.

2

THE BEST HOSPITAL

❁

For years, my father worked hard, saved money, kept talking about America, waiting anxiously for very important documents. A few times, he went to Palermo, the capital of Sicily, and once or twice to Rome. Finally, in 1960, he had all the long-sought crucial documents and was able to leave for America.

"I must go first," he told my mother and me. "I'll get everything ready. Then you'll come."

I was already twelve. I begged my father to hurry, worried that the older I got, the harder it would be for the American doctors to cure me.

My mother cried when my father left and every day after that. I wasn't sure whether she missed him or was afraid of the uncertain future that awaited us.

After a year, my mother and I were able to join my father. We went to Rome first, then flew to America on one of the new "jumbo jets." Since my uncle, who drove us to the airport, wasn't allowed to carry me onto the plane, the captain himself, the tallest man I'd ever seen, carried me. He deposited me in my seat, in what resembled a giant bus. There I sat, sick to my stomach and sucking on lemon slices for eight hours.

At the New York International Airport, my father had permission to carry me off the plane.

"You're in America, *gioia*!"

He was surprised to see how much I'd developed.

"Our little girl is a *signorina* now," my mother told him. I blushed, because being a *signorina* meant I was already getting my period.

"You won't need to be carried much longer." My father kissed me as he lifted me in his arms out of the taxi we took at the airport and carried me into our new home. "*Presto guarisci,* soon you'll be cured." He was triumphant.

He had rented an apartment in Brooklyn "*senza scale,*" without stairs, which he had furnished completely. He had found "*un buon lavoro,*" a good job, doing construction. He didn't mind having to work for a boss. It was the only way to get the best medical insurance for me, which was called Blue Cross. He took the card out of his wallet to show it to me: his Blue Cross card, my ticket to being cured.

Most important, he had found "*il migliore ospedale,*" the best hospital for me. Every day, as we waited for the call from the admitting office, he repeated, "*Presto guarisci. Presto cammini.* Soon you'll be cured. Soon you'll walk."

My mother was afraid… of this country so different from Sicily, of the tall buildings and wide streets, of all the people who spoke a language she couldn't understand. And she was afraid of what the American doctors would do to her daughter.

I knew the doctors would hurt me. The doctors in Italy had always hurt me. How different could the American doctors be? I didn't quite share my father's optimism. But, at the same time, I didn't share my mother's fear. I was too excited. I couldn't wait to find out what life in this new country had in store for me.

I didn't have to wait long. Less than a month after my arrival, I sat with my parents in the admitting office of the Hospital for Special

Surgery, in Manhattan, near the East River. My father struggled to answer questions, showing off the English he'd been learning in night school. My mother and I sat next to each other, anxious and confused.

"We have to wait before we can go up to the room," my father explained, when there were no more questions to answer. And we waited quietly, my mother and I afraid to talk to each other, as if we were in church.

Finally a nurse appeared. She was pushing a wheelchair. My father stood and started speaking in his tentative English. I was sure he was telling her we didn't need the wheelchair, because he could carry me. The nurse didn't understand or agree with him. She pushed the wheelchair right up to me and smiled. I smiled back and, lifting myself with my arms, with a swinging motion, managed to sit in it.

I'd never used a wheelchair before, never even seen one. But the feeling of moving on wheels was a familiar one. My mother had pushed me in my baby carriage, and when I started middle school, my father had bought me a bicycle with training wheels. He added a back to the seat, with a handle so I could be pushed.

I wasn't sure whether it was hard to get wheelchairs in Sicily, or whether my father didn't want to see me in one. He looked unhappy as he watched me get into the wheelchair. He rushed over and kissed me on the head.

"Don't be afraid of the chair. It's only until they cure you."

I wasn't afraid. As the nurse pushed me, I savored every second of the smooth ride. My parents had to walk fast to keep up with us. I couldn't keep my hands from moving down toward the push rims, knowing instinctively what they were for. The nurse must have guessed I was itching to push myself, because somewhere in the middle of a long corridor, she let go of the push handles and pointed straight ahead. "Go!" she said. I knew exactly what she meant. And I knew exactly what to do.

Without hesitation, I took off. Arms pumping, wheels turning. Go! For the first time in my life, I was moving on my own. No one carrying me, no one pushing me. I could go straight ahead. Or curve to the right, or to the left. I could go full speed or slow down to let my parents catch up. Stop and turn around to see how far I got. Then go again!

That day, in that long corridor in that American hospital, I fell in love—with the wheelchair. It was a heavy, ugly hospital wheelchair. Shiny chrome and green vinyl. But I loved it. Arms pumping, wheels turning. Go! On my own. Go! On my way. On my way to start my new life in America.

I was put on a floor with children and teenagers. Since I was thirteen, I went on the side with the teens. I felt very grown-up.

This hospital was different from hospitals in Italy. It was a cheerful place, with colorful pictures on the walls, kids in wheelchairs racing and laughing in the hallways, music coming from the rooms. Some rooms had four beds; some had two. I went to a room with two beds.

"*Non aver paura, gioia,* don't be afraid," my father repeated. But I was excited, not afraid.

Seeing the tears in my mother's eyes when she kissed me good-bye, I reassured her: "*Non ti preoccupare,* don't worry! I like it here."

My roommate's name was Rosa. She spoke some Sicilian, which she had learned from her grandmother. My being placed with Rosa was no coincidence. The thoughtfulness of the social worker, who knew I couldn't speak English, was behind it.

Rosa had polio, like me. She was older, already fifteen, and knew how to put on lipstick and set her hair on pink plastic rollers. She started teaching me English words—*pillow, blanket*—making me repeat them until I pronounced them right. When I made mistakes she called me *babba,* dumb. She said her grandmother called her that, so I didn't mind.

I made friends right away. I was ecstatic. In Sicily, I thought I was the only crippled girl in the world, and here I found myself surrounded by so many disabled girls and boys. The first English words I learned were the names of their different disabilities. Some of the names were difficult for me to pronounce: cerebral palsy, muscular dystrophy, spinal muscular atrophy… I was glad when I found out I could use acronyms: CP,

MD, SMA... The names of other disabilities sounded Italian and were easier to pronounce and to remember: dystonia, spina bifida, osteogenesis imperfecta...

"I don't understand how you can say osteogenesis imperfecta and not cerebral palsy!" complained one of my new friends, Jane—personally offended, since her disability was cerebral palsy. To make up for the offense, I told her how easy it was for me to understand her. Because of CP, her speech was wonderfully slurred, so I grasped a lot of what she said, while I couldn't understand the other kids, who spoke too fast. I was glad that in English my disability was called the same as it was in Italian: polio. I didn't know what I would have done if I had one of those hard-to-pronounce disabilities. I figured polio was the best disability for me.

There were quite a few kids whose disability was polio. When they had surgery and their legs were in casts, their braces stood at their bedsides. After the casts came off, they went down to physical therapy, PT for short, where they practiced walking with their braces and crutches. I was the only kid with polio there who didn't have braces.

"Don't worry, they'll give you braces soon enough," Rosa told me. She hated her braces with a passion. She talked about what she was going to do when she didn't need them anymore, after her surgeries: take them to the Staten Island garbage dump, throw them in the East River, melt them down with a blowtorch...

In the room across the hall, there was a beautiful girl named Audrey. When I first met her, I thought she, too, must have had polio as a baby, since her legs were small, like mine. But her disability was spina bifida. It had affected her from the waist down, so she had never walked, just like me. She had undergone many surgeries, and she was being taught to use braces and crutches in PT, though she wasn't at all eager to learn. Audrey and I were very grown-up; we had been getting our periods for almost a year, we wore bras and didn't need to stuff them with tissues, and we both instinctively had a way of making people notice us. We were the same age and the same size, but we didn't resemble each other.

I had dark hair and she had blond hair; I had brown eyes and she had blue eyes. Yet some of the volunteers asked if we were sisters. The other kids called us "the Bobbsey Twins" and teased us because we were always together.

In the morning, the one who got into her wheelchair first raced across the hall. Audrey had done her best to make her room more like home. The wall above her bed was covered with get-well cards. On the night table was her radio. On a small cart by the foot of the bed was her record player. Stacks of records and piles of magazines were on the windowsill.

I loved listening to records with Audrey. I couldn't understand the lyrics at first. I just enjoyed the music. But if the song was one I particularly liked, Audrey stopped the record and repeated the words slowly. She used dramatic gestures, acted out funny scenes, or drew stick figures, whatever she could think of, until she made me understand.

I learned a lot of English words by listening to Audrey's records. I learned about boyfriends and girlfriends, hugging and kissing, cheating, breaking up and making up again...

After only a week in the Hospital for Special Surgery, HSS for short, I knew at least a hundred English words, maybe more. The kids laughed at me when I made a mistake or, by mispronouncing a word, ended up saying something totally different. Because vowel sounds in Italian are rather uniform, I had trouble distinguishing between long and short, open and closed vowels. So I might say "peel" instead of "pill" and instead of "bedpan," I'd say "badpen."

My roommate, Rosa, couldn't stop laughing when, thinking I was asking for a sheet, I asked the nurse for a "shit." She told everyone about it. They were hysterical. But I didn't mind being teased by my new friends. Their laughter came at me like soap bubbles, bursting and disappearing in the air. It didn't jab me like the Sicilian children's derisive laughter had.

The American doctors, maybe a dozen of them, came to our floor in the morning and checked each one of us but talked only to one another. They bent and stretched our legs and checked the incisions of those who had just had surgery, but said nothing to us. Their visit was called "rounds."

"Get ready, the doctors are making rounds!" the nurses yelled.

After the doctors left our room, I asked Rosa, "What did they say about me?"

"I don't know what they said about you. I don't know what they said about me, either. I don't understand them."

"But you know English, Rosa!"

"Oh, they're not speaking English, believe me. They're talking medical mumbo jumbo."

I wanted the American doctors to acknowledge me, to notice how grown-up I was, and how quickly I was learning English. I wanted to get their attention by saying something intelligent to them.

"What can I say to the doctors?" I asked Rosa.

"Oh, you can say 'Fuck you!'"

"What does that mean?"

"It's like saying *piacere*."

Piacere is what Italians say when they meet each other—meaning "pleased." It seemed the appropriate thing to say to the American doctors. And the word was easy enough for me to pronounce. So the next morning, when they all stood around my bed, I gave the American doctors my biggest smile and, careful to pronounce it correctly, said: "Fuck you!"

One of the older, more important-looking doctors was talking. He stopped in mid-sentence. The look of shock on his face was not what I had expected. All the doctors seemed shocked, though the younger ones also seemed amused. One, in particular, was trying hard not to laugh.

I knew Rosa had tricked me. I wondered what I had said. I looked toward her, but her head was under the blanket. I wanted to pull the covers over my head, too. But then the important-looking doctor started talking again and all the others turned to listen to him. They talked to one another a while longer, as if I weren't there, then walked out of the room.

I expected everyone to laugh and make fun of me mercilessly. Instead, the kids treated me as if I were a hero.

"You said 'Fuck you' to the doctors? Wow! I wish I had the guts to do that!" It didn't matter to them that I hadn't known what I was saying.

Audrey explained to me the full meaning of the word *fuck*. She had to resort to gestures and drawings to make me understand. She couldn't believe how innocent I was for someone who looked so grown-up.

In Riposto, when the neighbor girls came to sit by our front door on summer evenings, they would tell sexy jokes. Then they'd look at me, as if suddenly remembering I was there, then look at one another and stop talking.

"Come on, finish the story."

"We're not supposed to talk about these things in front of you."

"Oh, please, I'm old enough."

"But you're a cripple, *ciunca*," the Sicilian girls said.

How could I argue with that?

Obviously, disabled American girls weren't told they couldn't learn about sex. The girls at HSS knew all there was to know. Often, when they came to listen to Audrey's records, after shimmying and bopping in our wheelchairs for a while, they all started talking about sex. I missed a lot of what they said because I didn't know English well enough yet. I nodded and blushed and giggled, too embarrassed to ask them to explain.

Some of the girls had boyfriends in the hospital. I heard about the "things" Rosa did with a seventeen-year-old boy named Jim, who had dystonia. Audrey liked a fifteen-year-old boy with CP named Joe. She dragged me along to his room at the other end of the hall. They didn't do much; he'd take her hand in his, which shook a little because of the CP. I smiled and looked around the room.

Joe's roommate, Bob, also fifteen, had MD. If he was in the room, he tried to take my hand.

"*Bella,*" he said. It was the only Italian word he knew.

During the first two weeks in the hospital, I had my muscles tested, my bones x-rayed, my blood drawn several times. None of those tests was pleasant, and some were painful. But what bothered me most was that a nurse or an orderly would come to take me down for another test when I was having fun, listening to records or trying to understand a story someone was telling. When I got back on the floor, I was so happy to be with my friends again that whatever discomfort I had endured seemed well worth it.

One afternoon, I was taken to a floor I'd never been on. A nurse told me to take my clothes off and put on a hospital gown. Then she left me sitting in my wheelchair outside a closed door. I waited until a young doctor came out, grabbed my wheelchair, and pushed me into a big room full of doctors. Some I'd never seen before; others I'd seen on our floor when they made rounds. I recognized the important-looking doctor who was shocked when I'd said "Fuck you!" He asked a lot of questions of the younger ones, some so young-looking, I didn't believe they were real doctors.

I was lifted by one of them onto an examining table. It was so high, I couldn't have gotten on it by myself. Still, the young doctor should have asked if I needed help before lifting me. They all looked at me. Some came over to the table to touch me. They made me lie on my back and bent and stretched my legs, while I kept pulling down the hospital gown, trying to keep covered. Then they made me sit up again. One of the older doctors pushed on my back as he talked. I understood the word *scoliosis*. Some of the kids had surgery for that. They were in huge body casts, so they couldn't sit in wheelchairs, but had to move around on stretchers.

Suddenly, I felt the hands behind me loosen the ties on my gown and push it off my shoulders.

"No!"

I thought I'd yelled loudly, but I didn't hear my voice come out. I crossed my arms to hold the open gown over my swelling breasts, which still felt unfamiliar. The doctors kept talking and touching my back and pushing on my shoulders. Then one of the older ones grabbed me from behind under the arms, lifting me up. Another doctor held my hips down. The gown fell to the floor. I was naked. I shut my eyes as tight as I could to make all the American doctors disappear.

Then I was back in my wheelchair. My eyes were still closed, so I didn't see who had gotten me off the table. When I opened my eyes, a woman doctor had picked up my gown and was helping me put it on. I had not noticed her before amid all the men. For a second, her eyes met mine. I thought she looked embarrassed. Maybe even guilty. Why did you let them do that? I wanted to yell at her. But she looked away so quickly, I couldn't be sure what I saw in her eyes.

I raced to Audrey's room the moment I got back on the floor. She wasn't there. I went looking everywhere, wheeling so fast in and out of rooms, bumping into medicine carts, almost colliding with another kid, almost running over a nurse.

"Watch where you're going! What's the matter with you?"

"Audrey! Where's Audrey?"

Finally, Chantelle stopped my wild run. A fifteen-year-old with skin like smooth, creamy chocolate and hair tightly pulled into a multitude of skinny braids, she had osteogenesis imperfecta and was small for her age, but she made up for her size with her sassy demeanor and her street-smart ways. She swiftly got in front of my chair with hers.

"Stop, girl, before you kill somebody!" she yelled in her high-pitched voice. "Do you wanna tell me what happened?"

"Where's Audrey?"

"You can't tell me? You can only tell Audrey? Okay. She should be coming up from PT soon."

PT. That's where Audrey was, of course. I went to Audrey's room and waited, rocking back and forth in my chair, arms crossed over my chest. When Audrey came back, I tried to tell her what had happened, but I couldn't think of the right words, and the words I thought of, I didn't pronounce right. I kept starting over with the big room and so many doctors. Audrey knew right away what I was talking about. She hugged me, and I buried my face in her long blond hair and cried.

"I know" was all Audrey said.

"But I'm angry!"

"I know."

"What they did was wrong!"

"I know."

"I know," Jane also said when Audrey told her what had happened.

"They've done it to Jane many times," Audrey told me.

Rosa nodded. "You'll get used to it."

Standing near us was Matthew, an older boy, who in place of arms had little wings—that's what they looked like. The doctors wanted to operate on him so he could wear artificial arms, which he didn't want or need, since he could do everything with his feet. He had been listening to us girls.

"I wouldn't mind being exhibited if they paid me," he said. "At least in the circus, freaks get paid."

"Don't listen to him, he's a smart-ass," Rosa said.

It was sassy Chantelle who managed to lighten things up. "Girl," she shrilled, grinning, "why didn't you say 'Fuck you'?"

My parents came that evening, as they did every evening. They came by subway from Brooklyn, and never got to the hospital before seven. My father looked tired, because he had worked hard all day. My mother looked lost. She missed her town, her family and friends, and couldn't get used to this new country. I couldn't tell my parents what had happened. I didn't want to make them unhappy. Besides, I was too ashamed.

At last, the doctors decided to start by releasing a tendon in my right leg and scheduled me for surgery.

"Great! After the surgery, they'll give you braces," Rosa said.

I was wheeled down on a stretcher at 9:00 A.M. , smiling and waving good-bye to everyone. Audrey was still in bed. "Good luck!" she yelled from her room. I couldn't see her, but I waved to her just the same. "Bye, Audrey!" I was not afraid. All the other kids had already had surgery; now I would be like everyone else.

I was taken to a floor that had a strange medicinal smell and left in front of a big closed door. When doctors and nurses wearing green gowns and masks went in and out, I tried to look through that door. All I could see was bright light.

Then a doctor and a nurse came over to me. The nurse held my arm and the doctor stuck a needle in my vein.

"Can you count backward from one hundred?" he asked.

I hadn't learned to count that high in English, let alone count backward. I wanted to explain, but I fell asleep before I could say a word.

I woke up in a strange place, with glaring lights above me and weird beeps and humming noises all around me. It felt as if my leg were in a meat grinder, flesh and bones being crushed and chopped and mashed into a pulp. I could never have imagined such pain.

I cried *"Aiuto!"* meaning "help," and called for my mother, *"Mamma!"*

The only words I could utter were in my native language. I couldn't remember a single one of the hundreds of English words I'd learned. A nurse's face appeared above me. She was talking to me, but I couldn't understand her. She gave me a shot and I went back to sleep.

The next time I awoke, I was throwing up, my whole body seized with violent waves, heaving and retching the most foul-tasting green poison. I was still in the recovery room, my leg still in the meat grinder. I felt terribly thirsty. But the English word *water* was nowhere to be found in my brain.

"Acqua," I cried. *"Acqua,"* I begged. But no one answered. No one came over to me.

Then I was back in my room and my parents were there. Was it evening already, or had they taken the day off from work? I was throwing up again and crying uncontrollably.

"*Mamma! Mamma! Che male!* How it hurts!"

My mother held me while I strained to bring up more foul-tasting green poison. She wiped my face with a cool, wet washcloth and put an ice chip in my mouth. And she cried right along with me. My father also seemed on the verge of tears.

Oh no! How could I make my parents so unhappy? They had been through so much for me already. I had to stop crying. I was a big girl, not a baby.

"*Sto meglio,*" I whispered, "I'm better," and smiled to make sure my parents believed me.

When I woke up again, my parents were gone. But someone was holding my hand. I turned my head on the vomit-stained pillow and saw Audrey. I squeezed her hand but could only speak to her in my mind. Oh, Audrey, I'm so sorry. I forgot all the English words you taught me. But I'm so happy you're here. My mother always told me there was a crippled girl like me living in another town. I didn't know you lived so far away, in America. But I knew that, wherever you were, I would find you. Audrey, my lost sister, my beautiful crippled sister. I'm so happy I found you. I love you, Audrey.

The English words all came back to me within a few days. The pain gradually subsided. The nausea lasted a whole week. I chewed ice chips until my gums, my tongue, even my teeth were numb. When I finally could get out of bed and into a wheelchair, I was so thrilled that I went racing up and down the corridor, yelling "Hello, everybody!"

Then I heard the music coming from Audrey's room. A few girls were in there, and others came in after me. Audrey had stolen some fat Magic Markers from the recreation room. With a red one, she wrote on the brand-new cast on my leg "LOVE, Audrey" as the girls crowded around, encircling me. They all signed their names and drew hearts and flowers, until my whole cast was covered.

The day before, my parents had brought me a box of chocolates. We passed it around as we listened to records. Some of the boys joined us, and soon we were all licking chocolate off our fingers and shimmying and bopping in our wheelchairs. My stomach got a bit queasy from the chocolate, and I felt kind of dizzy shaking my head to the music. But who cared? I was so happy to be with my friends. So happy to be in America. So happy my father had found the best hospital for me.

3

BLOOD SISTERS

❋

About a month after the surgery, I was discharged from the hospital and given a wheelchair. Rosa had been wrong about my getting braces. The doctors told my father the next step was to release another tendon, this time in my left leg. After that, my ankles would need to be fused. And other surgeries would be necessary—it was hard to predict how many—before I could be taught to stand and walk. My father agreed to it all, happy that I was getting the best care.

I barely had time to get settled at home before I had to go back into the hospital for more surgery. But I was happy to go. More surgery meant more pain, but it also meant seeing old friends and meeting new ones. Best of all, it meant being with Audrey.

Audrey and I always tried to be in the hospital at the same time.

"Tell the doctors you can't go in till next month. That's when I'm having my surgery," Audrey would say.

"Oh, please, see if they can do it earlier! I don't want to wait that long!"

We were best friends, though we never got to see each other outside of the hospital. Audrey lived on Long Island. Her parents had a car and drove her places, but I guess my home in Brooklyn was too far. We were happy talking on the phone every day. Usually, I waited for her to call me, since a call to Long Island was long-distance and expensive. Audrey's parents didn't mind the high phone bills.

I'd made no friends outside of the hospital. I went out only with my parents and not very often. Our apartment without stairs still had one step at the front door. I couldn't manage that step on my own in my wheelchair.

Audrey told me her house had a ramp, so she could go in and out without anyone's help. I asked my father to build a ramp for me. He told me he couldn't. Unlike Audrey's parents, who owned their house, we rented our apartment, and the landlord would never agree to a ramp.

"Don't worry, *gioia,* before long we won't need that wheelchair." Wasn't that the reason we had come to America? *Presto guarisci, presto cammini* was the refrain I heard every day.

If I could have gone out in my wheelchair, I wouldn't have gotten far, since none of the curbs had cuts, and there were steps going into most places. Besides, I wasn't brave enough to venture out on my own. I was still the shy crippled girl from the little town of Riposto.

When I went out with my parents, it was to visit our cousins Vito and Concetta and their son, Vittorio, or Victor, who was a few years older than I. They lived only a block away in an apartment on the second floor. My father carried me up the stairs.

Cousin Concetta had found a job for my mother in the factory where she worked, right in the neighborhood. They made ladies' coats and everyone there spoke some southern Italian dialect. They called the factory *fattoria,* which I thought was hysterical, since *fattoria* means "farm" in English.

"Are there cows where you work?" I asked.

She didn't appreciate the humor. She took her job very seriously. An expert seamstress, she was proud when her work was appreciated by her boss. And above all, she was happy to have found a place where people spoke her language.

My mother had not been going to church but didn't seem to miss it. Maybe there were no churches nearby. Or maybe after working Monday through Friday, she needed rest more than church services. I asked Audrey if she ever went to church and she laughed. Of course not! She was Jewish, she said. And she was not religious, and neither were her parents. I was glad to learn it wasn't necessary to be religious in America.

Both my parents left early in the morning to go to work, my father to his construction job, my mother to the factory. I was alone most of the day, but I didn't mind. It felt great to move around the apartment in my wheelchair—into the kitchen to get a soda or make myself a sandwich, into the living room to turn the TV on, and into the bathroom by myself. Although to get into the bathroom, I had to transfer to a stool, since my wheelchair didn't quite fit through the door. Taking a bath was tricky and I could do it only when my mother was there to help me. Audrey told me her bathroom was big; she could get her wheelchair right next to the bathtub and get in and out by herself.

TV was a novelty for me, since in Sicily only rich people owned one. I loved our set, encased in shiny dark wood, with a huge nineteen-inch screen. I watched game shows and *American Bandstand,* trying to remember the words of the songs I'd learned from Audrey.

One day, I turned on the TV and a bunch of disabled kids were going around on a stage, some with braces and crutches, and a woman in a low-cut dress was guiding them and patting first one, then another on the head—all this while a funny-looking man sang some sad-sounding song. I wasn't sure what they were doing. I got a strange feeling in my stomach, as if I was going to be sick. Maybe the ham I'd just eaten was spoiled.

"Send money so these unfortunate kids can walk," the man pleaded. I remembered that my father had told me how in America they collected money on television to find a cure. I felt as if I were one of those TV kids. I felt like I had in Sicily when people looked at me and clucked their tongues, got all teary-eyed, and murmured, *"Povera ciunca."*

"I'd rather not walk," I told the man, as if he could hear me. Saying that made me feel better. But I was glad my father wasn't there. When he asked that night what I'd watched on TV, I said game shows. But I told Audrey the next time she called, and she said she felt like puking, too, whenever she watched the telethon. That's what that show was called.

Twice a week, the home instructor from the Board of Education came. He was a nice man who brought me books and praised me for my progress in learning English. I liked his visits, but I wished I could go to school and meet other kids.

Audrey was now a freshman—which was a funny word for a girl—in a regular school with a ramp at the entrance. Her mother drove her there. There weren't many accessible schools, she told me. She was lucky to go to one, though she couldn't get into the auditorium and the science lab in her wheelchair. She had lots of friends, but she complained that they left her out of many things they did.

Sometimes I wished I could live with Audrey in her house with the ramp and the big bathroom, and go to school with her. Then I remembered how difficult it had been for my father to bring me to America, find a ground-floor apartment, and the hospital and the doctors I needed. I thought about how hard my parents worked, and I felt guilty for wanting more than they could give me.

Whenever Audrey and I were in the hospital together, and especially when we managed to be in the same room, we were thrilled. The first few nights, the two of us were so busy catching up, we wouldn't sleep at all.

"What's going on in here, a pajama party?"

Janet, the nice night nurse stuck her head in the room, trying to sound angry, but we could hear the laughter in her voice. If mean Miss Martins was on duty, we had to be careful and whisper and put our heads under the covers to muffle our giggles. She heard us anyway and came marching into the room.

"The next time I come in here, I'll give you each a shot."

"You can't do that without a doctor's orders," Audrey said, bravely challenging her.

"If I hear so much as a peep coming from this room, you'll find out what I can do!"

Audrey's favorite topic of conversation was Richard, a sophomore at her school. She had a major crush on Richard. She described the way he looked in the minutest detail—how his hair curled over his ears, his eyes slanted up when he smiled at her, his lips pouted just slightly.... When she described his cute butt, we'd both giggle so hard that if Miss Martins was on duty, she'd march in with her hands on her hips. If she was off, Audrey went on talking, both of us laughing harder and harder, until she got to the big bulge in Richard's pants. At that point, we'd be practically having convulsions under the covers, and that's when Audrey cried out, "Oh no, oh no, I'm wetting the bed!"

Because of her spina bifida, Audrey's bladder control was not the greatest, and she did have an accident once in a while, especially when she laughed too hard or got too excited. Though I couldn't see what she was doing under the covers, I knew her hand was between her legs as she tried to stop the pee from coming out. Polio had not affected my bladder at all. But I made believe I, too, was afraid of wetting the bed and I put my hand there and squeezed my legs together as tightly as my polio-weakened muscles allowed.

Audrey's relationship with Richard never went past his smiling at her, saying hello, and two or three times pushing her from the elevator to her classroom. Yet I was jealous. I wished there was a boy I could talk about with Audrey. But since I hardly ever went anywhere outside of the hospital, I never saw any boys who weren't handicapped, other than my cousin Victor.

In the hospital, Audrey and I were quite popular. But the boys in the hospital, as cute as some of them were, couldn't compare with Richard. Richard was a thousand, maybe even a million, times better. Because Richard was not handicapped. He was "normal." Audrey was sure that had she not been handicapped, Richard would have asked her out on a date, kissed her, and made out with her. It was a real tragedy that because of her disability she was missing out on Richard's love. But she kept hoping he would fall in love with her in spite of her disability.

Why normal boys were so much better than handicapped boys was not a question we ever thought of asking. Nor did we ask why normal boys didn't consider us—handicapped girls—worthy of their attentions. These were facts of life, unquestionable and unanswerable.

Every morning before breakfast, without even thinking we might want to wash our faces, Audrey got her makeup bag out.

"What color eye shadow do you want to wear today?"

I'd shrug, too inexperienced to make such a decision.

"What if I wear blue and you wear green?"

Any color was fine with me. She grabbed the side table, which was on wheels and could be pushed back and forth between our beds, and placed all sorts of tubes and jars on it. At first I didn't know what to do. I'd put on too much eye shadow, get it all smudged.

Audrey laughed. "You look like you got punched in the eyes!"

Then she'd show me how to do it right. I was a fast learner and before long I could apply makeup like a pro. What fun it was! Rubbing foundation on our noses and foreheads, defining our cheekbones with blush-on, carefully applying mascara on our lashes and frosty shadow on our lids. On our lips we'd wear light pink lipstick.

"You girls look like you're ready to go partying," the nurse's aide said when she brought our breakfast.

Audrey put all the makeup back into the bag to make room for her tray.

As soon as we were up in our chairs, we'd work on our hair. When I was a little girl, my mother had always kept my dark, wavy hair short. It felt great to have it reaching down to my shoulders, almost as long as Audrey's blond hair. I teased the top, puffed it up, and tried to get the bottom to flip—just like Audrey.

"Close your eyes," she'd say, holding her can of hair spray. The spray made my hair look shiny and smell like almonds. Then she handed me the can so I could spray her hair. I made sure I did it from the right distance.

We always had a *Seventeen* magazine open in front of us. The goal was to make ourselves look like the models on those glossy, sweet-smelling pages. Though, of course, we never fooled ourselves. We knew that no matter how hard we tried, we could never be like the models in *Seventeen*. We were handicapped and they were normal. That knowledge was a source of constant sorrow.

"Look, what beautiful legs!" Audrey would hold up the magazine. "And our legs are so ugly. They're shaped like sticks. And they're all covered with scars."

We looked at ourselves in the full-length mirror hanging in one of the bathrooms, seeing ourselves only from the waist up. If no one was around, we took off our tops and seductively moved our slender torsos—wearing our Maidenform bras—as if dancing to inaudible music, while keeping our lower bodies covered with sheets. We always tried to keep our legs hidden. We were happy when they were inside of casts.

One day, Audrey rushed into the room and grabbed the armrest of my chair, so I had to follow her. "Look at that girl's legs," she whispered, pointing at an older girl—at least sixteen—standing near the nurses' station.

I'd never seen the girl before. She wore a jade-colored A-line dress with a big bow a little above the waist, and pointed pumps of the exact same shade with little heels. Her legs were beautiful. By the way the nurses and some of the older kids were fussing over her, I deduced she had been a patient on the floor and was now visiting. She didn't look handicapped, though when she walked to the other side of the hall to get hugged by the head nurse, I noticed a limp.

"One of her legs is fake." Audrey was leaning on my armrest. "Can you guess which one?"

"No way," I said a little too loudly.

Audrey reprimanded me by slapping my shoulder. "She's an amputee. She lost her leg in a car accident. Can you tell which leg is fake?"

I couldn't. Both her legs were equally perfect. None of the kids I'd met in the hospital so far was an amputee. The boy with little wings instead of arms was just born that way.

"Amputees are better off than we are," Audrey said. "They get beautiful fake legs, and we get scars and more scars and horrid heavy braces. She looks normal, doesn't she?"

I had to agree. She looked as normal and dressed as fashionably as a model.

Audrey had found in *Seventeen* a picture of two long-legged models, a blonde and a brunette, standing with their arms around each other. The blonde wore a blue bikini with pink polka dots and the brunette wore a pink one with blue dots. Their smiling young faces vaguely resembled ours. Audrey had cut the page out and asked her mom to paste it on the wall between our beds.

"That's what we would look like if we weren't handicapped."

"But we're pretty, even though we're handicapped, Audrey. Everybody says so." I tried to make us feel better, but it didn't work.

"In a way, that makes it worse." She sighed. She looked so sad and serious, as if the weight of the world were on her shoulders.

I didn't argue with her. I didn't ask her to explain. I remembered the Sicilian women looking at me with such anguish whenever they said "*Che bella bambina!* What a pretty little girl! *Che peccato!* What a shame!"

The volunteer ladies who came to bring us candy had the same sorrowful looks on their middle-aged powdered faces.

"You're such pretty girls."

We knew it wasn't a compliment; it was pity. But what could we do? These were facts of life. Such beauty wasted on us, crippled girls!

Yet I felt so grown-up and glamorous when I was all made-up and my hair was fluffy and shiny from Audrey's hair spray. And when the boys in the hospital whistled to show their appreciation, it made me happy.

I had to make sure the makeup was off my face and my hair combed down by seven in the evening, when my parents came to visit. My father would have had a stroke if he had seen his little girl all made-up.

Sometimes I wished my parents were more like Audrey's parents. Audrey's mom bought the makeup and magazines for Audrey and taught her how to make herself look glamorous. My mom was beautiful, but she didn't know about makeup and hairdos. My parents came to the hospital straight from work, looking tired and unkempt. My father's clothes were covered with white dust from his construction job. Audrey's parents were so elegant and perfect. Her father, who was a dentist, always wore a suit and tie. Her mom looked like she'd stepped out of *Vogue*. Often, while we were making ourselves up or fussing with our hair, we had a 45 on the record player. Audrey no longer needed to do charades to get me to understand the lyrics. Now, just for fun, we both acted out songs, making dramatic gestures and pretending we were hugging and kissing some invisible normal boy.

In the evenings, all the kids came to listen to Audrey's records. We'd chip in and order pizza or Chinese food. We'd all be chewing, lip-synching, and licking sauce off our fingers or wiping it on one another's casts. We'd be laughing and choking and chasing one another, and doing the Twist and the Mashed Potato in our wheelchairs. We may not have looked like the teenagers on *American Bandstand*, but we sure could dance.

I loved those hospital parties. I couldn't imagine normal kids out in the real world having more fun at their parties than we had at ours. But Audrey said there was no comparison.

Of course, it wasn't all fun being in the hospital. Having to strip naked to be examined by doctors while they talked about me as if I weren't there; having every muscle prodded, every joint twisted, every inch of me poked, as if my body belonged to them and I had no say in what they did with it—none of that was fun. Neither was surgery: the disorientation coming out of anesthesia, the nausea and dizziness, and the unbearable pain. But all of it was worth it as long as Audrey and I could be together. Sometimes we managed to have our surgeries the same day, or a day apart.

Once, I woke up, disoriented as usual after surgery, and heard Audrey say, "Look, we're blood sisters."

I didn't know what she meant.

"Don't you see the bag of blood hanging from the pole?"

My eyes had trouble focusing, but, yes, there was a bagful of red blood hanging from the IV pole that stood between our beds.

"The blood from that bag is going into my veins and into yours," she explained. "We have the same type, O-positive, so they're giving us the same blood. That makes us blood sisters."

I believed her, of course.

I seemed to be having more surgeries than the other kids. The cast came off my leg after a tendon was released, and right away I'd go back into the hospital to have my ankle fused. The doctors never talked to me. Sometimes they talked to my father, who had complete faith in them. He believed each surgery brought me closer to being cured. He kept assuring me: *Presto guarisci, presto cammini.* Audrey, who had spent much of her childhood in hospitals, said I had to catch up after those years in Sicily, when I lived peacefully at home and never once got cut up.

I got used to the surgeries. As horrendous as the pain was, I knew it would go away, as would the nausea and dizziness. As soon as we started feeling better, Audrey and I resumed our daily routine: made ourselves up, partied, chatted with the girls and flirted with the boys.

The volunteer ladies came regularly, smiling and bearing gifts. One of them always talked religion to us. How unfair that children who never sinned had to suffer, she remarked. "You're right," Audrey countered. "We should start sinning, since we're already suffering."

The lady could tell I was easier prey than Audrey, and she asked me to pray with her. I got flustered and didn't know what to do. Audrey came to the rescue. "Come on, you had enough prayers in Sicily," she said, pulling me away. Then she turned to the lady and said, "No candies, either, thanks; we're watching our figures."

BLOOD SISTERS ❀ 43

Whenever I was in the hospital and Audrey wasn't, I felt lost. Her mother brought her to visit me and I was happy to see her, but all she talked about were her friends at school—all normal and wonderful. She sounded cheerful, yet she looked uptight. Was she faking? Did those normal kids treat her as well as she said they did? Did she really like them more than the handicapped kids at the hospital? I wasn't sure whether to be jealous or feel sorry for her.

When the doctors decided they had to fix my scoliosis and I went into the hospital for a spinal fusion, Audrey was all done with surgeries and hospitalizations. She came to visit me right after I was admitted. She was carrying a boxful of 45s on her lap. Her mother was lugging her record player together with its little cart. She had a stereo at home now, Audrey explained, sounding almost embarrassed, and preferred albums, since they took up less room.

She handed me an envelope. I pulled out a get-well card with a picture of a bunch of red tulips. In it Audrey had written, "To my blood sister with love." I asked her mother to tape the card on the wall over my bed. Then her mother moved my nightstand to plug the record player in the outlet.

"This'll be a long hospital stay and you'll need all the help you can get," Audrey said.

I put on a record, without looking to see which one. "In the still of the night, I held you, held you tight..." I crossed my arms in front of my chest, as if holding an invisible boy, and rocked back and forth to the music. Audrey only smiled, maybe too self-conscious to act out in front of her mother. I was jubilant! Now all the kids would come to my room to listen to music, dance, and have parties.

But there weren't going to be any parties.

I wasn't prepared for what was to come. I'd seen the kids in the huge casts that covered their bodies and went over their heads. They wheeled around slowly on stretchers, lying on their stomachs, with sandbags under their plaster-encased torsos. They looked so big and round, we called them the turtles. I knew when the doctors talked of operating on my back that I would be in one of those casts. I heard one of the doctors explain to my father that the cast would go on first, and there would be screws embedded. They would straighten my back by turning the screws every day. When my back was straight enough, they would operate.

I also knew they'd have to cut my long hair. Still, the night before the cast went on, when they shaved it all off, I cried.

"Your hair will grow back thicker and curlier," my mother said, trying to comfort me, kissing my bald head.

The next morning, they covered my entire body with stockinette, pulling it over my head, so I couldn't see what was going on, and placed me in some strange traction device, which stretched my back as much as possible. When they pulled my head all the way back, the same way they broke chickens' necks in Sicily, I started shaking.

"Are you cold?" they asked.

I whispered, "Yes."

But I wasn't cold; I was terrified. I kept shaking as they wrapped the hot plaster all around my body—around my thighs, around my head, covering my forehead, then under my chin. No plaster right on my face, only the stockinette. I couldn't see them working on me. I shook violently, but I was inside the cast now, hidden.

They finally cut the stockinette and uncovered my face.

"There you are!" they exclaimed, as if I could have been gone.

They wheeled me back to the floor on a stretcher, on my stomach, a huge turtle, helplessly shaking inside her thick new shell.

When my parents came that evening, I was still shaking, encased in the now cold, wet cast. My mother tried to kiss me but couldn't quite get to my face. She hugged my big plaster head and sobbed. My father's face looked stiff, his eyes not blinking. Maybe he was wondering if he should have given up on the idea of a cure. He kept leaving the room to go smoke a cigarette. Then he tried to make me laugh by telling me the white cast around my face made me look like Sister Teresina. She had been my favorite nun, but I didn't want to look like her. I started crying.

I was not a pretty girl anymore. What was Audrey going to say? Would she still want me as her blood sister?

But Audrey didn't visit me much. She was busy in high school, trying to get through math and win the attentions of some normal boy.

I cried on the phone to her. "I'm not pretty anymore."

"You will be again, don't worry," she said, comforting me. "You have to get your back straightened. You don't want to be a hunchback. It's bad enough you have ugly, useless legs."

I wasn't sure a straight back was worth going through such torture.

I made friends with the other turtle kids. Margarita, who spoke little English, talked to me in Spanish and I answered in Italian. We understood each other perfectly. And Ellen, smart and sophisticated, older than the rest of us, read aloud poems by Dylan Thomas. Both Margarita and Ellen only had scoliosis, no other disability. Audrey said they were going to be "practically normal" once their backs were straightened. They might have a protrusion—that was the nice word for hump—but they would be able to hide it with the right clothes.

One girl, Susie, didn't just have scoliosis; she had contracted polio as a baby, like me. I felt more of a bond with her, especially since she came from an Italian-American family. My father and Susie's would stand in the hallway, having conversations in Sicilian.

Every day the doctors turned the two big screws embedded in our casts. They kept taking X-rays, and when they were satisfied our backs were as straight as they could get, they operated and fused our spines. Some kids needed surgery only once, others twice. It depended on how many vertebrae needed to be fused. Susie and I, because of our polio, had to have most of our vertebrae fused, requiring three surgeries.

My brain erased the memory of the pain. Of the days following each operation, only segmented memories remained. My mother, who had taken a few days off from her job at the *fattoria*, stood by the sink opposite my bed and turned the water on full blast, in the hope that the gushing sound would make me pee. It didn't work. My bladder refused to empty and I had to be catheterized. And I couldn't forget the vomit, which got on the cast, right under my chin. As long as the stench lingered, the nausea wouldn't go away. My mother spoon-fed me tiny meatballs in a clear broth, her Sicilian cure-all recipe. But I couldn't manage to swallow more than two spoonfuls before starting to gag. We tried alcohol, baby powder, perfume, spray deodorant. It took many weeks for that smell to fade away.

The worst thing about being in the cast was losing the independence I'd recently acquired. I loved moving around in a wheelchair and was gratified to be able to tend to my own personal needs. Now, not only couldn't I sit in a wheelchair, I couldn't even turn in bed. When I had to go to the bathroom, a bedpan was slipped under me. A nurse had to wipe me because I couldn't reach down. When I got my period, a nurse put a sanitary napkin on me.

I'd just started to experience the tentative pleasure of exploring my body, looking, touching. Suddenly, my body was hidden inside the cast. I hated to feel a nurse's hands in my private places. The nurses touched me so boldly, as if their hands had every right to be there. Some of them were so rough, they hurt me.

"Not so hard, please."

But they laughed when I complained.

"Aren't you delicate! Aren't you the little princess!"

I tried to talk with the other girls in the big casts.

"I hate it, too" was all they said.

I couldn't mention this to my mother. She was already too burdened. I thought Audrey would understand. But when I tried to tell her on one of her rare visits, she started pondering out loud about how it would feel if Harry—that was the name of the boy she had a crush on now— ever touched her there, and whether it would hurt the first time. I wanted her to comfort me, to hug me; I wanted to bury my bald head in her beautiful blond hair. But how could I? I was just a big round turtle made of plaster. I didn't dare ask if we could still be blood sisters.

4

BLYTHEDALE

�֍

The big cast had to stay on for another six months after my spine was fused. Since my mother worked and couldn't take care of me at home, in July 1963, I moved from the Hospital for Special Surgery to Blythedale, a convalescent home in White Plains, about an hour and a half away. A few other girls, including Susie, went there also, as did the only boy, Edwin. I went gladly. I wouldn't have wanted to be at home, unable to move.

Blythedale was like the hospital, young children on one side and older kids on the other. Except no one had surgery there, and there were no doctors making rounds. You saw a doctor only when you got the flu.

Since I had no choice, I got used to being dependent and being handled by nurses and aides. In the big casts, we were not allowed to get up on stretchers, but our beds were pushed around by porters. We all lay on our stomachs, with sandbags under our chests, which lifted our torsos so that we could freely use our arms. Our beds got pushed to the recreation room, and to the schoolroom, where the one teacher, Miss Fox, treated us all equally, whether we were in first grade or twelfth.

"No talking or laughing!"

Our beds were also pushed outside, on the extensive Blythedale grounds. It felt strange but wonderful to be in bed under a tree. I hadn't seen so many trees since I'd left Sicily. During the last two years, I'd been indoors, either in our Brooklyn apartment or in the hospital.

I loved watching the squirrels chase each other and listening to the sparrows chirp. It was summer, so we stayed outside most of the day and sometimes into the evening. If Seth and Sarah, the two recreation counselors, could work late, we might have a campfire. Some in beds, others on stretchers and in wheelchairs, we formed a wide circle around the fire. Seth roasted marshmallows and Sarah played her guitar and sang. We all sang along.

I knew Audrey wouldn't be able to come see me in Blythedale. I had hoped to talk to her on the phone. But that wasn't easy. There was a pay phone in the recreation room, but I had to get someone to push me there, put the coins in, and dial the number for me. It took a lot of coins to call Audrey on Long Island. When I managed to call her, and told her about Blythedale, she said it sounded like the summer camp for handicapped kids she went to.

To talk to my parents, I had someone put in the coins, dial the number, let the phone ring once, and then hang up so I'd get my coins back. My parents knew it was my signal and called me.

Since Blythedale was so far, my parents could come only on weekends. That's also when Susie's parents came. Often my parents and Susie's met at the station and arrived together, carrying shopping bags full of good food: fresh mozzarella, prosciutto, dried sausage, crusty bread. We all sat together under a tree and had a picnic. Speaking the Sicilian dialect, our parents reminisced about their beloved island and its legendary beauty. They also talked about the poverty, the lack of education, the unemployment that forced many to emigrate. Sometimes my father recited Sicilian poetry. His favorite poet was Ignazio Buttitta. My father sounded angry and sad as he spoke of Sicilians being scorned for their dark complexion, their alleged uncleanliness and laziness. His voice got loud. Other kids' parents looked at us. "*Semu chiamati pi*

mjuria terroni; ca l'omini da Sicilia non semu genti boni. To insult us
they call us 'made of dirt'; Sicilians, they say, are not good people."

During the week, I spent the mornings studying. Miss Fox was not
much help, but the college students who came and tutored us were
great. They came from different schools—from nearby Westchester
Community College as well as from faraway New York University. I
loved to hear about their courses. To me, even midterms and finals
sounded like fun.

I studied American history, read about the colonies and the Revolutionary War, tried to memorize the names of the presidents, was fascinated by Abraham Lincoln, was horrified to learn about slavery. I read
about Franklin Delano Roosevelt, known as FDR, the president who
had polio. My book said he "conquered polio" to become one of our
greatest presidents. I asked my tutors if he was really cured, as my father
had told me. "No" was the answer, "but he couldn't have been president
if he had been seen as handicapped."

In the afternoon, we had recreation. We didn't glue tiles on metal
ashtrays like we did in the hospital. Seth and Sarah had us write poetry,
act in plays, and work on art projects. I adored them.

Sarah had very long, dark hair, wore sandals, and always carried her
guitar. She taught us folk songs. Folk songs were different from the songs
I listened to with Audrey. They were quieter and more serious. I didn't
like them at first, but when I listened carefully, I realized how much
meaning was in the words. The songs reminded me of my father's poetry.
They were about freedom, equality, solidarity, peace, not about boyfriends and girlfriends. We listened to Pete Seeger and Peter, Paul and
Mary on the stereo in the recreation room. I tried to sing along: "If I
had a hammer..." Sarah's favorite folksinger was Joan Baez. The first
time I heard a Joan Baez record, I was spellbound. I had my mother
pack all of Audrey's 45s and take them away.

Seth also wore sandals and had lots of curly brown hair. He talked
about Dr. Martin Luther King. Dr. King was not a medical doctor, but
a doctor of theology and a Baptist minister. Seth and Sara were both

Jewish, like Audrey. I knew kids of various Protestant denominations and a girl who was Hindu. Since in Riposto everyone was Catholic, I loved the idea of people having different religions, or no religion at all.

Dr. King, Seth told us, was a leader in the civil rights movement. I wanted to know all about the civil rights movement. I was outraged at the thought of racial segregation and discrimination. I was mesmerized by the story of Rosa Parks, who refused to sit in the back of the bus. I wished I could be a freedom rider. I pictured myself on a bus heading south, sitting next to Marcus, my favorite tutor, a very handsome black student from NYU. I wouldn't be afraid to get arrested, I told myself. I would be proud to go to jail with Dr. King. Nor would I be afraid of the Ku Klux Klan. I pictured myself holding Marcus's hand and confronting a man in a white hood.

Seth, Sarah, and Marcus had gone to the March on Washington on August 28. Hundreds of thousands of people from all over the country were there, they told me. How I wished I could have gone with them!

"Did Joan Baez sing?"

Of course, they told me. But the most exciting part of the rally had been Dr. King's speech.

"What did he say? Tell me everything."

They couldn't tell me without getting all choked up. Even Seth's eyes got misty as he recalled Dr. King's words: "I have a dream…" Sarah started strumming her guitar and humming softly. We all sang "We Shall Overcome."

The months passed quickly in Blythedale. In my bed in the big cast, I watched the leaves on the trees turn yellow and red, and dreamed of the time when my hair would be long like Sarah's. I would be a college student, go to folk concerts, and go to demonstrations in Washington and hear Dr. King speak.

One day in November, I was in the schoolroom, working with Marcus, when Sarah tiptoed in and whispered in my ear that there was a phone call from a friend of mine who seemed anxious to speak to me. I asked Miss Fox to excuse me and asked Marcus to push my bed to the phone.

It was Audrey. She started crying the moment she heard my voice. The boy she had a crush on had a girlfriend, a normal girlfriend, of course. I couldn't make out the boy's name, that's how hard she was crying—was it Harry? He had told Audrey he liked her but said there could never be anything between them, since she was handicapped. The boy wanted Audrey to meet his girlfriend, whose name was Margie or Marcie. He had introduced Audrey to his girlfriend as his "handicapped friend."

"I can't be his friend, period? I have to be his handicapped friend?" Audrey sobbed. "And you know what the little bitch had the nerve to tell me? That she sends money to the telethon, like I should be grateful for that!"

I listened in silence. I couldn't think of any comforting words to say. Finally, she stopped crying. "I didn't even ask how you are."

Since my mind was brimming with so many new ideas, I couldn't hold back. I started talking about the college students who tutored me, and about Seth and Sarah. I told her how I wanted to go to college, wanted to fight for civil rights, go to demonstrations, and hear Dr. King.

"I can't wait to be out in the real world!" I said.

"Oh, you're so naïve!" The bitterness in her voice hit me like a spray of snake venom. "You think they're all waiting for you with open arms in the real world! Don't you understand? No one wants anything to do with us because we're handicapped! The only thing the real world has to offer us is pity!"

Audrey was right. No matter what my father said, I knew I wasn't about to be cured. How could I go to college when I couldn't even get out my front door? How could I be a freedom rider when I couldn't ride on a bus? How was I going to get to a concert or a demonstration? And what good would a handicapped girl be at a demonstration? Or anywhere else, for that matter? For days I cried.

Before long, I wasn't the only one crying. About a week after Audrey's call, another call came, for Seth, while we were working on one of our art projects.

"The president's been shot."

Seth's face was as white as the sheets on our beds. He turned on the big TV set in the recreation room.

"The president's been shot," the nurses' voices echoed down the hallways.

In the following days, everyone crowded in front of the TV, crying. And I cried along with them. For the handsome president who was now dead, for his beautiful wife, who looked so sad, and for the two children, who would never see their daddy again.

I kept crying, even after everyone else had stopped. I cried because it was too cold to go outside, and the trees I loved were all bare. In Sicily, where the winters were mild, I'd never seen trees look so dead. I cried when it snowed so much that my parents couldn't come see me. And because I didn't like the food they served us and missed our summer picnics. I cried when the nurses were mean to me or too rough and hurt me. I cried when my roommates teased me because I was always crying.

Then the six months were up and it was time for the big cast to come off. Back in the hospital, they cut the cast with an electric circular saw down the middle in the back, rolled me over and cut it down the middle in the front, then forced it open with a pry bar. I came out of the cast naked and shaking, just as I had been when they'd put it on me.

"Your back looks nice and straight," one of the nurses said. "Do you want a mirror?"

But all I wanted was to be enclosed, hidden again. They put a smaller cast on me, which had to stay on for four more months. It covered my torso, from under my arms to my hips.

"What a nice shape that cast gives you!" Audrey said when she came to visit me in the hospital.

I hadn't seen her in over six months. She looked beautiful, with streaks in her hair—highlights, they were called—and her makeup so perfect. She said she had learned to accentuate her features without looking made-up. She seemed happy; she didn't talk about Harry, or whatever his name was. She brought me eye shadow and hair spray. I hadn't been wearing makeup all those months in the big cast, so I didn't even remember how to put it on. And my hair had grown back, but I didn't know what to do with it.

Audrey went to work.

"Your hair has grown in so nicely!" She played with it, teasing it on top, making it curl over my ears. Then she made me try on the eye shadow. "I knew it was your color! You look so pretty!"

I did feel pretty again. "Thank you, Audrey."

I hugged her, now that in the smaller cast I could reach her, and asked, "Are we blood sisters again?"

"Of course"— she laughed, hugging me back—"we're blood sisters forever."

I went back to Blythedale feeling pretty. In my shapely new cast, I wore jeans and bright- colored sweaters, instead of the triple X nightgowns that had been my exclusive wardrobe for many months. With my hair curly and shiny, and some makeup, only enough to bring out my features, I didn't feel like crying anymore. I could turn myself in bed now, though I still needed some help washing and dressing. I wasn't allowed to sit in a wheelchair, but I could wheel myself on a stretcher, on my stomach, a pillow under my chest. I became a pro at maneuvering, and, though it was still winter, I liked to sneak out the door.

In March, I looked for signs of the coming spring. It made me happy to discover grass growing where there had been none the day before, a violet shyly opening up to the mild sunshine, then the first tiny leaves appearing on trees.

Edwin, who had gotten his four-month cast a month before I did, also liked to sneak out the door. Two years older than I was, he was almost eighteen. We met outside and went all the way to the end of the path, where you could see the highway.

"That's a '62 Chevy Impala! That's a '61 Dodge Dart!" He pointed to the cars as they zoomed by.

I didn't care, but I tried to look interested.

When he got tired of looking at cars, he kissed me—clumsy, open-mouthed kisses that almost made me choke. Then he squeezed his hand inside my cast, but I didn't let him get in far enough to touch my breasts. Whenever his hand went toward the zipper of his pants, I got nervous, thinking I heard someone spying on us, and made him stop.

Audrey approved of Edwin. Since he had only scoliosis, no other disability, he rated pretty high in her book.

"Maybe he won't have much of a protrusion on his back when he's done," she said.

The morning after our first campfire of the season, I hurried to the pay phone with a bunch of coins I kept under my pillow and called Audrey. I told her how Edwin and I had parked our stretchers right next to each other's and shared a heavy blanket. Seth had some trouble getting the fire started, but once it got going, it was the most beautiful fire ever. Trembling from the excitement, and the still-chilly weather, I'd let Edwin guide my hand to his crotch under our blanket. I touched something hard and throbbing.

Audrey got so agitated, she wouldn't let me tell the story.

"You held it in your hand? Wow, how big was it? How long? How hard?"

"It was big," I told her, though I had no basis for comparison.

I think for the first time Audrey was jealous of me.

I never found out how much of a protrusion Edwin had. He went to HSS to get his cast off and I never heard from him again.

"Of course," Audrey said. "Now that he's practically normal, he wouldn't want anything to do with a handicapped girl."

"I didn't love him anyway," I declared.

When my turn came to get my cast off, I was nervous. I'd already been fitted with braces while at Blythedale. At HSS, they would teach me to stand and walk. I'd seen kids walking with braces and crutches. It didn't look easy.

It was even harder than I'd thought. I exhausted myself every day in

PT, determined to learn to walk as well as I could. Unlike Audrey, I felt I had to walk. My father had brought me to America so I could walk. I wanted to repay my parents for all the sacrifices they had made. But now I understood what Audrey meant when she talked about those who had only scoliosis being "practically normal." I watched my Blythedale roommates come into the hospital, shed their casts, and walk out looking gorgeous.

When Susie joined me at HSS, I was so happy. Her cast came off and we went to PT together. But Susie had learned to use braces and crutches when she was a little girl. It didn't take long for her to get back in practice. She went home, while I was only starting to take tentative steps.

I felt so awkward and clumsy, though my therapist generously praised me for my progress.

"Leave your braces on and take the crutches to your floor, so you can practice walking on your own," she said one afternoon.

"I don't think I'm ready," I stammered.

She just smiled as she secured the crutches to the back of my wheelchair.

When the elevator doors opened on my floor, my favorite nurse was there.

"Congratulations!"

That evening, she helped me get ready to surprise my parents. She picked the loosest pair of pants I had and put them on me, pulling them over my braces while I lay in bed on my back. She assured me the braces hardly showed when I stood leaning on the crutches, full of trepidation. I waited at the door of my room until she announced, under her breath, as she quickly walked away, "They're here."

I saw my parents heading toward my room, and I started stepping, right crutch, left foot, left crutch, right foot, very carefully, trying not to shake, hoping not to fall. My parents stopped in the middle of the hallway and watched me. I got within a few feet of them. My mother had tears in her eyes, and my father had a big smile on his face.

"Look how tall you are!" my mother exclaimed.

Then my father spoke: "I'm sure before long you'll be able to walk without those sticks."

My heart sank. It had been so hard to learn to walk with crutches, and now he expected me to learn to walk without them? How was I ever going to do that? Can't this be enough? I wanted to yell. But suddenly, I felt so exhausted. I knew I couldn't walk back to my room. When I turned and saw the nurse had brought out my wheelchair, I was so grateful.

A few days after, I fell in PT and fractured my right knee. They sent me back to Blythedale for six weeks, to give my bone time to heal. I was grateful for the reprieve. Though I kept saying I couldn't wait to get out, in all honesty the thought scared me. What was I going to do when I went home? What was I going to do in the "real world"?

5

THE REAL WORLD

❁

"One thing you'll do when you're discharged is go to high school," the hospital social worker kept telling me. And I did, when I finally left the hospital, if only for a few months, the last few months of my senior year. I went to Grover Cleveland High School in Brooklyn, wheelchair-accessible by 1960s standards. Access was through the basement and there was an elevator to get to the class-rooms. Though I'd learned to walk with braces and crutches as well as I could, I had trouble with distances. So I used the wheelchair most of the time in school.

A dozen or so of us rode the "handicapped bus" every day and, when we didn't have classes, we sat around in the "handicapped homeroom" with our teacher, Mr. Maloney. I quickly made friends with my disabled fellow students. I also quickly fell in love—with Frankie. He'd had polio but walked with braces and crutches much better than I did. Tall, with curly brown hair and deep-set eyes, he was the handsomest boy in the world. But he didn't seem interested in me.

"What's wrong with you?" Audrey shouted on the phone when I told her about Frankie. "Why do you have to fall in love with a handicapped boy? Why can't you get a crush on a normal student?"

One day, Frankie and I found ourselves alone in homeroom. Everyone else was in class, and Mr. Maloney had gone to the rest room. I kept my eyes somewhere in the middle of page 57 of the biography of Madame Marie Curie and pretended I couldn't feel Frankie's eyes on me. Then he was beside me, his arm around my shoulders, his warm breath on my face and his lips finding mine. I kissed him back with all the passion and awkwardness of young love.

On the bus going home that day, Frankie sat next to me. I was beaming. I wanted everybody to know we were now "an item." But that's not what Frankie had in mind.

"You're a beautiful girl. Even though you're handicapped, you look good enough to attract normal guys. You know, I've gone out with two normal girls already. Don't get me wrong... I really like you. You're the most beautiful handicapped girl I know. But why should we settle for each other when we can both do better?"

I wanted to say, Frankie, I don't think I could do better. You're the handsomest boy I know, period. But who was I to argue? I tried to ignore Frankie after that revelation, and I stopped talking about him with Audrey. I never told her about his kiss.

Thanks to Mr. Maloney's recommendation, I was admitted to St. John's University in Jamaica, Queens. The Office of Vocational Rehabilitation, a governmental agency that assisted disabled people in becoming employable, approved payment of full tuition. My father was so proud, he told everyone.

To be closer to the college, we moved to Queens. My father bought a house in Bayside. He'd worked hard to save enough for a down payment. "*La nostra casetta,*" he called it, "our little house." My mother loved the backyard, where she planted rosebushes.

My father promised to buy me a car so I'd be able to drive from our new house to St. John's, which wasn't far. I'd been learning to drive with hand controls. The device, which could be applied to any car, was surprisingly simple. All I had to do was pull up on the lever to accelerate and push down to brake.

Audrey was accepted at Hofstra University, on Long Island. Hofstra had a better reputation than St. John's, and was known to be easier to navigate in a wheelchair. Her parents would be paying Audrey's tuition, higher than St. John's, undoubtedly. She had gotten a car on her birthday: a Mustang—bright blue, to match her eyes.

"I'm so glad you live in Queens now," she said the first time she drove to visit me. "I don't think I'd trust myself to drive to Brooklyn." But she looked so sure of herself behind that wheel, she probably could have driven not only to Brooklyn but to Manhattan and even to the Bronx. She came over two or three times a week. She'd blow the horn and I'd come out of the house and get in her car.

We rode around for hours. Northern Boulevard, Utopia Parkway, cruising along, back and forth. If we were in the mood to speed, we'd get on the Long Island Expressway, then get off at one exit, make a left turn, and get back on. Seeing us in the car, no one could tell we were handicapped. We were two hot chicks, a blonde and a brunette, out joyriding. Guys on the street whistled when we stopped at a light; from other cars, some men blew us kisses, while others made lewd remarks— the kind of behavior women in consciousness-raising groups around the country were calling offensive and demeaning.

Not us. Audrey and I soaked in every lustful look. We savored every obscene word.

I thought we were just having fun. But then Audrey would say, "All I have to do is park, get the chair out, and they'll run the other way so fast! We're both beautiful… we could have it all. Why do we have to be handicapped?"

I didn't have an answer to that question, but I don't think she expected one. She went on: "I don't want to live as a handicapped woman. I want to be a real woman; I want a real life; I want happiness. Don't you?" She did expect an answer to that.

I didn't know how to argue with her. I nodded in sad agreement. Of course I wanted a real life. Of course I wanted happiness.

"Why do we have to be handicapped?" Audrey asked again. And sometimes she sighed and said, "We'd be better off dead."

Whenever people said "better off dead" when talking about disability, I tried to shield myself by pretending I didn't hear. But I couldn't with Audrey.

"I hate when you say that! I don't like the way we're treated, but I don't want us to be dead. That's really scary!"

"Chicken!" Audrey muttered.

I got my own car when I started college. It was a brown secondhand Mercury, the best my father could afford. Audrey still came by on weekends, or on days when neither one of us had classes, to take me for a ride.

"My car is the kind people look at, and when they look at the car, they see us," she said.

I was glad my car wasn't the kind people looked at. I didn't want to be distracted by people's looks. I wanted to fully enjoy the freedom I experienced behind the wheel. It was the same sensation I experienced when rolling in my wheelchair, multiplied ten times, a hundred times. In my car, I was completely independent. There were no steps, no stairs, no barriers on the road. Once in the car, I never needed anyone's help, never needed to be pushed or lifted. I was equal to every other driver in every other car. I could go anywhere, go everywhere. With nothing to stop me. On my own. On my way.

In college, I began to understand what Audrey had been going through trying to fit into "the real world." There was no "handicapped homeroom" at St. John's. If there were disabled students, I didn't see them.

I was eager to make friends. But none of the college students seemed interested in me. The guys ignored me. The girls were nice enough, smiled and asked how I was or if I needed help. Sometimes I sat in the lounge with girls I knew from my classes and listened to them talking about their boyfriends. They never tried to include me in those conversations. Sometimes they looked at me, as if suddenly realizing I was there, looked at one another, and stopped talking. Just like the neighbor girls back in Sicily.

I spent the long breaks between classes in the ladies' room, or sitting in my parked car if the weather was good. I'd started smoking, thinking it would help me fit in. But I never liked it. I lit a cigarette, took a few puffs, and put it out.

I was exhausted all the time. Since the campus was not very accessible, I left my wheelchair in the car and walked with my braces and crutches. I struggled up and down steps. I walked slowly in the long corridors, praying I wouldn't get knocked down by a student hurrying to get to class. I fell at times, nearly dying of embarrassment. Halfway through the semester, I fell going up the steps to the library and hurt more than my pride. I broke my knee and ended up in a hospital in Queens.

This hospital was nothing like HSS. There were no children or teenagers. I was the only girl on the floor. The men there—the orderlies, the janitors, the interns, and some of the patients—all seemed quite appreciative of my youth and prettiness. I mentioned that to Audrey when I called her to tell her what had happened.

"Of course, they don't know you're handicapped; they think you just have a broken leg."

I didn't care what they thought. After being ignored by the college men at St. John's, it felt good to get some male attention. I flirted shamelessly.

I was in the hospital for just five days. The last night I was there, I woke up from a deep sleep, to see a man standing at my bedside. He had pulled the curtain halfway around my bed. But the light coming in from the open door was enough for me to recognize the good-looking orderly I'd flirted with in the evening. His penis was out of his pants. It seemed huge. He was holding it in one hand and his other hand was at his mouth, his index finger pressing against his tightly closed lips.

I was too shocked to utter a word. He smiled at me when he realized

I was going to keep quiet, but he kept his index finger in front of his lips. He was stroking his penis faster now. I watched, not sure whether to be frightened or fascinated. Then he grabbed his penis with both hands, arched his back, and semen squirted over my bed.

Oh no! How was I going to explain the sticky sheet to the nurses? He smiled as he put his shrunken penis back in his pants, pulled up his zipper, and went out the door.

I was discharged the next morning. The bed was left unmade. No one noticed the spots on the sheet. I called Audrey as soon as I got home.

"He didn't make you take it in your mouth?"

"No!"

"Or even in your hand?"

"No!"

"Would you have done it?"

"Audrey! Of course not! I didn't want him to do what he did!"

"But you didn't scream. You could have screamed."

She was right. Why hadn't I screamed? Had I liked watching him? Would I have taken his penis in my hand had he asked? I had flirted with him, after all.

"That's true; I could have screamed."

"Oh, no, you don't have to feel guilty on top of it." Audrey's voice was suddenly soft and comforting. "It's okay. Men usually don't even see us. They don't think of us as women because we're handicapped. So we have to be glad for any attention we get."

I went back to St. John's in my wheelchair, with a cast on my leg. I needed help getting the chair in and out of the car. I waited by many doors, sometimes in rain and snow, for someone to get me up the steps. Certain buildings I just couldn't get into. I couldn't use many of the rest rooms. But at least I could zoom up and down the corridors and didn't have to be afraid of getting knocked over.

Because I wasn't exhausted all the time, I was able to try harder at making friends. I became more outgoing. I didn't wait to be included in conversations, but joined in at the right moment with an appropriate remark. Men weren't standing in line to ask me out on a date, but they seemed to notice me now. I didn't have to wait long before someone volunteered to get me up or down steps.

One guy often appeared at the right time, when I needed help. I figured we had the same schedule. He was nice-looking, with dark hair and brown eyes. His name was Paul.

"Ready to earn your brownie points?" I joked as he grabbed the push handles of my chair.

"How about a kiss instead?"

"Okay. But you'll have to take an IOU, because I'm late for class."

I kept using the wheelchair after the cast came off. If asked why I wasn't walking, I had lots of excuses: I was afraid to fall again; the weather was nasty; my leg still hurt. I didn't mention that when using the wheelchair, I had more energy for socializing.

I made friends with a girl from my English class, Jenny. We had lunch together at least twice a week. She was pretty and popular, and had a gorgeous boyfriend named Tom. Jenny loved to talk about their relationship, which was a stormy one—lots of fights and reconciliations. I listened patiently, nodding a lot and being as sympathetic as a friend should be.

Once, after a long lunch, which ended with Jenny crying over her strawberry ice cream while I patted her arm with sisterly affection, she asked, "Aren't you glad you don't have to deal with this stuff?"

"What stuff?"

"You know, this boyfriend stuff!"

"Well, since I don't have a boyfriend right now, I don't have to deal with it. But I'm sure I will in the future."

She looked at me as if I were speaking a foreign language. "Do you think you'll ever get a boyfriend?"

Like everyone else, Jenny believed relationships were not possible for me. She had generously told me about hers, so I could have some vicarious experience. We left the cafeteria without speaking.

I stopped having lunch with Jenny and started having lunch with

Anna. She was friends with Paul, the guy who was collecting IOUs from me. She'd come along one day as Paul was getting me up the steps to the library, and she casually grabbed the footrests of my chair to help. Anna was the opposite of Jenny—not that pretty, and though she had friends, male and female, she wasn't popular and didn't have a boyfriend. Nor did she show much interest in being popular or having a boyfriend. We talked about serious issues—civil rights, women's liberation, the war in Vietnam... I was reluctant to end our conversations.

Anna also loved folk music, and we planned to go to a concert together. "Maybe we can ask Paul to join us. Does he like folk music?"

Anna didn't answer.

"Paul, your friend, do you know if he likes folk music?"

She was looking at me as if I'd turned into a Martian.

"Yes, he does," she whispered finally.

"Well? Do you think he would go with us?"

She sighed. "It's not fair."

I was puzzled. "What's not fair?"

"It's not fair that you're handicapped."

"You're telling me!" I laughed.

"It's not fair for you, and it's not fair for Paul, who's in love with you."

"Paul is in love with me?"

I was astounded. Other than a little teasing, there had been no sign of any love interest. He showed up at the right time to help me get in and out of inaccessible buildings—that was all. The IOUs for kisses had remained unclaimed.

"How do you know Paul's in love with me?"

"We're friends. He confides in me." She sounded burdened. "It's very painful for him, you know, to be in love with you, knowing nothing can come of it. I understand him so well. I know all about love that cannot be. I was once in love with a priest."

What the hell was she talking about? Love that cannot be? In love with a priest? Oh, yes, of course. Like being in love with a cripple. Knowing nothing can come of it.

"I understand him so well," she repeated, and sighed. "Poor Paul!"

I couldn't stand it. "Come on! You don't expect me to feel sorry for him!"

"Well, you could try to be more considerate of his feelings. The priest I was in love with tried to stay away from me..."

I'd had more than I could take. "I don't want to know about the priest, Anna. Good-bye."

I called Audrey from a pay phone. She was home from school that day. "I can't believe this!" she kept saying as she listened to my story. When I stopped talking, she asked, "Do you have any more classes?"

"American history at three."

"Cut it. Get in your car and drive out here."

"I don't know..."

"Drive out here," she insisted. "I've got a story, too, very similar to yours. You're not going to believe it."

She was waiting for me in her car. She pulled out of her driveway and motioned for me to pull in. I parked, got out on my crutches, and went to sit in her car. She told me her story while driving around the neighborhood. I listened as I looked for signs of the coming spring: daffodils ready to bloom in front of one house, violets around the lawn of another...

"What are you looking at? Are you listening to me?" She got annoyed when she didn't have my undivided attention. Her story was better than mine. I'd learned about Paul's love from a third party. She'd learned from the guy himself, who confessed his love for her and his anguish at knowing nothing could come of it.

"To me, you're like a nun," he had declared.

And Audrey had replied, "I can't be a nun! I'm Jewish!"

That struck me as outrageously funny. I started laughing and couldn't stop. Audrey was soon laughing, too, so hard that she couldn't drive anymore. She parked the car on a quiet street, in front of someone's newly planted lawn, and we both grew hysterical, laughing harder and harder, hitting each other, then hugging, shaking and hiccupping, mascara-stained tears running down our cheeks. Until we weren't even sure if we were laughing or crying.

Later that day, I called my mother to tell her I would be spending the night at Audrey's. Then we got all made-up and dressed to kill. She wore a skintight electric blue sweater and I wore a skintight hot-pink one—one of hers. We put both our chairs in her car, which was always a feat, and drove out to a club that had no steps. She parked in the "No Parking" zone in front of the door.

"You'll get a ticket," I said.

"Fuck it!"

"You have a foul mouth."

"I know." She laughed.

While struggling to get our chairs out of the car, we couldn't help but notice a group of young people on the sidewalk—staring at us. I tried to concentrate on securing my leg rests. Audrey, sitting straight in her chair, pushed her long blond hair back with a flick of her hand, raised her head defiantly, and stared back.

"Like the show? Wanna give us a round of applause?"

I knew she was in top form.

We'd been to that club before, but we'd never attracted so much attention as that night. Was it the skintight sweaters, the way we were moving to the music in our wheelchairs, or the vibes we were sending out?

Audrey started it. "If I wasn't handicapped, you could come home with me and fuck me all night," I heard her say to a guy with longish blond hair who'd bought her a drink. He must have whispered "Let's do it anyway," because she said, "Oh no, believe me, you don't want to risk falling in love with me! It would be very painful for you because nothing can come of it. A handicapped girl is like a nun."

I caught up quickly. I wrapped my arm around the arm of the guy who had just handed me a drink and whispered, "Isn't it a shame I'm handicapped? I could be dancing with you, rubbing my breasts against you…"

"Do you give money to the telethon?" Audrey was asking.

"If you give enough money, we'll get cured, and then you'll want us to be your girlfriends," I chimed in.

We kept the game going all night—or at least until our bladders got too full. Accessible rest rooms were unheard of. When we couldn't hold it anymore, we had to leave.

"I'm gonna wet my pants in five seconds," Audrey whispered as we rolled out the door.

There was a ticket stuck under her windshield wiper. She left it there. Once in the car, our chairs folded and jammed into the back, she handed me the jar she kept under the seat for emergencies.

"Don't you want to go first?" I asked.

"Too late for me."

I saw her pants were all wet. I peed in the jar, emptied it out the door, and we headed back to her house.

Audrey's mother had opened the foldaway bed for me. I got undressed quickly, took off my braces, and lay down. I was tired. I needed to get at least a few hours' sleep. I wanted to drive to St. John's in the morning and not miss my nine o'clock English class. I unfolded the blanket Audrey's mother had left for me and got under it.

But Audrey kept moving around in her wheelchair, not at all eager to get in bed. She was still wearing her sexy electric blue sweater but had taken off her wet pants and underpants and sat there bare-assed. From her hips to her knees, her thighs, lacking muscles, formed a soft flattened V against the wheelchair seat. Her skinny legs, lined with pink scars, dangled, her bare feet, not quite reaching the footrests, pointing straight forward from surgically fused ankles. We both made a point of looking at our naked bodies in the mirror only from the waist up, but we were so familiar with each other's bodies. Looking at Audrey's legs now was like seeing my own in a mirror.

She was fumbling with her jewelry box, which she had taken out of the bottom drawer of her dresser and unlocked with a tiny key.

"Want to see what I've got?" She didn't sound mischievous, which she usually did when she asked that question.

"Sure." I was too sleepy to show much enthusiasm.

She took out a pill bottle and held it up to me. There were quite a few pills in it, judging by the sound it made when Audrey shook it.

"What are they?"

She twisted the cap off and let some pills fall into her palm. She smiled as she stuck her hand in front of my face. It was full of red capsules.

"What are they?" I asked again.

"Se-con-als." She enunciated each syllable.

"Sleeping pills?"

She nodded, still smiling.

"Where did you get them?"

"From my mother. I ask her for one now and then, saying I can't sleep. And I steal one or two when I get the chance. I've been hoarding them for months." She spread them all out on her bed and started counting.

"How many do you think I'll have to take to die?"

"I don't know."

"I don't think I have enough yet." She shook her head.

Though still exhausted, I wasn't sleepy anymore. "Would you really do it, Audrey?"

"Do you want to live, just to be treated like a leper?" She was good at answering a question with a question.

"The guys at the club weren't treating us like lepers, Audrey."

"Did any of them ask you for a date?" She had a point there. "Men notice us because we're beautiful and act sexy. But that just makes us more freakish, don't you see? When they're attracted to us, men feel like they're not normal, and they resent us for that. I guess if we were homely, things would be simpler."

She was playing with the pills, scooping them back into the bottle, then making them fall out onto the bed again.

"Oh, come on, Audrey! You make it sound like we don't have a right to be attractive. The way I see it, if men resent us, it's their problem." I pulled the blanket over my shoulders.

She sneered at me. "Oh, yeah? It's their problem? But we're the ones who will never have a real relationship, get married, have a family, be happy…"

I'd been learning about the women's liberation movement, had even read Betty Friedan's *The Feminine Mystique,* so I proclaimed, "I don't need a man to be happy."

"Oh, excuse me! Are you going to become a lesbian? I doubt it would be any easier with women."

"Nothing wrong with being a lesbian, but that's not what I meant, Audrey."

"Oh, forgive me; I forgot. You're going to have a career! You think that when you graduate, they'll be waiting for you with all kinds of job offers. That's why you study all the time. Are you going to make the dean's list?"

I didn't answer. Instead, I asked again, "Would you really do it, Audrey?"

She had put all the pills back in the bottle and was putting it back in her jewelry box.

"What do you think?" Again she answered with a question. "Do you think I'm chicken, like you?"

I did make the dean's list. Audrey's average was barely above a D.

What's the use? Why waste the time? That was Audrey's attitude. Was she right? Was I wasting my time trying to get good grades? What job prospects were there for handicapped girls? I had decided to major in English. According to Audrey, I wanted to prove I'd gotten over my "language difficulty." And I was minoring in Italian—to show some loyalty to my native tongue, again according to Audrey.

My father was thrilled when he got the letter of congratulations. He had it engraved onto a gold-colored metal plate and mounted. He hung it up on the living room wall. Anyone who entered our house was escorted straight to it. "*Leggi qua!* Read here!" my father ordered. And they had to read the whole letter, couldn't just read the first sentence, say "How wonderful," and walk away. If the visitor couldn't read English, my father translated the whole letter, adding a few superlatives here and there. Though embarrassed, I was happy to see that my father was proud of me.

But I knew my success in college didn't make up for my not being "cured." I saw the sadness in my father's eyes whenever he looked at me struggling with my braces and crutches. I noticed the angry way he handled my wheelchair when getting it in or out of the car—as if he wanted to smash it on the ground. I knew I was not to blame; still, I felt I had failed him.

My father didn't tell me how he found the new doctor. I knew he had been calling hospitals. We went to see him, and he said a series of muscle transplants might help. Since the muscles used to bend my legs were stronger than those needed to straighten them, they could be repositioned, so I could use them to lock my knees and stand. This type of surgery worked best on children, but with a lot of therapy, I might be able to get rid of the braces. No guarantee, of course.

Following the examination, his secretary explained that though the hospital expenses would be covered by Blue Cross, the doctor's fee was a little high. "No problem," my father said, interrupting her. He told her that he would make up the difference, work overtime if he had to.

What could I say? That I didn't want to get cut up anymore? That I wanted to take the Shakespeare course the next semester? Wasn't I happy to be given the chance to get rid of the braces? Wasn't I grateful to my father? I went into the hospital in the fall of 1966, as cheerful as ever.

The hospital was drab compared to HSS. Very few of the patients were young. The few who were never stayed long. They had broken bones, mostly. None were disabled like me.

Usually, in my room were women in their nineties with broken hips, who slept constantly. A few times, I rang my bell to call a nurse, suspecting my roommate was dead. But the nurses knew I needed urgent care only if I'd just had surgery. The best I could hope for was a "Can I help you?" over the intercom.

"I think my roommate passed away!"

"Okay, I'll be there in a minute!" the voice on the intercom told me. I knew it would be at least a half hour. Luckily, no one died.

I read to pass the time, anything from Shakespeare to Harold Robbins, from *Rolling Stone* to *True Confessions,* and watched the soaps on TV.

I was in and out of that hospital for almost a year. I missed a year of college. I missed two big NYC demonstrations against the war. I didn't go to San Francisco during the Summer of Love. I did wear flowers in my hair, which was probably all I would have done had I been out of the hospital. I had transplant after transplant—four or five or six. My mind erased the memories of pain associated with the surgeries. Pleasant memories of my time there were retained: my mother spoon-feeding me her tiny meatballs in broth; my father reciting poetry in Sicilian; Sarah, my Blythedale counselor, visiting me and playing her guitar.

Other memories of that hospital would have been better forgotten: being pushed in my chair to therapy by an orderly and feeling his hard penis pressing against my back and the nape of my neck; waking up in the middle of the night because my breasts were being fondled or a man's hand was between my thighs.

I was young and enjoyed male attention, especially since outside of the hospital I didn't get much. Often I flirted without realizing I was doing it. I flirted with the orderlies, the X-ray technicians, the interns. Then, when they did things that shocked and humiliated me, I didn't know how to react and resist. I passively submitted, feeling it was my fault.

A cute intern often stopped by my room to tell me how beautiful I was. He asked what I was reading or what I was watching on TV. He said he wanted to take me out on a date when I got out of the hospital. I smiled a lot, told him he was cute.

One night, I woke up from a deep sleep—especially deep due to the sleeping pills the nurses generously and indiscriminately handed out every night. The intern was by my bed. My young body was responding to the skillful movements of his hands. Then he was on top of me, and before I knew what was happening, he was penetrating me.

When he was done, he lay on top of me for a few minutes, and I lay quietly under the weight of his body. Then he got up and left. I pulled a tissue out of the box on my nightstand and wiped between my legs. There was blood mixed with his sticky semen. My blood. He had gotten all the way inside me. I definitely was not a virgin anymore.

Was it rape? Or was there consent? I didn't scream. I responded to his caresses while half- asleep. And I had been flirting with him. Was it "free love"? Or was I a slut? Everyone said I was such a nice girl, a cheerful girl. Such a good patient.

A scalpel or a penis. What was the difference? I'd gotten used to strangers touching me, handling me, manipulating me, doctors cutting me up, over and over again, inflicting pain. Pain or pleasure. What was the difference? Did it matter what they did to me? After all, what claim could I have on this defective, damaged, disabled body? Wasn't I supposed to be grateful to the doctors who were trying to fix it? Wasn't I supposed to be grateful to any man for any attention I could get?

After the intern's nocturnal visit, I tried to call Audrey. I needed the comfort of her voice. I wanted her to tell me I wouldn't get pregnant. I hadn't seen the intern put on a condom, but it was dark in the room. Surely a doctor would have been careful. Still, I worried. To whom could I confide but my blood sister? I couldn't upset my mother. And I was afraid anyone else would have blamed me for what had happened.

Audrey hadn't been to see me at all. And we hadn't been talking on the phone as much. I assumed she was busy in college. When I called her house, her mother answered.

ापतितेल

She sounded surprised to hear my voice. "Audrey? Audrey's in the hospital."

In the hospital? What hospital? What for? Audrey was all done with hospitalizations. Her parents had long ago stopped being obsessed with the cure. Why was Audrey in the hospital? Her mother seemed reluctant to answer.

"Do you have a phone in your room? I'll tell Audrey to call you as soon as she feels better."

I gave her my room number and hung up. Only then did I remember the red pills. I doubled over in my chair, as if I'd been punched in the gut. Oh no! I should have warned her mother. But how could I have ratted on Audrey? She showed me the pills because we were blood sisters and she trusted me.

"Oh, please, Audrey, don't die," I repeated over and over. "I don't want you to die. I don't want you to leave me."

Her mother had said she would have Audrey call me. That meant she wasn't going to die. But why wasn't she calling me? I waited for three days, too afraid to call her mother again. I hardly left my room, because I didn't want to miss Audrey's call. But then, when the call came at nine in the morning, I was so sure it was my mother, who always called at that time, I answered in Italian. *"Pronto."*

"I fucked it up, but I'll do better next time." Audrey's voice sounded weak and hoarse.

I couldn't talk. I held the receiver with both hands and cried.

Her mother had gotten up in the middle of the night because she couldn't sleep, Audrey told me. She had looked in on Audrey and noticed she was breathing funny. She'd awakened Audrey's father, who had taken her pulse and immediately picked her up in his arms and carried her to the car. Still in their pajamas, her parents had rushed Audrey to the hospital, where they pumped her stomach.

I listened, breathless, to Audrey's dramatic story. It was as if she wasn't talking about herself. She could have been describing the last episode of our favorite soap opera.

"Your parents must be so glad you didn't die."

"I'll have to plan it better next time."

"I'm sure glad you didn't die, Audrey!" My voice shook. I was afraid she'd get mad and hang up.

"I love you, Audrey," I whispered into the receiver.

"I love you, too," she whispered back.

She came to visit me two weeks later, looking more beautiful than ever. Her hair was longer and blonder, her eyes bluer and brighter. Everyone had been supportive, she told me. Even the psychiatrist she was now seeing was sympathetic. Her college friends all understood why she had tried to kill herself. In her place, they, too, would want to die.

"But aren't your friends glad you didn't die?"

She didn't answer.

"I'm sure glad you didn't die!"

This time, she answered. "I know." Her voice was dreamy, and as soft as melted butter. "If only life could be as simple as it was when we were at HSS with all the other kids. If only we didn't have to live in the real world."

6

BETTER OFF

❖

I hadn't been able to spend much time with Audrey since the start of the fall semester. I was carrying eighteen credits, trying to gain back some of the time lost while in the hospital. The muscle transplants had made my legs stronger, so I could walk farther without getting too exhausted. But I still needed braces and crutches. I went for physical therapy twice a week, and did my daily exercises religiously. I acted as if I still believed I could get rid of the braces. But I knew it wasn't going to happen.

Audrey's mother called on a Saturday afternoon, while I was studying.

"We had to take Audrey to the hospital again."

I knew what she meant. I got in my car. I didn't leave a note for my parents, who were out shopping. I wouldn't have known what to say.

Audrey's mother was standing at the door of the hospital room, looking tired and not so glamorous. She waved me in. The hospital bed was so neat, the covers so tightly drawn over Audrey's slender body, it almost looked empty. In the dim light, Audrey's face, so pale and still, was almost indistinguishable from the white sheet. The only recognizable feature was the mass of blond hair spread out like a golden halo on the pillow. I wanted to touch Audrey's hair, smooth it out, but I was afraid to wake her. She was hooked up to a beeping machine, probably a heart monitor. I stood leaning on my crutches by the bed, counting the beeps.

Thanks for coming. Audrey's mother mouthed the words without making any sound.

I nodded. And we stood side by side in silence, watching Audrey sleep.

I wanted Audrey's mother to tell me what had happened. How many pills had Audrey taken and how did she get them? Did she steal them from her? Of course not! After the first attempt, her mother would have made sure the pills were out of Audrey's reach. Did the sympathetic psychiatrist write her a prescription? He couldn't have, knowing what she planned to do.

Audrey's mother's eyes were probing me. She assumed Audrey always confided in me. What could I say if she asked me what I knew? That this time Audrey had not shown me any pills? That she didn't trust me, since I'd told her I didn't want her to die?

I didn't ask Audrey's mother any questions and she didn't ask me any. The machine kept beeping. Audrey slept. After about an hour, I left.

The next morning, the phone rang. "How rude of me to sleep through your visit yesterday!" Audrey's voice was hoarse but clear.

"You sure sound awake now! Do you promise to stay awake if I come see you today?"

"I'll try if you try not to be boring!"

During the next few days, everyone who visited Audrey tried to be as cheerful as possible. As if by tacit consensus, no one made reference to the reason Audrey was in the hospital. We acted as if she were recovering from a bad bout of flu.

"Audrey's doing great!" one of her college friends said as we both waited for the elevator. "She is such a brave girl!"

I wondered about the meaning of that remark. Was Audrey brave because she had tried to kill herself? I gave Audrey's friend a puzzled look. She gave me a big sad smile.

"You're brave, too!" she said.

"Not me. Audrey always says I'm chicken."

Did Audrey's friend think I was brave because she imagined I, too, wanted to commit suicide? Or were we both, Audrey and I, brave simply because we were handicapped? Brave if we lived, maybe even more brave if we died.

It wasn't until Audrey was home from the hospital and I went out to Long Island that I learned the details of what had happened. She told me the story while driving around her neighborhood. Sitting in the passenger seat, I listened as I admired the colors of the autumn leaves. She had gone to a new doctor and had easily gotten him to write her a prescription.

"I just said I couldn't sleep because I was depressed over being handicapped," she said, chuckling.

When her parents decided to go to the Catskills with some friends, she thought the timing was perfect. She had been to the Catskills with her parents many times, always spending a night or two at the Concord Hotel. But this time she couldn't go, she told them; she'd been invited to a party, this of all nights, the event of the season, not to be missed. One of her friends would sleep over afterward. She was so convincing, so improved with the psychiatrist's help, her parents never suspected. So why had they changed their plans? Her father ate something that didn't agree with him and they headed back home, stopping at every rest station so he could go to the bathroom.

"My luck, can you believe it? Now I'm back at square one!" Audrey had parked the car on a quiet street and was lighting a joint. I didn't ask her how she'd gotten it.

She took a drag, then handed it to me. "Don't be a party pooper. Have a toke."

I took a drag and the harsh smoke burned my throat. I started coughing. She took the joint from my hand, took another drag, then put it out. I wanted to yell at her, shake her, hit her.

"You're my blood sister."

She put her arms around me and we hugged in silence.

The following year, 1968, was traumatic for the whole country.

We lived through two assassinations. On April 4, in Memphis, Dr. King was shot. I heard the news on my car radio, on Grand Central Parkway, on my way home from St. John's. Unable to go on driving, I pulled off the road and cried, until a police car stopped and a young black officer knocked on my window. Every time I'd hear the police called "pigs" in the future, I would remember this young officer's hand on mine and the kindness in his voice.

Two months later, on June 5, Bobby Kennedy was killed. He had just won the California Democratic primary, giving his young supporters renewed hope that he might become our next president.

That year also saw the escalation of the Vietnam War and the Mỹ Lai Massacre. And we watched the police acting as true enemies, attacking demonstrators outside the Chicago Democratic Convention with truncheons, Mace, and tear gas.

Audrey and I now sported long patchwork skirts, which conveniently hid our legs. We discarded our bras, which at age thirteen we'd been proud to wear. Around our necks we piled love beads and silver chains with peace symbols. When Audrey came over, I'd get in her car, but instead of driving around aimlessly, we headed for Greenwich Village. It was the mecca, the place where being different was valued, not scorned. Among the hippies, we almost felt like we belonged. We hung out in Washington Square Park—joined in a protest if one was going on, listened to the folksingers who congregated there, bought a nickel bag of grass. I was the more political one, more vehement in my opposition to the war. I quoted Dr. King, whose picture I had on the wall above my desk. Audrey could sing just like

Janis Joplin. I always wanted to go to demonstrations; she wanted to go to rock concerts.

During the first part of the year, I'd broken my left knee, and soon after my right ankle. Unfortunately, the muscle transplants did nothing to prevent the falls and breaks. I broke my knee when I fell going down the stairs to the cavernous Gaslight Cafe, probably the most inaccessible folk-music club in the Village. I broke my ankle when I slipped in the bathroom at home. Both times I was hospitalized briefly, then had to wear casts—six weeks for the knee and four for the ankle.

"Your legs are a lot more trouble than they're worth," Audrey commented.

"You're right; I should have them cut off," I joked.

"Or stop walking."

Audrey had never wanted to walk with braces and crutches. She didn't think it was worth the effort. I would have agreed if I hadn't felt duty-bound to walk. With a broken leg, I could use my wheelchair without feeling I was being lazy.

Neither one of us had much trouble getting someone to help us, but I had more trouble asking for and receiving help. Maybe because I'd been so dependent as a little girl in Sicily.

That summer, after we both turned twenty, we went to a Planned Parenthood clinic to be fitted for diaphragms. "We can't always rely on a guy to wear a rubber, and besides, those things can break. A girl has to take responsibility and make sure she's protected." Audrey was very persuasive. Perhaps she wanted to convince herself as well as me that we were "real women." She wanted the Pill, but I'd heard rumors of health hazards, so we settled for diaphragms.

"Why are you here?" The nurse at the front desk acted surprised.

"For the same reason other women are. We don't want to get pregnant," Audrey replied.

"Really?"

She kept staring at us while we waited to go into the examination room.

The female gynecologist, who saw Audrey first, then me, didn't comment about our disabilities, but our concurrent impressions were that she was trying a bit too hard to appear professional and casual.

We practiced putting our diaphragms in and taking them out whenever we slept at each other's houses. "Wanna play with the yarmulkes?" That's what Audrey called them.

We learned to handle them like real pros, but we weren't getting much use out of them. We both had one-night stands with guys we met in Washington Square Park. They promised to call but never did. I wasn't too disappointed, since the experience for me wasn't as "groovy" as Audrey told me hers had been. At least what I remembered of it wasn't— I'd gotten so high in order to go through with it, my groove sensor might have been a bit off.

In the fall, at a concert at the Nassau Coliseum, Audrey met Ray. I hadn't gone with her; I didn't have time for concerts at the start of a new semester. Six or seven years older, Ray had been an accountant or something sensible like that before letting his hair grow and becoming a draft dodger and a hippie. They had a few dates, and soon Audrey was referring to him as her boyfriend. We started spending less time together. I was busy with school; she was busy with Ray. I did meet him once. Though not terribly handsome, he was attentive to Audrey. Yet something seemed askew. Maybe I was jealous, since I didn't have a boyfriend of my own.

Then Audrey told me stories that made me like Ray even less. He carried her up the stairs of inaccessible places, but when she wanted to leave, he refused to carry her down. He made her beg and cry. If they were in a place where she needed help to use the bathroom, he made her wait until she wet her pants.

"He says he likes me because I'm handicapped," Audrey told me. "He's never nasty; he just wants to play games."

The end of the semester was approaching, and I was studying for exams when Audrey called me to tell me she was in the hospital. Her voice didn't sound weak or hoarse. She had not taken pills this time; she had slit her wrists.

"I wanted to try something different," she said, as if talking about ordering takeout. "But it was a mistake. Too messy."

The thought of the blood made me dizzy and nauseous. I squeezed my eyes shut to blot out the image.

"But at least I didn't make the mess at home. I did it at Ray's."

Apparently, she'd had enough of the games. When, after a take-out dinner at his place, she wanted to leave and he refused to carry her downstairs, she threatened to break up with him. He got furious.

"And who else do you think will have you?" he said.

She locked herself in the bathroom and used his razor on her wrists. It was an impulsive act, not a planned attempt like the other two. He had to unscrew the doorknob to get the door open. He wrapped a towel around her arms and carried her down and into his car. Then he brought down her chair and threw it into the trunk. He left her in the emergency room while she was being bandaged, before her parents got there.

She never heard from him again. I wanted us to confront Ray, call him a sick coward. But Audrey just gave a dismissive wave of her hand. "My fault for being a sucker."

I concentrated on getting through the spring semester. Having to spend another year at St. John's was a drag. I wanted to be where the action was, at Columbia or at New York University.

I broke my leg again in the summer of '69, when I tripped over a tile my father had left in the hallway after replacing the kitchen floor. I blamed my carelessness, not wanting him to feel guilty. Once in a while, he still talked about looking for a better doctor, but it was now too hard to keep up the pretense.

That August, Audrey and I watched on TV as half a million young people danced in the rain at Woodstock.

"It's your fault we aren't there. If you hadn't broken your leg again, we could have gone."

"Sure, we'd have fun stuck in the mud in our wheelchairs!"

The fall of '69 was unusually cold. But I convinced Audrey we should go to Washington on November 15 for what would turn out to be the largest demonstration against the war in Vietnam. We took off in the morning in Audrey's car. It was still pitch-dark, and freezing. We took along two guys we knew from various protests. But Audrey didn't trust them to drive. They slept in the backseat, their legs stretched out over Audrey's folded chair, which lay between them. Mine was in the trunk. Audrey and I took turns driving, stopping every hour or so and climbing over each other to switch seats.

I was the one to drive us into D.C. The traffic was at a crawl, and throngs of people were on the sidewalks. We had planned to park in the Union Station garage, but Audrey spotted a space and yelled at me to pull in. I pointed to a sign that said NO PARKING, AUTHORIZED VEHICLES ONLY.

Audrey laughed. "Just park the fucking car!"

Our friends pushed us in our chairs in the huge crowd starting to move toward the Washington Monument. There were cops all around.

"Why did you bring them? It's not safe for them here." The officer was addressing our friends.

"What makes you think they brought us?" Audrey pointed her chin up at him. "We brought them, from New York. They slept in the backseat of my car while the two of us drove."

The cop walked away.

Some of the marchers stared at us; others thanked us for being there.

"What are you thanking us for? We're here because we're against the war, just like you." Audrey was annoyed.

I was too excited to let anything bother me. I'd been dreaming of going to a big demonstration in Washington since my Blythedale days, when I'd listened spellbound to Seth and Sarah talk about the 1963 march. At the rally, Pete Seeger led the crowd in singing over and over "All we are saying is give peace a chance." I loved John Lennon's song but still preferred "We Shall Overcome." Though by midday it warmed up, the temperature never reached forty degrees, and it was breezy. Shivering from the cold and the intense emotion, I cried for all those who had died in the war, American and Vietnamese. And I cried because whenever I'd thought of going to a demonstration in D.C., I'd always envisioned Dr. King speaking.

That whole year, Audrey didn't talk much about killing herself. At times, though, she'd repeat certain things she'd heard—at a party, someone had said he'd prefer the electric chair to a wheelchair; during a class discussion of Darwin's theory of survival of the fittest, a girl said it was amazing disabled people were alive, and then after class she told Audrey how much she admired her. Audrey also liked to talk about a young man from Massapequa, another Long Island town, a marine who had returned from Vietnam paralyzed.

"Everyone says it would be better if he'd died in the war."

One day in early April 1970, the title of an article in the *Daily News* caught my attention: "You Can Be President, Not Teacher, with Polio."

The article was about a young woman named Judy Heumann, who had contracted polio as a baby and used a wheelchair. She wanted to be a teacher and had graduated from Long Island University, in Brooklyn, with a degree in education. She passed all her exams with flying colors. All but one: Because of her disability, she failed the physical. She was therefore denied her license to teach.

Most of us would have gone home and cried our eyes out. But Judy Heumann refused to accept the commonly held opinion that a disabled woman could not be a teacher. She knew she was fully qualified and believed she had a right to pursue her chosen career. She accused the Board of Education of discriminating against her, and decided to fight back and sue.

I was in awe of this young woman. I never would have had the guts to do what she was doing. It would never have occurred to me that I could sue. I was so impressed that I cut out the newspaper article and taped it to the wall above my desk.

By sheer coincidence, that same day, I received in the mail a brochure about the graduate program in Italian at New York University. One of my professors had recommended the NYU program, seeing how much I enjoyed his classes. I'd sent away for the information, thinking it might be interesting to take a few graduate courses in Italian literature. NYU's main attraction was its location, Greenwich Village. After class, I could hang out in Washington Square Park.

Looking through the brochure, I saw under the heading "Financial Aid," a subheading, "Graduate Teaching Assistantships." An assistant-ship provided full tuition, plus a small salary. It allowed you to teach Italian under the supervision of an experienced instructor. It was a great way to develop language-teaching skills while paying for your courses, the brochure explained.

I had not considered teaching at all—not since as a child I'd fallen in love with my third- grade teacher. But, on impulse, I taped the page about teaching assistantships alongside the newspaper clipping about Judy Heumann.

I called Audrey to tell her about the article and also about the possibility of my going to NYU and becoming an Italian teacher. She didn't seem interested in either topic.

"You could hang out with me in Washington Square Park after my classes."

No response.

A few days after that one-sided conversation, I got a call from Audrey's mother. I had a 9:00 A.M. class and was rushing to get ready to leave. I was less than a month away from graduation.

"Can I speak to Audrey?"

"Audrey?"

"Yes, isn't Audrey there?"

"Here?"

"Yes, there. Audrey left home yesterday, saying she was sleeping over at your house."

I couldn't speak. I got very cold, though it was springtime, a bright sunny day in April. I shivered and clenched my teeth while Audrey's mother yelled, "Answer me! Do you know where Audrey is?"

"I don't know; I haven't talked to Audrey in a couple of days," I finally managed to murmur.

"Oh no!"

Audrey's mother sounded so distraught, I felt I had to say something helpful. "Maybe you misunderstood. She must be staying with another friend."

"What other friend?" There was a hint of hope in her voice.

"Oh, Audrey has so many friends! It could be anyone." And I tried to make myself believe that.

But that terrible cold feeling stayed with me as I drove to school. I got there too late to go to my 9:00 A.M. class. I sat in the students' lounge and shivered. I went to my ten o'clock Twentieth-Century Poetry class but couldn't pay attention. I shook violently as the professor talked about Sylvia Plath.

"Maybe you're getting a fever," a classmate commented.

I called Audrey's house from a pay phone as soon as I got out of class. A voice I didn't recognize answered. She said Audrey's mother was busy at the moment, and asked if I could call later.

I called late in the afternoon, after I got home, and Audrey's mother came to the phone.

"We've notified the police. They're checking the hospitals in case she was in an accident."

That's it, I thought. Audrey was an excellent driver, but she liked to speed, and she liked to smoke pot. She could have gotten herself into an accident. Hopefully, she wasn't hurt too badly.

That night, I dreamed I was back in Riposto. Audrey was with me. The *Addolorata* was beckoning us.

"This is your destiny." I heard Sister Angelica's ominous words, "You can never be happy." A strange darkness was closing in on both of us crippled girls. In my dream, we hugged in silence, as we had many times.

The next day, the police found Audrey's lifeless body lying on the bed of a motel room in Long Beach, not far from her home. Audrey had checked in using her own name. Her car was parked right outside her room. She had hung a DO NOT DISTURB sign on the doorknob, and bolted the door from the inside. The police were called when the maid, who had decided that after two days the room should be cleaned, couldn't get the door open. The coroner determined the cause of death was ingestion of at least sixty Seconals.

A friend of Audrey's mother called to give me the news. I didn't cry. I shivered and shook, as I had for two days. It turned out I really did have a fever. But I insisted on going to the funeral service. My father drove me, since I was too sick to drive myself.

I couldn't cry at the funeral, either. The rabbi said Audrey now had stopped suffering. She had suffered bravely all her life, he said. What a sad life hers had been; she had been so unhappy. And all the people nodded and wiped their eyes.

No, no, I wanted to scream, Audrey was a lot of fun! Audrey and I had been so happy so many times!

I wanted to scream, but I couldn't. I just shivered and shook. I was angry. Angry at Audrey for dying and at myself for being unable to stop her. Angry at the rabbi for spreading lies about her life. Angry at the people wiping their eyes in silent complicity. Angry at the real world, such an inhospitable place for us. Angry at everyone who had made Audrey believe she was better off dead.

I ran a high fever for quite a few days. I slept and the nightmare overtook me. I woke and the nightmare did not end. I shivered and I burned up and I shivered again. And then I cried. Audrey, my blood sister, my beautiful crippled sister. Why did you have to leave me? What will I do without you? What will I do now, Audrey?

7

A PLACE WHERE I NEVER
WANT TO GO BACK

❃

Everything that happened right after Audrey's suicide is mercifully blurry in my memory. Somehow I managed to take my finals. I didn't attend the graduation ceremony. My diploma was mailed to me.

The St. John's Office of Career Planning set up a few job interviews for me. I didn't go to any of them. I told myself I'd go to the next one. But when the day came, I decided I wasn't feeling well enough and stayed in bed, or sat on the lounge chair in the backyard, watching my mother's roses open up big and beautiful, only to drop all their petals and die.

If it rained, I watched the soaps, not even knowing which, *All My Children, General Hospital...* It didn't matter; the plots were all the same, and the actors all looked the same. All so perfect, even when they were supposed to be dying. And when they died, you knew they would come back, if only as their own twin brother or sister.

The best thing about the soaps was that the stories weren't real. It was easier to look at the clean-shaven faces of fake doctors than at the real pictures of the four students killed in May by the National Guard at Kent State. It was easier to admire Susan Lucci's flawless eye makeup than see the anguish on the Vietnamese women's faces, shown regularly during the news hour. Or on my own face in the mirror.

The dreams were the worst. Audrey was always waiting for me to get ready to go with her. *You look gorgeous. Stop messing around; let's go.* I kept fussing with my hair and makeup, reluctant to follow her. Yet, in the dreams, I never quite remembered the reason for my reluctance. Sometimes I dreamed we were in Riposto. Audrey was wearing a nun's habit and beckoning to me.

"You can't be a nun! You're Jewish!" I'd yell, and wake up half laughing, half sobbing.

Even awake, during the day, I'd hear her saying, *Let's go, let's go have some fun,* as if she were right beside me. I'd shake my head, hit it with the palm of my hand a few times, repeating, "Audrey's dead. Audrey's dead."

The days were getting shorter, the sun setting earlier, when the devastating news came that first one, then another of our beloved icons had died of overdoses—Jimi Hendrix in the middle of September and, less than a month after, Janis Joplin. The thought of her dying alone in a hotel room, just like Audrey, ripped my heart apart. For at least a week, I couldn't get out of bed.

Audrey could sing just like Janis. "Take another little piece of my heart..."

My worried parents called their kind, old-fashioned Italian doctor, who made house calls, Dr. Conetta. He arrived with his black bag, and after washing his hands, he stuck a thermometer in my mouth and made me sit up in bed so that he could listen to my lungs with his stethoscope. I obediently breathed in and out. Then, his round, freshly shaved face so close to mine that I could smell the minty sweetness of his aftershave, he took the thermometer out of my mouth and looked straight into my eyes.

"Smile! Doctor's orders. Think of all you've got to smile about!"

I couldn't think of a single thing, but I smiled.

"There! You have a beautiful smile." And he walked away, patting my mother's shoulder.

Dr. Conetta recommended I see a psychologist. To appease my parents, I agreed to it.

The psychologist was nice enough. I hated the chair he had in his office. It was so soft, I sank into it and had a hard time getting up. There was a box of tissues on a side table. I knew people were supposed to cry when they went to psychologists and psychiatrists, but I didn't feel like crying in front of him.

"I have symptoms of severe depression," I said, showing off what I'd learned in the psychology courses I'd taken in college, and trying to make his job easier by providing him with a ready-made diagnosis.

"Tell me how you feel," he insisted, and I stammered, "I don't know…"

I remembered that Audrey had told me she rehearsed before an appointment so she could put on a good show. Had she been alive, she could have coached me, so I, too, could have been an interesting case for the psychologist. But Audrey couldn't help me. She was dead.

I was glad when the holidays came, because the psychologist went on vacation. With the temperature dropping into the twenties, I had a good excuse not to go out. My father brought home a Christmas tree, which my mother decorated with golden glass balls and ribbons. I hated having that tree in our living room. It should have been left alive in the woods, not cut down. I hated knowing that beautiful tree was dead.

My cousins came over for Christmas and again for New Year's, and my mother made my favorite dish, *falsomagro,* a stuffed beef roll cooked in tomato sauce. We had panettone and Sicilian cannoli for dessert and sipped amaretto liqueur. I forced myself to eat but couldn't force myself to enjoy it.

Right after the holidays, I fell in the bathroom and broke my right knee. With a cast on my leg, and the weather getting colder each day, I couldn't be expected to go to the psychologist's office. I spent most of the day in bed. The kind Dr. Conetta, with his black bag, arrived regularly to order me to smile, and I did my best to oblige.

Once in a while, I halfheartedly thought about calling disabled friends from the hospital or from high school. But whenever I opened my little red phone book, looking for numbers to dial, it was the *A* page that appeared first. And every time, my eyes went right to Audrey's name and number. Underneath her home number, which I didn't need to have written down, since there was no way I could have forgotten it, there were other numbers—numbers of hospital rooms where Audrey had stayed after her suicide attempts. It always surprised me to see Audrey's name still on that *A* page, as if it should have disappeared, like Audrey had disappeared by dying. Yet I wouldn't cross it out or white it out. And I never thought of getting a new phone book.

When the cast came off in the beginning of March, I still had no desire to go out. The approaching spring, the time of year I always looked forward to, now carried with it a sense of dread. I did go to physical therapy, but only once a week, having convinced my therapist I could exercise daily on my own. Because my parents were so worried, I agreed to start seeing the psychologist again. I arranged to have my session on the same day as my physical therapy, so I only had to get dressed and put on makeup once a week.

I went to the psychologist in my wheelchair, using my still-not-healed knee as an excuse, and remained in it throughout the session—much better than sinking into that dreadful cushiony chair.

He always asked how I felt about everything.

"My best friend killed herself because she thought she would never be happy."

"How do you feel about that?"

"I'm afraid I will never be happy."

"How do you feel about that?"

On the side table, the box of tissues sat, unnecessary and unused.

In April, to make the psychologist feel successful, and make my parents worry less about me, I decided to go to job interviews. Interesting listings had to be ruled out because the workplace was up flights of stairs or there was no parking available nearby. After many phone calls, I managed to find one or two possibilities.

I sat in the elegantly decorated office of a magazine editor, an attractive woman with platinum streaks in her expertly cut, perfectly coiffed short hair. As friendly as could be, she kept praising me—for my looks, my intelligence, my accomplishments. She had me read an article about the rewards and, at the same time, the strains of pursuing a career while raising a family. It was not an article I would have chosen. She had me proofread parts of it, try to improve on the language of certain sentences. She seemed pleased, repeated we were on the same wave length, said she believed we could work beautifully together, then added, "You could proofread from your own home."

"Oh, I drive. I would have no trouble getting here." There was even a parking garage under the building, which meant I wouldn't waste time trying to find parking close to the entrance.

"I think it would be best," she said, nodding repeatedly and forcefully, though not a hair of her perfect hairdo moved. "This is such a high-profile office."

High-profile? Suddenly, I understood. In my mind, I heard Audrey laughing: *Get real, why would she want a cripple around her fancy office?*

I told the lady editor I would think about her proposal, but I never got back to her. I went to a couple of other interviews, and each time the interviewer was nice but didn't offer me a job. One guy told me the company would be glad to hire me when I got better. Better? Did he mean I needed more education, experience, training?

"Yes, when you'll be able to walk well."

I didn't bother telling him I would never walk well.

I was complaining about the useless aggravation of going to job interviews one day at the dinner table, and noticed my father smiling. My words were anything but cheerful, yet his smile kept growing brighter. Then he announced we were going on a trip to Italy. He was entitled to a two-week vacation on his job, he said. We would go at the end of May or at the beginning of June.

I feigned enthusiasm and got busy helping with the preparations. I got so busy that I couldn't very well keep appointments with the psychologist or go on job interviews. I feigned enthusiasm so well, I almost fooled myself. And I certainly fooled my father. His smile grew ever brighter as the day of our departure approached.

The trip wasn't as beneficial as my father had hoped.

We decided not to take my wheelchair, to better show off how well I could walk on crutches. At the airport, I was made to sit in a chair with little wheels, impossible for me to push, and taken in it to the gate. I walked to my assigned seat on the plane and didn't get up until we landed in Rome. I was too afraid to move while in the air, and the rest room was too minuscule to navigate on crutches.

Had I brought my wheelchair, it wouldn't have been of much use. My relatives' houses all had steps and stairs. On my crutches, I dragged myself up and down. When I got too tired, I got carried—by my father, uncles, and cousins, just like when I was a child. Except I wasn't small now and the braces I wore made me heavy and awkward to carry. Bathrooms seemed to always be up or down a flight of stairs. I solved that problem by not taking in any fluids unless I knew there was a bathroom nearby. The dehydration made me feel all the more exhausted.

But I enjoyed being in Rome, even as I remembered how afraid I was as a child being taken to hospitals and doctors. We stayed with my cousins. I didn't get to go inside St. Peter's or see the Sistine Chapel or any of the museums. But my cousins drove me around, and it was enough for me to see the Eternal City from the car. I even enjoyed getting stuck in traffic and hearing the Romans curse at one another. We drove around the Colosseum, unable to stop anywhere near it. But we were lucky enough to find parking close to the Trevi Fountain, so I could walk over to it, lean on the rail, and toss in my coins.

We went by train down to Sicily. My father helped me on, grabbing me under the arms to lift me, causing me great embarrassment when my shirt kept riding up. We didn't stay in Riposto, but in Giarre with my father's family. My mother's parents, the grandparents we had lived with, were dead. First my grandfather and then my grandmother had died shortly after we left for America. I'd been in the hospital, undergoing surgery after surgery, at the time and didn't have a chance to mourn them. Now it felt as if I'd just lost them. Never again would I hear my grandmother calling me *picciridda,* or taste the cherries my grandfather brought home for me.

The old house in Giarre smelled of my aunt's freshly baked cakes and cookies, just as I remembered. My grandmother had gotten even shorter and chubbier. She moaned about her failing eyesight while criticizing me for wearing makeup. My aunt complained that I ate like a bird.

"These were your favorite cookies."

"They still are, but I'm stuffed."

"You never got stuffed when you were little."

I nibbled on another cookie while my father smoked and ranted about the unchanged situation in Sicily, the injustice of national policies that caused it to remain the poorest region in Italy. He struck the table with his fist, frustrated by his people's failure to fight back.

The weather was hot and humid. On an extremely muggy day, my cousin Giuseppe drove us in his Fiat from Giarre to Riposto. My parents had been to Riposto a few times already. It was a short walk across the train tracks, but too far for me on my crutches.

I had not met Giuseppe before our trip. He had married one of my favorite cousins. He was nice but a bit peculiar. For instance, he had a fear of drafts.

That day, sitting in the backseat of Giuseppe's Fiat, my mother and I kept rolling down the windows, and he made us roll them back up. "Do you want us all to die of pneumonia?"

"We wouldn't die, Giuseppe; they have penicillin today," my father, who was sitting in front, joked. My mother and I winked at each other as we fanned ourselves with the magazines bought at the store by the railroad.

Giuseppe also drove much too slowly. "You can speed up a bit; we're not following a hearse," my father told him, and my mother and I covered our mouths to muffle our laughter.

The streets in Giarre seemed narrower than I remembered. The streets in Riposto seemed narrower still. As we kept creeping along, the streets were getting narrower and narrower, the buildings along both sides getting closer and closer together, almost leaning toward us, closing in on us. I worried that Giuseppe's Fiat, with us in it, would get stuck and be crushed between the buildings. I knew that kind of fear was irrational. Was I catching phobias from Giuseppe? My mother kept fanning herself and didn't notice the narrowing streets. My father kept joking.

Then I saw faces at the windows, and behind the glass panels of front doors—strange, eerie faces. They were all mouthing something. I was certain they were saying "*Che peccato!* What a shame!" as they had always done. But they couldn't see me inside the car, could they? My mother pointed to a few of the faces, evidently thinking I should recognize them. She was repeating people's names, trying to jog my memory. But her voice sounded faint and far away and I made no effort to understand her.

I was feeling more and more frightened but didn't know why. This was the town where I was born and had lived for thirteen years, yet it felt as alien as a ghost town in the TV show *Twilight Zone*. I felt nauseated. Was I carsick? I used to get carsick when I was a little girl. But I was not a little girl anymore. I was a young woman. I'd been driving for years in New York, and I'd driven to D. C. with Audrey. Only lately, I hadn't been getting out much.

It must be the heat that's making me sick, I thought. Damn Giuseppe and his irrational fear of drafts! I was getting more nauseated and dizzy, and the buildings on each side of the street were touching the car now, squeezing us inside it. I'll suffocate if I stay in this car; I'll die in this car. I gotta get out of this car, I gotta get out of this car, I gotta get out of this car. The mantra was filling my spinning head. I'll throw myself out of the car, I'll get hurt, but at the speed we're going, I won't die, I thought. I pulled on the handle. Luckily, the door didn't open. Cautious Giuseppe had made sure the doors were locked.

Then suddenly, I knew where we were. Right in front of us was the

convent of the Addolorata. On the right was the old house where we
had lived. The street was Via Libertà. Across that street, my mother had
carried me from the door of our house to the door of the convent, to
hand me over to the nuns. A warm, quivering burden to be passed
around from arms to arms. A pathetic little crippled girl. *Ciunca*.

There were people coming out of the church. Was the Sunday Mass
over? But I didn't think it was Sunday. Funny, I couldn't remember what
day of the week it was. The people were all dressed in black. Someone
must have died, I thought; this must be a funeral. And I looked around,
expecting to see a hearse parked by the church, waiting for the coffin to
be carried by pallbearers out of the church doors and down the steps.
The people's faces were ghostly, all gray. Everything I looked at was gray.
Something was wrong with my eyes. Was I going blind?

"Do you want to get out?" My father had opened the car door and
was standing there holding my crutches. "Do you think you could make
it up the steps by holding on to me and Giuseppe?"

I shook my head, though shaking my head made me feel dizzier.

"Look, there's Nunziatina with her daughter Pinuccia." My mother,
who had gotten out of the car on the other side and was now standing
near my father, was pointing toward two female figures. I recognized
the names of our old neighbors, but I was too afraid to look at the dark
shapes moving toward the car.

"Don't you want to go into the church and light a candle to the
Addolorata?" The question came from Giuseppe, but I couldn't see him.
He must have been standing behind the car.

I shook my head more and more vehemently, making myself dizzier
and dizzier. The *Addolorata*. The mere mention of the *Addolorata* filled
me with dread. I shut my eyes as tight as I could. But I saw in my mind
the statue of the grieving mother holding on her lap her dead son. She
was beckoning to me. Light a candle for the *Addolorata*. I kept shaking
my head. "No, I don't want to go into the church. No, no."

Then I opened my eyes and saw the nun. She was coming down the
steps, her long black habit billowing in the breeze. She was coming to

get me. But I was big now. She could never take me in her arms and carry me away.

"Is that Sister Teresina?" my father asked.

"No," my mother replied, "it's Sister Angelica."

I started shaking. I was the little crippled girl in the nun's arms, hearing her say, "You poor child, you will never be happy."

I had struggled to get away from the nun's ominous words. Why had I come back? I was so frightened, I was shaking uncontrollably. I knew I was really sick, and I tried to tell my mother: "I want to go home!" And home meant New York, our house, my car, my books, even the job interviews I hated. Home meant far away from this town, this church, these people, this nun. "I want to go home!" But my mouth was shaking so badly, the words came out all scrambled. Then everything went black.

The next thing I knew, we were back in the house in Giarre. I had a wet cloth on my forehead and my aunt was holding a tall glass of water. "Drink some more. You don't drink enough; that's why you had heatstroke."

I grabbed the glass with both hands and swallowed as fast as I could, drinking like someone who'd been lost for days in the desert.

My grandmother replaced the cloth on my forehead with a wetter, cooler one. "*Stai meglio?* Do you feel better?"

I felt confused and disoriented. Most of all, I felt embarrassed. I wondered what had happened. Had I fainted? In front of the nun and all those people? I didn't want to think about it. "I feel much better," I told her. And I did. I felt much better away from Via Libertà, the convent, the nuns, the *Addolorata*. I knew I'd feel even better once I was home in New York. And I knew I never wanted to go back to Riposto.

PART II

Fighting Back

8

WE CAN FIGHT FOR
OUR RIGHTS

❊

Glad to be home in New York, I decided to reach out to some disabled friends. How were they managing in the real world? I wondered. We had brief phone conversations; I made no effort to see them. Then during a call, my friend Susie told me about a meeting of disabled people she was planning to attend. The name of the organization holding the meeting was PRIDE, which was an acronym. According to Susie, it stood for People for the Rehabilitation and the Independence of the Disabled Through Education. A mouthful. I liked the acronym better than the full name. The meeting was in Queens, conveniently enough. And what was it about? Getting special parking permits, Susie told me, so we could park where other people couldn't, like in "No Parking Anytime" zones.

"Far-out," I said, remembering how Audrey used to get tickets, which her wealthy parents didn't mind paying.

Lately, I hadn't been driving much. But when I ventured out to a library or a store, I usually got so disgusted waiting and going around the block, I just went back home. If I had a job interview, I gave myself an extra hour to find parking.

"I'd love to have a special permit," I said. "And I'd love to see you."

"There'll be other people you know, and Judy Heumann will be there."

Judy Heumann. The name rang a bell. Why, yes, she was the young woman who sued the Board of Ed when she was denied her license to teach. I looked at the newspaper clipping still taped to the wall above my desk. It was starting to turn yellow. Susie told me Judy had won her case, or settled or something. Anyway, she was teaching now.

After I hung up, I stood and, leaning across the desk, read through the article. Then, since it was taped next to it, I went on to read the page from the NYU brochure about assistantships. I remembered how excited I'd been when I called Audrey to tell her about Judy Heumann and about wanting to teach Italian.

The meeting was in the living room of somebody's house. I recognized a few faces when I walked in with my braces and crutches. There weren't many people there—I counted eleven; someone else might have come in after me. Six were in wheelchairs. I was glad I wasn't; there wouldn't have been room for another one. I sat in a high-back dining chair. There were newspapers piled up on the table. Rather than listening to what was being said, I kept looking around me—dark, heavy furniture, some pushed against the walls. I stared at a pretty girl with blond hair sitting across from me in a wheelchair. I wondered if Audrey would have attended this meeting. Why couldn't I stop thinking about Audrey? How could I make my mind stop wandering and start paying attention?

I recognized Judy Heumann from her picture in the paper. But I had expected her to look more formidable, like someone capable of taking on the Board of Ed. Instead, she was cute, bright-eyed, and small. Maybe she looked small because her wheelchair was big. She wore a fashionable peasant-style dress with short puffy sleeves.

When the meeting was over, I decided to introduce myself to Judy.

"It's a pleasure to meet you!" She gave me a sparkling smile and held out her hand.

Standing with my braced legs far apart for maximum balance, I slid the crutch out from under my right arm and grabbed it with my left hand, tightening the muscles of my left forearm to keep the other crutch secure under it. I was able to bend down just enough to give Judy's hand a hearty shake.

I wanted to ask, How did you muster the strength to fight back? How did you arrive at the realization that being denied a license to teach was an act of discrimination, when the rest of us accepted such verdicts as the inevitable outcome of being disabled?

But I didn't ask those questions. We talked about what had been discussed. The Department of Motor Vehicles only agreed to issue us permits to park in front of our schools or places of work. They didn't think we should have any desire for frivolous activities such as going to a movie or a restaurant. I told Judy I agreed with the people who argued in favor of holding a demonstration in front of the DMV.

"Then you should come to meetings of my organization. It's called Disabled In Action. We hold demos and do civil disobedience."

"Okay!" I exclaimed.

Then out of the blue, I found myself telling her about the Italian graduate program at NYU and about teaching assistantships. I told her I received the brochure with the application in the mail the same day the first article about her came out. I even told her that the newspaper clipping and the page from the NYU brochure were taped to my wall, side by side.

"I've been thinking of applying. I'd like to teach Italian."

What the hell was I saying? I hadn't been thinking about doing much of anything lately.

Judy grabbed my right arm and almost threw me off balance. I hadn't put my crutch back under it.

"So what are you waiting for? Apply!"

I laughed, trying to keep my balance.

"Promise you'll apply!"

I could tell she wasn't going to let go of my arm unless I promised. "Okay, I'll apply."

"Right away!" She let go of my arm and pointed an admonishing finger toward my face.

I didn't apply right away. I missed the application deadline for the fall semester of 1971. I told myself I'd aim for the spring of 1972.

I did, however, start going to meetings, both of PRIDE and of Judy's organization, Disabled in Action. I liked DIA more than I liked PRIDE, which, in spite of the great acronym, seemed a bit tame. DIA meetings were often held in Brooklyn. But it was worth the drive. I listened in awe to Judy.

"It is not our disability that handicaps us; it is society that handicaps us. . . . Disability only becomes a tragedy for us when society fails to provide the things we need to lead our lives. It's a tragedy when we're discriminated against, kept out, treated as inferior." She spoke the most amazing truths in such a sweet-sounding, girlish voice. She was a true revolutionary, our Angela Davis.

I thought my parents would be happy I was going out. But I could tell they weren't so enthusiastic about my interest in disability activism. Once, back from a meeting, when I started talking about Judy and some other disabled people I admired, my father interrupted me.

"I wish you'd make normal friends."

His words felt like knives stabbing me. I went into my room, slammed the door, threw myself on the bed, and cried.

My mother knocked after a few minutes. I didn't say "Come in," but she did anyway. She sat on the bed and stroked my shoulders. "Your father didn't mean it."

"Didn't mean what?"

"He didn't mean to imply you weren't normal."

I sat up in bed and yelled, "I don't care! Maybe I don't even want to be normal! Maybe I don't even like normal people!"

She put her arm around me and I shrank away from her. "It's just that having handicapped friends makes it harder for you to get over... to forget..."

I turned around to look her in the eyes. "Forget what? Forget who?"

She said her name in a whisper. "Audrey."

I yelled even louder: "I don't want to forget about Audrey; I never want to forget about Audrey!"

My parents were really tickled, though, when my picture, taken at the demonstration in front of the DMV, was in the *Daily News*. My father must have gone around to every local store and newsstand. Every relative, every friend, in the United States and in Italy, got a newspaper clipping. In the picture, I was standing with my crutches, holding a sign I'd made the night before the demonstration.

I was very proud of my sign. Some had made fancy ones, using boards and markers of various colors, drawing pictures of cars. Mine was simple: block letters in black Magic Marker on a white board. It read:

IF YOU THINK WE'RE HELPLESS
WE GOT NEWS FOR YOU, MAN!
WE CAN FIGHT FOR OUR RIGHTS
JUST AS WELL AS YOU CAN!

Susie couldn't stop laughing. She thought "man!" was funny. "Sooooo hippie," she kept murmuring, shaking her head.

But, hey, it rhymed. Others criticized my sign for being too general.

"This way, I can reuse it," I said. "I'm lazy. I'd rather not have to make a new sign every time we have a demonstration."

But really, I wanted my sign to do more than demand a parking permit. I wanted those few words on that twenty-four-square-inch board to present, in a nutshell, what I saw as the big picture, our common struggle.

It was amazing to discover how similar our experiences were, once we started comparing notes. Until then, we had all considered our disabilities to be the problem. We believed we were supposed to "cope" as best we could. As we talked, we realized the disability itself was not that big a deal for us. We had all learned to accept our physical limitations. What made life difficult was not the disability, but the lack of services and support, the lack of accessibility, the unfair and stereotypical ways in which we were treated, the pity doled out for us all our lives. Often, after a meeting, I wrote my thoughts down in a notebook. "It's not my fault that I'm disabled, yet I've been made to feel that it is," I wrote. "My polio never made me unhappy; people made me unhappy. Ever since I was a little girl, people have always made me feel I was no good because I was disabled. From the Sicilian women and the nuns to the doctors who couldn't fix me, to my fellow students and prospective employers... and even my own parents." As I wrote, my tears fell and stained the pages—tears of anger, of relief, and of new hope.

I was thunderstruck by the realization that as a disabled person I had "rights." I'd been hearing and talking and getting excited about "rights," and never before had it dawned on me that the same arguments could apply to me, to us, disabled people. There were rights for black people, rights for women, rights for Native Americans, for immigrants, for workers, for gays; there were even animal rights. But I'd never before heard anybody talking about rights for disabled people. They talked about benefits and cures and charity for us, not rights.

I got so fired up at the mere notion of disabled people "fighting"— instead of asking pretty please, instead of begging, and of sitting around wishing and hoping and praying to be cured. The message that we weren't "helpless," as everyone seemed to believe and as everyone wanted us to believe, was one that I wanted to shout to the four corners of the earth. The best I could do for the time being was to print it in big black letters on a white board.

I got to reuse my sign a few times. When we went on a march to the UN, I rolled in my wheelchair with the sign hanging around my neck, hitting my chin or covering my face when I went over a bump or a pothole. And I used it in October, when we blocked Madison Avenue to protest Nixon's veto of the Rehabilitation Act. About eighty people took part in that demo. We were even joined by some disabled Vietnam vets. Judy and a few others got summonses from the police. My heart was beating fast, but I wasn't nervous, despite the police all around us, just excited.

At other protests, I was often the only disabled person—except when Audrey went with me when she was alive—and had to endure the stares and the pats on the head, and the warnings to be careful, and the "So sorry!" and "Thank you for being inspirational!" all reminding me that fighting for a common cause didn't make my presence any less of an oddity. At "our" demonstrations, among so many disabled like me, I felt right; I felt strong and powerful. Here we were all together as one, finally fighting back.

Sometimes, when I drove into the city for a meeting or a protest, I found myself heading down to Greenwich Village. I'd stop near Washington Square Park and sit in my car. I tried to spot the NYU graduate students: those who looked older, carried heavier books, and seemed rushed, unlike the hippies hanging out in the park. I had trouble imagining myself among those students. How would I fit in? I decided to start going on job interviews again rather than apply for admission to NYU. If I find a job I like, I told myself, I'll forget about graduate school.

By the way the interviews were going, I didn't think I had a chance. Then toward the end of the spring, I got an offer—to work in the Benefits Review Department at the Social Security office in Queens. I knew immediately I didn't want that job. I knew it when I walked into the office on my crutches and was greeted by Richard Nixon. A huge picture of him was hanging on the wall opposite the front door. Apart from the picture, which, hopefully, would be replaced soon, I couldn't see myself sitting all day reading people's applications for Social Security. Better if I applied for Social Security disability benefits myself and stayed home and watched soaps for the rest of my life. I thought my father would agree. Instead, he was upset.

"A government job offers security and good benefits!"

Was he thinking that, being disabled, I had to settle for whatever job I could get? Maybe he was right. The building had an elevator and a parking lot for employees. I might never get another offer that included such amenities. But why take a job I didn't like? I had rights. I wanted to be able to make choices in my life.

While I kept pondering and deliberating, my parking permit arrived in the mail. I was thrilled. When my parents got home from work, I showed them the laminated green card with the stamp of the DMV, brimming with pride.

"Well, now you can go anywhere you want and park right in front of the door!" My father laughed.

"Not exactly, but the permit will make life a bit easier for many of us," I tried to explain. "I got this permit because we came together and fought for it. And what we accomplished will benefit many disabled people. This permit is a small example of the power we can have when we organize and fight for our rights."

"Yes, and it should make it easier to find a job you like."

My first reaction was anger. My father had not been listening to me; he didn't understand how important my activism was. Then I realized the permit gave me a way out of settling for a job I didn't want. I saw my father's smile and smiled back.

I went into my room and picked up the phone, then paused, my hand on the dial. The person I wanted to call was Audrey. I hit my head a few times with the palm of my hand, as I always did when I found myself acting as if Audrey were still alive. I just wished I could have shown her my new parking permit, told her about my sign, about our protests, our meetings, about all the new ideas in my head. I wondered if I could have gotten Audrey excited about joining us and fighting for our rights. I wondered if I could have gotten her excited enough to want to stay alive.

I loved using the pronouns *we* and *us* in contrast with the pronouns *they* and *them*. "They treat us as if we're sick, as if we can't do anything. We won't take any more of their bullshit."

"But who are they? Who are these bad guys?" my father asked. He'd never had any trouble naming bad guys—the fascists, the greedy, the idle rich, the mafiosi, the corrupt politicians. It bothered him that my use of the pronoun seemed to include everyone who wasn't like me and my friends—who wasn't disabled.

"What about your mother and me? Do you think we're bad guys?"

Judy liked to refer to "us" as a minority. Like members of other minorities, we were treated as inferior, kept in the margins of society, denied equal rights and opportunities. However, in most minorities the children resembled the parents. Being disabled, I was different from my own parents. That realization made me want to cry.

"Of course you're not bad guys; you're my parents!"

I wished I could explain my feelings to my father. But how could I when I didn't fully understand them myself? What I knew for sure was that it felt good when "we" succeeded and made change happen. And it felt good to belong, to be part of something. I wasn't sure what that something was, but I knew I wanted to be part of it.

9

JUST ONE OF THE
GRADUATE STUDENTS

❧

I stood, my right hip leaning against the desk, carefully peeling off the wall the yellowed newspaper clipping about Judy Heumann.

Nica, the black-and-white mutt with floppy ears I'd adopted the year before, stood on her hind legs, pushing her strong little body against my braces, helping me balance. She knew just how to do it.

My cousin Victor's wife, Josie, had picked Nica, which is Sicilian for "little," out of a litter of puppies her neighbors were giving away. I fell in love with the tiny fur ball the second she jumped out of Josie's bag. It was taking my parents longer, but they were falling in love with her, too.

I'd already removed other newspaper clippings from the wall. The article announcing the withdrawal of all U.S. troops from Vietnam and the one about the *Roe v. Wade* Supreme Court decision, which established throughout the country a woman's right to a safe and legal abortion, came off easily—they had been up only since January.

The clipping about Judy Heumann was over three years old. It was yellow and brittle. But I managed to remove it all in one piece. Then I started working on the page about assistantships at NYU. The brochure paper, being thicker and glossy, had not aged as badly and detached quickly. I would let my father, who had decided my room needed a fresh coat of paint, deal with all my posters and prints. But I didn't trust him to handle these delicate items.

Judy had asked, the last time I'd seen her, what had happened to my idea of becoming an Italian teacher. I didn't know how to answer. I'd accepted a job the year before doing translations for an international firm. The money was good and I translated some interesting material—articles, book proposals, abstracts for film scripts. But I worked mostly from home. Though Nica appreciated that, I didn't. I needed to get out more. I went to DIA meetings and demonstrations, and hung out with disabled friends. My parents were right. I needed to meet new people.

As I looked at the page from the NYU brochure, a telephone number in bold letters jumped out at me. After three years, the info was probably outdated. What the heck. I sat down and dialed the number.

"I want to apply for a graduate assistantship and teach Italian."

The female voice at the other end told me I couldn't apply for an assistantship without first applying for admission to the Graduate School of Arts and Sciences.

"Okay, then, I'd like to apply for admission."

The woman took down my name and address. "I'll send you the full package. You'll need to have the college where you got your bachelor's send us your transcripts, and you'll need three letters of recommendation from professors."

Cool. My grades at St. John's had been good. Since I'd been their only disabled student, my professors would remember me.

"But you missed the deadline to apply for the '73 fall semester. You'll be applying for the spring of '74."

Oh no, now that I'd taken the plunge, I wanted to start right away. "I can't wait until '74."

"Why can't you wait?"

Good question. I'd been procrastinating for years; what difference would another few months make?

"What program did you say you're interested in?"

"Italian."

"Well..." the woman said, as if talking to herself, "the program isn't large. They're happy to get new students... What you can do"—now she was addressing me—"is go in person to the French and Italian Department; the two programs are together. Get all your papers ready; make copies of everything. Send the originals to us and take the copies to Professor DuBois, the chair of the department. The Graduate School may admit someone after the deadline if a department chair intervenes."

I blew the woman a kiss after she hung up.

I straightened my long skirt, checked my makeup, smoothed my hair, walked out the door on my crutches, and got in the car. Nica barked and barked. She didn't like being left alone. I was already in the Midtown Tunnel when I realized I didn't have the address of the French and Italian Department. I'd ask around; someone around NYU would know.

The first person I asked told me to go to 19 University Place, sixth floor. Amazingly, I found a parking spot in front of the door. And the door was level, no steps at all. I took the elevator, and when I got out, there were two young women standing there speaking Italian. This was my lucky day. Everything would work out like magic.

"Do you know if Professor DuBois is in?" I asked in Italian, using the *tu,* the familiar form of address, as if I belonged in that office, as if I were one of the graduate students or even one of the teaching assistants.

"He should be in his office," one of the young women said, pointing to a door across from us. The other one asked, "*Ch'è successo?* What happened?"

I wasn't sure what she meant. Did she think I was there to report on something that had happened? Then it dawned on me that, of course, she wanted to know what had happened to me, why I was on crutches.

I recalled Audrey's saying that when they asked what happened, it was because they didn't think you were hopeless. "They don't ask if they can tell you're a cripple and always will be."

With my long skirt hiding the braces, especially if I was standing still, not struggling stiff-legged to walk, I might pass for someone who was hurt, not disabled.

"*Storia lunga,* long story," I replied as I headed for Professor DuBois's office.

"Yes, may I help you?" I hadn't anticipated a secretary stopping me in my tracks.

"I'd like to see Professor DuBois."

"Are you one of his students?"

If I lied, would she let me into his office? I decided to tell the truth.

"No, I'm applying for admission in the Italian program. I was told by the Graduate School to come to this department."

"Do you have your application, transcripts, and recommendations?"

How embarrassing. The woman on the phone wanted me to go see Professor DuBois after I had all my papers together, not come rushing in totally unprepared.

"I don't have everything; I'm still waiting for one more letter," I said, lying now. "I had some health problems and missed the deadline."

Had I no shame? Where was my sense of integrity? The secretary looked me over. She had a full face and inquisitive eyes.

"What happened to you?"

This time, I deserved it. I didn't have to bring up the "health problems." In my mind, I saw Judy point an admonishing finger. And I heard Audrey laughing. I remembered how Audrey shamelessly pulled the disability card when convenient. "Lighten up," she'd say when I acted self-righteously annoyed. "They're always using the disability against us; if once in a while we can use it to our advantage, what's the harm?"

Just then, the door of the office opened and a tall man with graying hair and a well-trimmed beard strode out.

"Professor DuBois!"

The bearded man looked at me, puzzled. The secretary took over professionally. She explained why I was there, speaking succinctly but making sure to mention the health problems.

"Maybe it would be better if you waited till spring." The professor nodded. "Give yourself time to heal and get rid of the crutches."

Okay. If I really wanted to study and teach here, I would have to tell the truth.

"I'm not going to get rid of the crutches; I had polio when I was a child and this is the way I walk."

Complete silence. In the background, the two young women had stopped chattering in Italian.

The secretary spoke first. "Oh, I'm so sorry."

"But I manage very well, and I'm an excellent student."

Then Professor DuBois spoke: "Get me a copy of everything, transcripts, letters of recommendation, everything. And if you're as good as you say you are, I'll make sure you start this fall."

"Thanks! *Grazie! Merci!*"

He walked away so fast, I didn't think he heard me.

I had taught Nica to bring me the mail. She ran to the door when the mailman dropped envelopes through the slot, picked each one up, and carried it over to me. No matter what I was doing, I had to take it from her mouth and make a big fuss.

"Good girl, Nica!"

She wagged her tail, waving her round butt from side to side, jumped up and down a few times, then ran to the door again to get another piece. She never bit through the paper, never tore it or got it wet with saliva.

I recognized the envelope with the NYU logo—a torch, which to me looked more like an ice-cream cone.

"Good girl, Nica!"

Her round brown eyes followed the movements of my hands as I pulled out the letter.

"We are pleased to inform you…" I read the words and yelled. Nica got so excited, she jumped on my lap. Her paws on my shoulders, she licked my cheeks, my nose, my eyes. I grabbed her soft furry head and planted a kiss between her floppy ears.

"We've already assigned the assistantships," Professor DuBois's secretary, whose name I'd learned was Cathy, said. "It's August, you know. School is starting in a few weeks."

I held in my hand the letter from the Graduate School. How stupid of me to have gotten excited. How stupid to assume I would get an assistantship automatically if I was admitted.

"But you can start taking courses in September and apply for an assistantship next year."

Start taking courses? The assistantship was supposed to cover tuition. How was I going to pay for courses? I couldn't appeal to the Office of Vocational Rehabilitation. The only time they paid for graduate school was if you wanted to become a rehab counselor. Disabled rehab counselors got hired to work in hospitals, schools, and nonprofits. There was somewhat of a demand, however small, for disabled rehab counselors. Quite a few of my friends had gone that route, including Susie. But I didn't want to make my disability a profession. I wanted to be an Italian teacher. Unfortunately, there was no demand for disabled Italian teachers.

"I can't start taking courses. I can't afford to pay tuition."

Cathy gave me a sympathetic look. "Can your family help?"

No way! I couldn't ask my parents to pay for me to go to NYU. I didn't even know how many thousands that would be.

"There may still be a chance of your getting a scholarship, you know."

No, I didn't know.

"Sometimes, at the last minute, a scholarship becomes available."

"Really?" Was Cathy trying to humor me? Did she feel sorry for me?

Cathy wasn't just humoring me. I did get a scholarship and was able to start taking courses in the fall.

Not getting an assistantship turned out to be a good thing. I had a great amount of reading to do for each course, and thirty-page research papers to write. My classmates were brilliant and spoke Italian impeccably, even the American-born students; it was hard to keep up with them during class discussions. I couldn't have handled teaching and taking courses at the same time. Yet the assistants didn't have any trouble. Graduate classes started at 6:00 P.M. because most of the students worked during the day. They complained to one another about being tired when they arrived. I was always exhausted, but I didn't feel I had a right to complain.

I drove into the city in the early afternoon and went to the impressive, and to me intimidating, new Bobst Library. I got dizzy when I entered the enormous atrium, whether I looked up into the twelve-story-high void or down at the black-and-white optical-illusion floor. Once, my crutch slipped on the shiny marble and down I went. Luckily, I didn't break any bones. After that, I was always nervous until I got into the elevator. I was okay upstairs—as long as I didn't walk too close to the rail and look down. Most of the Italian books were on the fourth floor. I got friendly with the work-study students who carried books from the stacks to a table for me. There I sat reading until it was time for class.

Though the library was just a few blocks from the buildings where my classes were held, I got in my car and drove there. If I left the car parked in front of Bobst, I would be too tired to get back to it after classes, especially with the bagful of books hanging from one of my crutches. With my parking permit, I didn't have to worry about "No Parking" zones or putting coins in a meter every hour. I thought of how my disabled friends and I had fought to get those permits.

Using my wheelchair never seemed an option. It was hard for me to get it in and out of the car, especially when I was tired. Also, most buildings had a step at the entrance. Even a low step would be a problem when using my wheelchair.

Make them ramp these steps! the budding activist in me urged every time I went in and out. But I was too timid, too new at NYU and too new to disability rights activism. There was another reason for not wanting to use my wheelchair. I knew my professors and fellow students would have thought of me as more disabled and would have had more trouble accepting me. Would Judy have said I wasn't "liberated"?

Maybe. But I longed to be accepted by my nondisabled peers. I wanted to "belong" at NYU.

I'd stopped going to DIA. I was always too busy or too tired. I wondered if being a graduate student at NYU was worth my having to miss the meetings and demonstrations that had become an important part of my life. Was it worth not being with my disabled friends?

In my first semester, I couldn't make any friends. My classmates were nice enough, but they exchanged phone numbers and never asked for mine, laughed at private jokes, and talked of private matters. They made plans to go after classes to the Cookery, a piano bar and restaurant at the corner of University Place and Eighth Street, and never asked me to go along.

"I wish you'd make normal friends." I remembered my father's words, and how angry they'd made me. But my father had a point. What was wrong with me that I could make friends only with other disabled people? Was I this way because of Audrey?

Don't you fucking blame me for your inadequacies! I heard Audrey say in the middle of my wondering and self-doubting.

"Oh, I'm not blaming you, Audrey!" I answered out loud. "Man, you still have a foul mouth even though you're dead!" I laughed. And although laughing made me question my sanity more, it made me feel better.

In my second semester, things got easier. I felt more confident, both academically and socially. I'd gotten all A's in my first semester and was no longer afraid to speak in class. And I was more outgoing. I offered my fellow students my phone number and got theirs. I laughed at their jokes and told some myself. Some evenings, no matter how exhausted, I followed them to the Cookery for hot buttered rum and jazz.

I was doing something right to make others more comfortable around me. I was starting to feel like I belonged, like I was just one of the graduate students.

"I don't think of you as disabled," Alexandra, one of my classmates, said to me one day. She had been curious about my parking permit, and I told her how we'd demonstrated in front of the DMV. Then I found myself talking about Judy, her suing the Board of Ed, my involvement with DIA. Alexandra's changed expression told me I was making her uncomfortable.

We were sitting in her studio apartment on Thirteenth Street. I loved her apartment, though it was up a few steps. I dragged myself up those steps because I liked visiting with her.

"I don't think of you as disabled." What did she mean? Was I supposed to take her remark as a compliment? Is that what I needed to do to make able-bodied friends? Make them forget I was disabled? Is that what I'd been doing? Trudging behind them, dragging myself up steps, never making a big deal of it, never mentioning how hard it was for me, never showing how tired I was, hiding the braces under bell-bottoms or long skirts, not talking about friends who, like me, were disabled. Trying to make everyone, including myself, think I was just another graduate student at NYU.

I didn't know how to respond to Alexandra's remark. I sipped the instant coffee she'd made for me, which was strong and bitter. I asked for some sugar. She gave me a packet of Sweet'n Low.

I shouldn't let such things bother me, I told myself. Not when I was finally feeling happy. Spring had come; the magnolia trees were in bloom. Instead of sitting in the library, I now sat with my books in Washington Square Park. I sat with my books, waiting for Ennio.

I'd met Ennio in the park in March, on one of the first warm days of the year. He saw me on a bench in the sun with my Italian books and sat beside me and started talking in Italian. Immediately, I loved his voice and his heavy Roman accent. I kept my eyes on my book. He told me he had a degree in architecture and was visiting New York. He was living in a loft on Great Jones Street with two other guys.

I turned toward him, but not enough to get a good look at his face. I told him I was a graduate student at NYU. We kept talking, sitting side by side on the park bench, until he asked, "Are those your crutches?"

He stood up and faced me. He was so tall and thin. I had to tilt my head back to see his face. He had smiling dark eyes and curly dark hair.

"Yes, they're my crutches," I said, and waited for him to ask, "What happened to you?" But he didn't. He helped me get up from the bench and walked me to my car.

The day after, he was sitting beside me again. Whenever I sat in the park, there he was. One afternoon, I accepted his invitation to go see the loft on Great Jones. It was up a flight of stairs. I started going up the stairs, both crutches under one arm, the other arm on the railing.

"Oh, come on, that looks hard to do."

Before I knew what was happening, he had lifted me and was carrying me up. He cradled me like a baby, or a bride, while managing to hold my crutches, too, in one hand. I held on to him, my arms locked around his neck. When we got to the top of the stairs, he leaned the crutches against the wall, but he didn't put me down. He kissed me, and the most natural thing for me to do was kiss him back. Then he lowered me to the floor and I grabbed my crutches. He unlocked his door and we went in.

"Looks like my roommates are out."

The loft was huge, sparsely furnished. "I'll show you my room," he said, and I followed.

There were neat piles of books and record albums on the floor and a mattress covered with an Indian spread—rows of elephants in orange, yellow, and brown tones. It looked new, the lines where it had been folded still showing. In one corner, a vase with daffodils sat on a milk crate. My favorite spring flower. How did Ennio know? Maybe I had told him.

He took an album from one of the piles on the floor and went out of the room with it. I stood leaning on my crutches. There was no place where I could sit. Then I heard Fabrizio De André start to sing "La Canzone di Marinella." My favorite Italian song. My favorite Italian singer/songwriter. How did Ennio know? He came back with a Coke in his hand, but he didn't give it to me. He just put it down on the pile of books next to the mattress. He grabbed me at the waist and I let my crutches fall to the floor. While we kissed, he let himself drop onto the mattress, and I went down with him.

He undressed me slowly. What will he say when he sees the braces? I wondered. All he said was, "Help me take these off." What will he think of my ugly skinny legs and all my scars? He didn't seem to notice.

My sexual encounters until then had been instances of abuse, or, at best, halfhearted submission on my part. I couldn't believe how much I desired this young man with the heavy Roman accent and the smiling dark eyes.

I didn't notice when or how Ennio undressed himself. His body was all long, hard bones and muscles. The most natural thing for me to do was let him press his naked body against mine. Using every muscle that worked, my body rose to press against his as I welcomed him inside me. Fabrizio De André was singing: "Only the spring flowers could see Marinella's skin trembling under the king's kisses."

It was a beautiful spring. I was happy sitting in the park with my books and with Ennio. When it was time for class, Ennio walked me to my car, took my crutches, threw them in the back, and sat in the passenger seat. I parked as close to the building's door as possible; he got out and got my crutches, then walked me to class. If it was early, he waited with me until the professor arrived. I introduced him to my classmates. I could tell they were impressed I had a boyfriend—and such a good-looking one. Further proof I was just like them. More reason for them not to think of me as disabled.

Sometimes Ennio picked me up after classes and we went to the loft on Great Jones. I'd seen his roommates only a few times, as they were hardly ever there. Whenever I spent the night with Ennio, I told my parents I was staying with Alexandra. I felt guiltier about Nica's whining and waiting all night for me to get home than about lying to my parents. I would have been glad to have them meet Ennio. We could have sat around the dining room table, speaking Italian. But Ennio showed no interest in meeting them.

"Sometime you can come out to Queens with me."

"*Vediamo,* we'll see."

He didn't talk about his family, other than to refer to his parents as *i vecchi,* the old folks, and to say they were *noiosi,* boring. He had a younger brother who was just an annoyance, *una seccatura.* I knew he would be going back to Rome soon. I told him I had cousins in Rome.

"Can I call you if I'm in Rome sometime?"

"*Vediamo.*"

"Will you come back to New York?"

"*Vediamo.*"

You're making a fool of yourself! It was as if Audrey were saying that to me.

So what. I was happy sitting with Ennio in the park. Even if I suspected my happiness wouldn't last long. I figured I was just an interesting diversion for him. It was okay for him to be with a disabled girl when far away from home. But I wasn't someone he'd want to introduce to his old folks.

The spring semester was almost over. I'd worked hard and was hoping to get A's. I'd applied for an assistantship for the fall. I made sure I put the application in early. Now that I'd gotten used to being a graduate student, I felt ready to try my hand at teaching.

I wasn't quite awake when the phone rang. Since I'd finished and handed in all my papers, after a few sleepless nights and a few pots of espresso, I wanted to sleep late. I answered the phone. It was Cathy.

"Can you stop in the office one day this week? Professor DuBois wants to talk with you."

"Sure, anytime, even today."

"Okay, two o' clock."

Now I was awake. I wondered what Professor DuBois wanted to talk about. Could it have to do with the assistantship?

It did. I walked into the office, and two Italian professors were with

DuBois. The three of them were sitting in a row with frozen smiles on their faces. DuBois was puffing on his pipe. The others were smoking cigarettes. The smell had never bothered me before; I'd grown up with it. I'd even tried smoking at one time. But now the smoke was stifling. It contributed to the sinister atmosphere in that room.

DuBois spoke first. "I understand you've applied for an assistantship. Do you think you'll feel comfortable in front of a classroom of students?" Then the others began asking questions. "Are you able to keep your balance and write on the blackboard?" "In some classrooms, the teacher's desk is up on a platform. Can you step up to it?" "What if a discipline problem should arise?" "What if the students feel uncomfortable with a handicapped teacher?" I couldn't tell who was asking what question.

This felt like an interrogation. Worse, an inquisition. I was afraid I'd start crying. I had done nothing wrong. Why were they doing this to me? I'd thought they liked me.

I answered each question as best I could. "I'm sure I'll love being in a classroom full of students." "I can hold the crutches under my arms while I write on the blackboard. I'll show you if you'd like." "It would be best if I was assigned a classroom that didn't have a platform." "I hope not to have to deal with discipline problems, but I'll do my best if I run into any. I'll get advice from experienced teachers. Do you have any advice for me?" "I'm good at making people feel comfortable around me. I've had a lot of practice. Have I made you feel uncomfortable?"

But I felt that no matter what I said, they had already decided not to give me the assistantship. I was convinced. No chance in hell. Fine, I didn't want it anymore. I just wanted them to stop badgering me. I wanted to get out of that damn office and away from the smell of smoke. I walked out while they were thanking me for my time.

Back in my car, I started crying. I did want the assistantship. How dare they treat me like a criminal because I wanted to teach! What could I do? Didn't I have rights? Wasn't this discrimination? I was sure they didn't interrogate the other applicants this way. Could I sue?

I'll call Judy, I thought. But I'd heard Judy had moved to California.

I'll get advice from disabled friends. But were they still my friends? I hadn't seen them in quite a while. I felt I'd betrayed them. I'd been hanging out only with able-bodied people who didn't even think of me as disabled. And I had an able-bodied boyfriend.

Suddenly, I wanted Ennio. I wanted him to hold me, to comfort me. I wanted him to make love to me. I parked my car and went to sit on the bench where we always sat together, near the statue of Garibaldi, the champion of the oppressed, the hero of both worlds, Italy and the Americas. I sat waiting for Ennio. But he didn't come. I waited for hours. The sun was starting to go down. I found it difficult to get up from the bench. I'd gotten used to Ennio's helping me. All I have to do was call him, I thought. If I call him, he will come.

I walked to the pay phone on Washington Square South and dialed Ennio's number.

One of his roommates answered. "Oh, it's you. Don't you know? Ennio left last night. He went back to Rome."

I hung up. How could he leave me without saying good-bye? Then I recalled asking if we could do something special before he went back, maybe go to the Metropolitan Museum. He had said he didn't like good-byes.

I was walking toward my car, tears blurring my vision, when my foot got caught on a big bump on the sidewalk. As I went down, I remembered that the roots of an old tree had made the concrete buckle on that spot. On any other day, I would have been careful. I knew as soon as I hit the ground that my left leg was broken, and I knew it was a bad break—not a dislocation or a simple fracture. The pain shot up my leg, and I screamed, "Fuck!" It seemed like the perfect word under the circumstances. This had to have been the most fucked-up day of my life.

You sure have a foul mouth! Suddenly, hearing Audrey, or the thought of her saying that to me, made me laugh. I was on the ground with a broken leg, I was sure my dream of becoming an Italian teacher had gone up in smoke, and my boyfriend had left me without saying good-bye. I felt defeated and abandoned, I was in excruciating pain, and yet I couldn't stop laughing. If that wasn't crazy, then what was?

No one who knew me was around when the ambulance arrived and the EMS guys lifted me off the ground, strapped me to a stretcher, and, with the siren wailing, took me to the NYU Medical Center. I decided at that moment not to let any of my professors and fellow students know what had happened. Why? Maybe I didn't want them to feel sorry for me, or didn't want to remind them I was "disabled." What did it matter? Let them think I'd gone to Rome with Ennio.

I had a complex break, which required surgery and hospitalization. In the hospital, my roommate was a feisty, funny older woman who had had both legs amputated below the knees due to complications of diabetes. She had bright auburn hair, "Out of a bottle, darling!" She wore lots of green eye shadow, big silver earrings, and jade beads over her silk nightgown. She was having difficulty learning to walk on prostheses but took it all in stride.

"I'm happy to have these gorgeous gams." She lifted her gown in a comic seductive gesture. "My real legs never looked so good, not even when I was young. Lately, they were scary-looking and much more trouble than they were worth."

"I guess mine are, too."

"Yours are what, darling?"

"My legs are more trouble than they're worth. My best friend used to tell me that."

I spent most of the summer at home, with a thick cast covering my whole leg. I had convinced myself I had no chance of getting an assistantship. I'd heard nothing from anyone at the department after the day of the inquisition, and made no effort to contact them.

I wanted to call my disabled friends. But I was too embarrassed, after almost a year of silence. I wished I could go to a meeting or a demonstration. But I wouldn't have fit behind the wheel with such a big cast, or been able to get my chair in and out of the car.

I saw no point in reading the works assigned for the fall courses. So I read romance novels, and a book I'd picked up at the library about amputations and prostheses. I copied paragraphs from different chapters onto a pad, tore the pages off, stapled them together, and put them in a folder containing articles about amputees running marathons, skiing, and performing other amazing feats. I had no desire to run a marathon, but I was interested in amputees. I remembered, so many years before, how Audrey had pointed at the girl in the jade-colored dress, with her perfect-looking legs. "Amputees are better off than we are."

I watched the downfall of Richard Nixon on TV, and played with Nica. When the mail came, she ran and got it, one envelope at a time.

"Good girl!"

I noticed the ice-cream-cone logo in the return address, and as I took the envelope from Nica's mouth, I had the impulse to tear it in half. But I didn't want to hurt Nica's feelings. She sat at attention in front of me. That meant she had already brought all the mail.

"Okay. I'll open it. But it's not good news."

Nica watched fixedly as I pulled the letter out.

"We're glad to inform you that you have been awarded a Graduate Teaching Assistantship for the fall 1974 semester." I read the sentence again to make sure I was reading it right.

"Nica, I'm gonna teach Italian."

I was surprised at the dull tone of my voice.

10

THE HANDICAPPED TEACHER

❁

There was no way I could sleep that night. The next morning, for the very first time, I would be entering a classroom as a teacher. If Audrey had been alive, she could have given me some Valium to calm me down. Better not think about Audrey. But what would she have thought of me being a teacher? I also wondered whether Judy would be proud of me, or pissed at my desertion of DIA.

I decided I had to go to the bathroom, and debated whether to use my wheelchair or put on my braces. I was afraid with the wheelchair I'd make more noise, so I put on the braces. At the foot of the bed, Nica was sleeping soundly. My leg hurt when I stood up and walked. The cast had been off for almost three weeks. I had fought with the orthopedist to remove it ahead of schedule, so I could attend the first meeting of the graduate assistants. What else could I do? I couldn't show up in a wheelchair with a cast on my leg. They might have changed their minds about the assistantship.

At the meeting at NYU, the pain in my leg had been excruciating. Everyone had greeted me and congratulated me, as I walked—very slowly—into the room. I wanted to cry out with every step. I sat at the conference table with the brace locked at the knee, knowing I wouldn't have been able to bend and straighten my leg without crying out.

I learned I would be assisting two instructors, teaching two Beginning Italian classes. Language classes at NYU were intensive. They met five days a week. The instructor taught three days, introducing new grammatical points. The assistant taught two days, reinforcing the grammar, doing drills, and going over exercises. The first day, the instructor and the assistant were to conduct the class together. I listened, hoping no one would notice my stiff leg under the table.

Since that meeting, I'd been having physical therapy. The pain was now bearable. There had been another meeting and a few phone conversations between instructors and assistants.

When I got back from the bathroom, Nica was awake. It was already 4:30. The class started at nine. I wanted to leave early to avoid the rush-hour traffic. As quietly as possible, I walked to the kitchen to make a pot of espresso, shushing Nica, who followed closely behind me.

I was standing near the door, waiting for the instructor.

"Do you want to sit here?" The spindly young man with long, stringy brown hair was pointing to a seat. He thought I was a student.

Just then, the instructor rushed into the classroom and motioned for me to stand beside him in front of the class. He began by saying, "*Io mi chiamo Giuseppe Italiano.*" That was his real name, quite appropriate for an Italian teacher. A few students giggled. I'd memorized the lesson plan and felt very confident. Still, my heart was beating fast. Giuseppe, or Joe, as he was known outside of the classroom, turned toward me and winked inconspicuously. I was grateful for that sign of encouragement. "*E lei come si chiama?*"

Were they wondering why I was on crutches? Did they think I'd gotten hurt, or could they tell I was permanently disabled? Did they want to ask "What happened to you?"

We went through a brief dialogue. Then Joe handed the written version to the students. He went to one side, I to the other. We approached each student and asked, *"Lei come si chiama?"* They caught on quickly and tried to say their names in Italian. We helped with pronunciation.

"Carlo!"

"Margherita!"

I shook each student's hand. *"Piacere!"*

Each time I let go of the crutch with my right hand, putting more weight on my left leg, I felt the pain shoot up from my foot to my hip, but I ignored it. I was okay. I felt relaxed. I was even starting to have fun.

I couldn't believe how much I loved teaching. I was always nervous before I walked in, but once in the classroom, I relaxed and felt there was no other place in the world I'd rather be. My students liked me, I could tell.

"The students have no problem with my being disabled; they're very comfortable with me as their teacher," I told Professor DuBois when we found ourselves in the elevator together.

"I knew you'd be fine." He nodded and smiled.

Then why the inquisition that day, I wanted to ask. But I didn't. I didn't tell him that on that infamous day my spirit, my heart and my leg were broken. And while my spirit and my heart had healed, my leg still hurt. Instead, I exclaimed, "I love teaching!"

"I love teaching," I told everyone, including Nica, who wasn't at all interested. My father, on the other hand, was thrilled. He told relatives, friends, and acquaintances that his daughter was now a *professoressa*.

"Not quite, *Papà;* I'm only in training."

I also loved my office. It was the size of a closet, with no windows, but I loved it. I put a poster of the Trevi Fountain on the wall facing my desk. It covered the whole wall; that's how small the room was. There were two chairs, one for me, the other for a student. If two students came together, one of them had to stand, or sit on my desk.

I loved it when students came to my office. They came to get help with Italian grammar but always ended up telling me about their lives. I loved hearing it all.

Only once, a student said very politely, "If you don't mind my asking…"

I didn't wait to hear the obvious question. "I had polio when I was a child."

"Oh."

I was glad she didn't add "I'm sorry." She didn't seem to want more information.

"We all think you're great."

I smiled and opened the textbook to go over Italian verbs.

Even when no students came, I loved sitting in my little office, reading over the work we would be discussing at night in my graduate class. Sometimes I'd close the door to concentrate on my reading. But I could still hear students talking to one another in the hallway.

"Are you taking French or Italian?"

"Do you like your class?"

Did I recognize the students' voices? Were any of them coming to see me?

"And who is your teacher?"

"My teacher…"

I lifted my head from Dante's *Vita Nuova, The New Life,* and listened. He sounded like one of my students.

"She's the handicapped teacher."

I felt like I'd been punched in the gut. I pushed against the desk to move my chair back just enough that I could reach the door and turn the knob to lock it. I was the handicapped teacher. That's how they thought of me. Not just the Italian teacher, but the handicapped teacher. When I heard the knock, I held my breath. I could tell the student was trying to turn the knob. They all knew I never locked the door when I was in my office.

"I saw her just a little while ago."

"Well, I guess she left."

I waited for the voices to move away, then started crying. A few minutes before, I'd been so happy. I'd felt I belonged in this department, in my closet of an office. I believed I was accepted by my students, well liked. "We think you're great." I'd taken it as a compliment. Suddenly, I suspected what the girl had meant was "We think you're great to be teaching even though you're a cripple."

I could never be just one of the teachers. Like I could not be just one of the graduate students. Like I was never just one of the girls. *Ciunca.* I didn't know if I was sad or angry, or both. Dante's *Vita Nuova* was still open on my desk. I picked it up and hurled it at the Trevi Fountain. Nothing was new in my life. This was how it had always been and how it would always be. No matter what I did, no matter what I accomplished, I would be known for my disability. I would always be the different one, the handicapped one.

"Well, hello stranger!" That's how my old friends greeted me when they saw me at the DIA meeting. I was embarrassed but, at the same time, happy to be with them. A lot had changed, including many of the faces. Even without Judy, DIA was going strong, while the first organization I had joined, PRIDE, had fizzled out. The time for pride had not yet come.

Judy had been gone for over a year. She was in Berkeley, California, the best of all possible places for disabled people. That was thanks to the work of a guy named Ed Roberts, who'd had polio and couldn't move at all, couldn't even breathe on his own. He used a respirator and slept in an iron lung, someone said. Ed and his friends, who, like him, were paralyzed but probably could breathe on their own, called themselves "the rolling quads," and had been fighting to make Berkeley very accessible—curb cuts at every corner, ramps in front of every building. And now Ed had started some kind of center for disabled people. Judy was working with Ed.

"What kind of center?" I asked.

"An independent center," my friend Susie said.

"An independent living center," a man who seemed older than the rest interjected, correcting her.

"What kind of center is that?" I was curious to know more.

"I'm not sure." Susie shrugged. "It's some kind of place where disabled people can learn to be independent."

"Yes, be in charge of their lives," the man said. "Ed says that no matter how disabled you are, you gotta call the shots. You shouldn't have some doctor or social worker say you need to be taken care of, treat you like you're sick, or lock you up in some hellhole of a nursing home. Even if you can't move at all and need things done for you, as long as you decide who does what and how, you're in control, you can live your life on your own terms."

"And I say you shouldn't have your parents or other relatives doing it all for you, thinking they know what's best," a young guy interjected.

"If everything is accessible, you can live on your own where you want, work, get married, whatever," the older man continued. "That's called independent living."

It made perfect sense. Luckily, I could do most things for myself, but I remembered how dependent I'd been as a child in Sicily, and later, when in the big cast, how I'd hated the way nurses and aides handled me. What help I'd gotten was always on their terms, not mine.

"At the center in Berkeley, they have people like Ed who know the ropes and show others the way. And they fight to make things better and better."

I wanted to find out all I could about what was going on in Berkeley and about Ed Roberts's work. I wished I could join Judy and Ed. But at least I was here at this meeting, among the people I felt most comfortable with.

I expected the older guy to run the meeting. But a woman in a power chair rolled up to the front. She had a round face and a twinkle in her eyes, and was using some kind of respirator. A ventilator, Susie said it was called. I wondered if it was similar to the one the guy in Berkeley used. Her voice was loud when she started talking; then, as she went on, it got lower. She stopped talking for a second and sucked on a hose held by a gooseneck device near her mouth, and her voice got louder again. It was a bit disconcerting, but only until you got used to it.

A small woman came in as the meeting was about to start and sat next to me. She walked with braces and crutches much better and faster than I did. She had a long braid and the biggest, brightest, friendliest smile in the world.

A main topic on the agenda was the telethon. I wondered if they were talking about a specific one? The Muscular Dystrophy Association one? United Cerebral Palsy?

"The telethon contravenes what our movement is all about. We want rights, not pity," the woman with the ventilator was saying.

I was getting more excited by the minute.

During a break, I turned toward the small woman sitting next to me. She was wearing pants over her braces. Her pant legs had ridden up, and I could see her braces were just like mine. She was older than I was. I asked her if she worked, and she told me she taught math at the New Jersey Institute of Technology, in Newark, New Jersey. I was so happy to hear she was a teacher. I told her I'd just started teaching Italian as a graduate assistant at NYU. Then I found myself telling her what had happened, how upset I'd been to hear a student referring to me as "the handicapped teacher."

She flashed her amazing smile and leaned toward me. "Let these kids remember ten or twenty years from now that they had a handicapped teacher in college. Then they will treat the disabled people they meet with more respect."

Her words made sense. Maybe it wasn't so bad if students saw me as "the handicapped teacher."

I wanted to hug this woman who seemed so wise. But I didn't even know her name. I held out my hand and introduced myself, apologizing for not having done so sooner. She said her name was Frieda Zames.

Frieda. I loved her name as much as I loved her smile. I repeated it a few times. Frieda, Frieda. Maybe what I liked was that it sounded so much like *freedom*. At that moment, I felt free—free to be myself. It was wonderful not to have to pretend, not to have to work hard to belong. I was so happy to be sitting next to Frieda, so happy to be in this room with "my people."

11

AMPUTATION

❋

"At what age did you contract polio? When was the spinal fusion done? What other surgeries have you had?"

The nurse wrote down my answers quickly. She was maybe thirty, attractive and pleasant. She smiled a lot.

"And what are you in for this time?"

Didn't she know? Had she been sent to take my history without being told what I was in for?

"I'm here for a knee disarticulation. I'm going to have both my legs amputated at the knees."

She was looking straight at me and smiling. But the smile was now frozen on her face; her eyes were blank. I was afraid she was going to faint. She was a nurse, for goodness sake! She couldn't faint just because my legs were going to be amputated. Wasn't she supposed to be used to this sort of thing? She must have had other patients whose legs were amputated. But maybe not. She was young.

I felt guilty for having been so blunt. "It's all right." I tried to sound reassuring. "It's a decision I made. A difficult decision. But I believe it's the right one."

She got hold of herself. "Oh, I'm sorry. You seemed so cheerful and carefree. I thought you were in for something minor this time. You've been through so much already."

Oh, yes, I'd been through so much already. Tendons released, muscles transplanted, joints rebuilt, whole spine fused. Not to mention all the broken bones that had to be set. She'd written it all down—all I'd been through. Yet here I was so cheerful and carefree.

"But why are you having your legs amputated?"

Did she need to write that answer down?

Why?

Because my legs keep breaking. I fall and break my knee. I fall and break my ankle. And always at the worst-possible time—at the beginning of the semester, or when I have to give midterms or finals, right before my master's exam, or when I've moved into a new apartment. Every time a bone breaks, it's another break in the progress of my life, the life that's been put on hold so many times. It's hospitals again, and X-rays and casts, and months of not being able to walk, and having to use a wheelchair.

I'm a teacher. How can I teach if I keep breaking my legs? I'm afraid I couldn't teach sitting in a wheelchair. I couldn't write on the blackboard. I'd make my students and colleagues uncomfortable.

Why?

Because the general consensus is that walking is better than using a wheelchair. Because I've been brainwashed into believing that I must walk, no matter how heavy the braces are, no matter how difficult it is to balance on crutches, no matter how many times I fall and break my bones, no matter how much my legs hurt when, after I take the braces off at night, I allow myself to feel the pain. No matter how good it feels to use a wheelchair.

My disabled friends tell me I shouldn't struggle to walk. In the disability movement, we believe we have to fight for our rights as disabled people. And I want to fight. I want to fight to change the world. Still—I can't help it—I also want to be accepted, to fit in.

Why?

Why must I walk? Because it's my duty. I owe it to everybody, my professors, my students, my friends who don't want to think of me as disabled, and most of all to my parents. My father worked so hard to get me to America, so I could walk. My mother gave up so much, her family, her friends, her town, where everyone spoke her language, to come to a foreign land so far away, just so I could walk. All through my childhood, I heard my father say, "In America, you'll be cured, In America, you'll walk." Well, the doctors didn't cure me. But they did get me to walk. So I must keep walking.

How can I let my father down? Though this was not what he had in mind. I hadn't talked to my father about this decision, this operation—I wouldn't dare use the word *amputation*. I start talking and he clams up, walks away. My mother says he'll come around afterward. She says it's because of experiences he had in the war, seeing soldiers with their legs blown off... I believe with my mother that he will come around, that he'll be happy and proud of me when he sees me walking on my new legs.

Why?

Because at this point, I've wrecked my polio legs trying to walk. My poor polio legs, which while I was growing up in Sicily knew nothing of surgeons and scalpels and casts. Oh, my father took me to the best doctors in Italy, and they stuck me with needles, burned me with electric shocks, always hurt me and scared me, but never cut me, never tried to reassemble or reconstruct me, never made me walk with braces. The best therapy my legs knew back then were my mother's tender caresses, and the heat of the sun, the burning sand, and the soothing coolness of the Ionian Sea.

Why?

Because the doctors believe I'll be able to keep walking, and walk better on artificial legs. The doctors, the therapists, the prosthetists at the Institute of Rehabilitative Medicine have been testing me and studying me for almost a year. They had me kneeling inside casts, with

attached pylons and rubber feet. They took pictures of me balancing
on those strange contraptions, holding on to my crutches in my purple
Danskin tights, big smile on my face. Cheerful and carefree.

Why?

Why do I want my legs to be amputated? Because they're useless.
They're nothing but trouble; they've caused me nothing but pain.
They're too short for my body, too skinny and ugly and full of scars.
I've always been ashamed of them. I hate them. And I hate the braces,
the shiny metal, the worn-out leather straps. And the ugly shoes I have
to wear. My body is defective and will still be defective. I'll still be disabled. But I'll look more normal with my new legs. I'll wear normal
shoes on my new feet; I'll go shopping on Eighth Street for pretty high-
heeled shoes, sexy leather boots, open-toe sandals. On my new legs I'll
wear stockings, flesh-colored nylons, black silk, fishnet. I'll wear miniskirts to show them off. They'll be so long and shapely and smooth and
soft; they'll look so real, my new legs.

It wasn't easy to decide. I wanted the doctors to tell me what to do.
I first asked the question a year ago. I asked the orthopedist. "What if
I had my legs amputated? Would I be able to walk with prostheses?" I
never expected to be taken seriously.

"It's an option you have if you want to keep walking."

And before I knew it, I had a whole team working with me until they
were satisfied I would be able to walk well with prostheses. They'll make
me immediate prostheses after the surgery. I'll be walking in no time at
all, they said.

They've made me feel like a star this past year. These American doctors who wouldn't pay attention to me unless unknowingly I used a
curse word, who saw only my disability, acted as if I didn't exist as a
person. Now they all know my name. The head of every department
has taken my case to heart. The head of orthopedic surgery will perform
the amputation. The head of prosthetics will make my prostheses. The
head of physiatry has prepared my rehab plan. The head of the whole
institute, Dr. Howard Rusk, the founding father of rehabilitative

medicine, examined me himself, and came to watch me walk on my weird contraptions. He tells me how much he admires my courage. The doctors are writing articles about me. All are anxious to see how well I'll walk after the amputation, how much my quality of life will improve. They need to confirm their prognosis is right; they want to finish writing their articles. I owe it to them to go through with this. Though none will say I must.

"It's your decision. It's an option you have if you want to keep walking."

It wasn't easy to decide. I never "decided" to have all the other surgeries. For years, it was my father who signed the consent forms, so happy that the American doctors knew how to help me. I signed for the last muscle transplants, since I was already eighteen. But I didn't feel I was making a decision. I always felt I had no choice.

It wasn't easy to decide. I've been seeing a psychologist twice a week for the past three months. What are my motives? Do I really want to do this? Am I making a mistake? Will I regret this for the rest of my life? It's my decision. It's an option I have if I want to keep walking.

The nurse was waiting for me to sign the consent form. Not the nurse who almost fainted in the afternoon, another nurse, much older and not so attractive. She didn't smile. I wondered if she knew what I was in for. If she knew what I was consenting to. She was probably used to this sort of thing; many patients had their legs amputated. She was definitely not the type to get emotional, unlike the young nurse earlier. I could tell she was getting annoyed now. She had other duties, other business to attend to. I'd wasted enough of her time. I signed my name on the dotted line neatly with a steady hand.

"Here!" I smiled as I handed her the form. She didn't smile back.

At 11:00 P.M., the same nurse brought me a sleeping pill and watched while I swallowed it. I fell asleep almost immediately.

It was still dark outside when I woke up from a deep yet restless sleep. I'd been dreaming but didn't remember the dream. Had I dreamed of

Riposto? I pulled the string hanging above my head and turned on the light. I was grateful the other bed in the room was empty. I didn't have to worry about disturbing a roommate. I looked for my watch, which I thought I'd put on the nightstand. But I couldn't find it. Why didn't I leave it on my wrist? The surgery was scheduled for 8:00 A.M. They would be coming to get me ready at six, if not before. I wished I knew what time it was.

I pushed the covers off of me. I bent my knees and pulled them up against my chest and sat with my arms around my legs, hugging them.

Forgive me for what's about to happen to you. Forgive me for all the hurt. Forgive me for hating you.

Suddenly, I wanted to know exactly what was going to happen to them. What will they do with my legs when they're amputated? I wondered for the first time. Why had it never occurred to me to ask? Will they throw them down the incinerator? Together with gallbladders and cancerous kidneys? My poor polio legs, which my mother used to massage so tenderly, religiously, when I was a little girl. I wanted to call my mother and ask her to hurry to the hospital and massage my legs one last time and kiss them good-bye.

I didn't realize how loudly I was crying until I heard the nurse's voice asking, "Are you all right?" and saw her alarmed young face in front of me.

She was the nurse who had taken my history the day before. She put her arm around my shoulders, and I was so glad she was there.

"Thank you," I tried to say between sobs. I was so grateful to her for not being used to this sort of thing, for being unprofessional and emotional and human.

"You can still change your mind, you know. If you don't want to go through with it, it's all right." Her voice was like melted butter.

"Oh, I'll go through with it. I'm fine, really. I just needed to say good-bye."

When they came to take me to the OR, I had washed my face with cold water and combed my long hair, twisting it in back of my head so that it would fit neatly under the blue cap. The young Hispanic man who helped me transfer from the bed onto the stretcher had a round, pleasant face. He smiled at me as he covered my legs with a blue sheet.

"Are you ready to go?"

I gave him the biggest smile I could muster. "As ready as I'll ever be!"

12

YOU DO WHAT YOU HAVE
TO DO

❁

The year I had my legs amputated, 1977, was an important year for disability rights. A great battle was waged across the country to get the regulations issued for Section 504 of the Rehabilitation Act of 1973, which Nixon had signed after vetoing the proposed bill twice.

Section 504 of the law, which we hailed as our first civil rights statute, made it illegal for any agency, institution, or service receiving federal funding "to discriminate solely by reason of handicap." The list of agencies and institutions receiving federal funding, throughout the country, was practically endless. Realizing the vast scope of the law, the Department of Health, Education, and Welfare (HEW), after four years, had still not issued regulations. Without regulations, the law could not be implemented. When Jimmy Carter was elected president, our hopes were raised. But though the regulations had been written at this point, Joseph Califano, the new HEW secretary, was in no hurry to sign them.

I was admitted to NYU Medical Center on March 8, International Women's Day, and had the amputation surgery on the ninth. I was in the hospital for about three weeks. The only pain I suffered was immediately following the surgery. I had no trouble with swelling, or phantom feelings. They put casts on my stumps, and pylons with rubber feet, so I was able to stand and walk with my crutches within days of the surgery. When the casts came off, I was moved to the Institute of Rehabilitative Medicine (IRM), on the north end of the NYU Medical Center complex, which stretched from First Avenue to the FDR Drive and from Thirty-first to Thirty-fourth streets. There, every day for many hours, I worked hard learning to walk on prostheses.

IRM in the 1970s was full of young people, most of them with spinal cord injuries. The joint was jumpin'. When they were discharged, these young men and women would face the difficulties of adjusting to life as paraplegics or quadriplegics, and to a once-familiar world suddenly full of barriers, physical and otherwise. For now, with their families and friends assuring them they would be cured and walk again, they figured they might as well horse around, drink beer, and blast their boom boxes.

On April 5, at 6:00 P.M., I was resting after a hard day in PT, when I got a call from Susie, who urged me to turn on the news. My roommate, a nineteen-year-old whose neck had been broken in a car accident, was listening, at earsplitting volume, to Rod Stewart singing "Tonight's the night." Her eyes closed, her lips curved into a blissful smile, she was in a trance of pre-accident ecstasy.

I could hardly hear my friend, and couldn't make out a word the reporter was saying when I turned on the TV in the room. But I could see disabled people demonstrating at the NYC HEW office. I deduced that it was about the regulations for Section 504.

Lifting myself with my arms, I jumped into the wheelchair that was alongside my bed—still amazed at how easily I could transfer without legs—and rolled to the pay phone in the waiting area, hoping it'd be quieter than my room. I called the one person I was sure could explain things to me: Frieda. No answer. She wasn't home. Of course, she was at the demonstration.

I had not been as active in DIA as I would have liked. I was busy studying and teaching or recovering from fractures and breaks, or, in the last months, seeing doctors and therapists and trying to come to a decision about amputation. I'd also been busy looking for an apartment, and in May 1976, I'd finally moved out of my parents' house.

I'd searched the whole Village, driving around, stopping at buildings that had no steps but didn't look too fancy, asking if there were apartments for rent. Looking through ads in newspapers was a waste of time. The word *accessible* had no meaning to realtors and landlords.

Finally, I'd found a studio in a building with a level entrance and an elevator, right on Bleeker Street. Although small and dark, with the only window facing a brick wall, it was smack in the middle of the Village, where I'd always dreamed I'd live.

When I first told my parents, they both looked so worried. I thought they'd start warning me about the dangers of living on my own. Instead, my father asked, "Do you have to pay a month's rent in advance and a month's rent as a deposit?"

I told him I'd been saving and had the money.

He took out his checkbook and wrote me a check.

"*Ecco, gioia,* here! Use the money you saved to buy some furniture."

My mother hugged me. She cried while repeating how happy she was.

One sad note was leaving behind my precious Nica. I solemnly swore to her on a box of dog biscuits that I'd see her at least every weekend.

The other problem was that, though the apartment was otherwise accessible, the bathroom door was too narrow. If I used my wheelchair, I had to transfer onto a stool to get in. Two months after moving, I fell while transferring and broke my right leg. That fall weighted the scale in favor of the amputation.

Now I had no legs to break and transferring was much easier for me. I couldn't wait to get back to my little "hole."

I tried to call Frieda again the next morning, April 6, and still no answer.

Though I had not been able to attend DIA meetings regularly, I'd tried my best to go to demonstrations. Now I wished I was with Frieda and the other DIA activists at the HEW office.

For years, I'd been—and indeed still was—terribly conflicted. I wanted to be around other disabled people, with whom I felt most comfortable, be part of our movement, and fight for our rights. At the same time, I wanted to be accepted in the nondisabled world; I didn't want to be seen as different. I'd discussed my feelings in depth with my psychotherapist, while trying to decide about the amputation. It had been at times unbearably painful to dig deep inside myself and uncover hidden motives, confront rational and irrational fears, distinguish between my own wishes and outside pressures.

I'd talked to Frieda while trying to decide. She couldn't understand why I didn't just use a wheelchair if I couldn't walk anymore, or a scooter, like the one she had recently gotten. Judy might have questioned whether I was "liberated" enough. Frieda, however, was never one to analyze or judge. "If you feel that's what you have to do, then do what you have to do."

I finally reached Frieda on the morning of April 7. The American Coalition of Citizens with Disabilities had staged a sit-in at the HEW headquarters in D.C., Frieda told me, and had called for protests and sit-ins at regional HEW offices. DIA had held a demonstration of about fifty people outside of the HEW office, while she and eight other DIA members had gone inside. They had occupied the NYC office for thirty-three hours. There was no way they could have stayed longer. She, for one, had to get back to her teaching. In D.C., they lasted only twenty-eight hours, she added, as if to make herself and the other DIA members look better. But in San Francisco, disabled activists were still occupying the HEW office. Judy Heumann was there with at least a hundred people who either worked at the Berkeley Center for Independent Living (CIL) or received services there. They were planning to stay as long as it took. Ed Roberts, though not staying in the HEW office day and night, was overseeing the protest. He was now a big shot. He had been appointed by the governor of California, Jerry Brown, to head the state's Department of Rehabilitation.

As the San Francisco sit-in continued, I called Frieda almost daily from the hospital for updates. "Are they still in there?"

"Yes, they're holding strong."

Strong was not a strong-enough word to describe those extraordinary activists. I wished I could have been in that building with them. At the same time, I questioned my ability to do what they were doing.

Frieda reported, "The Black Panthers are bringing them food... The Butterfly Brigade [a gay group] got walkie-talkies for them..."

I was moved by the support the sit-in was getting from such disparate groups.

Finally, on April 28, the good news: Califano had signed the Section 504 regulations. We could now start using the law to fight against discrimination.

The protesters didn't leave until April 30, after they had examined the document. The sit-in had lasted twenty-five days. It was the longest sit-in ever in a government building. It showed the effectiveness of civil disobedience. It gave our struggle for disability rights recognition and validation as a real movement. It also established a tradition of solidarity between disability rights activists and other groups fighting for social justice—a solidarity that at times would, however, be put to the test.

Shortly after the San Francisco protesters victoriously marched out of the HEW building, I walked out of IRM on my long, shapely prosthetic legs. I wore stockings, pretty shoes, and a short skirt. I was still a bit unsteady, but I had the whole summer ahead of me. I would work hard in physical therapy, and by September, when I was planning to go back to NYU, I'd be a real pro and feel like I'd been born with gorgeous fake legs.

I had asked for a leave of absence from NYU "for personal reasons," after making sure my health insurance would remain active. I'd been worried about whether the insurance would cover the surgery, the prostheses, the rehab, the lengthy hospitalization. At times, I still questioned whether my father's treasured Blue Cross policy had been enough to cover the endless surgeries and years in various hospitals, or if telethon money had supplemented the quest for my cure—I vaguely remembered that my father had mentioned the March of Dimes. Later, in the hospital with a broken leg, having aged out of my father's Blue Cross policy, I recalled being asked by a social worker to sign a paper attesting to the fact that I had no income or resources of my own. There were no coverage problems throughout my stay at the hospital and at IRM.

My professors, colleagues, and students didn't know about the amputation. They probably guessed I'd gone to the hospital. I hadn't been able to keep my falls, fractures, and casts secret. I'd been forced to cancel classes, couldn't finish my papers on time, got incompletes, postponed my master's exam. Now I was planning to take the exam in September, and apply for an instructorship. I was afraid that if I disclosed my latest surgery, I'd blow my chances of advancement at NYU. Professor DuBois said whenever he saw me, "Hope you're getting better!" If he'd known, he would have thought I was getting a lot worse.

I'd learned that amputation freaked people out. Friends—disabled and nondisabled—had reacted negatively to my news. Later, they were supportive, though some, including Susie, never visited me in the hospital.

"I'd rather wait and see you when you're out," they said on the phone.

What hurt most was to see my father so distressed. When my parents visited me right after the surgery, my mother rushed into my room ahead of my father to put a pillow under the blankets where my legs no longer were.

"It's so hard for your father…"

Every time they came, whether I was in bed or in my chair, I made sure I was well covered. I hoped my father would get over his grief once he saw me walking. But the first time I showed off my prostheses, wearing a short skirt, my father wouldn't even look at me.

"*Come sei bella!* How beautiful you look!" My mother hugged me. But her admiration couldn't make up for my father's rejection.

"He'll come around," she kept telling me, and I kept hoping he would. One of the reasons for my decision had been to make my father happy, by being able to walk, rather than needing a wheelchair, which I knew he hated. Ironically, I had succeeded in making him more unhappy.

I worked hard in PT all summer. I still needed crutches for balance, because my trunk muscles were weak, but I could walk much better and faster. While with braces I'd walked stiff-legged, with prostheses I was able to bend my knees and take natural-looking steps. I'd gained a few inches, and my friends said I looked like a fashion model. I surprised even the doctors who were writing articles about me with how well I'd learned to walk.

In September, I went back to NYU. I explained I'd had surgery to strengthen my legs. It wasn't that much of a lie. My "new legs" were by far sturdier than my polio legs. I promised there would be no more accidents and absences. I took the master's exam and passed it with honors. With the degree, I was awarded an instructorship.

I attended DIA meetings as regularly as I could. There was a lot of excitement about what Section 504 meant for us. Since those with mobility impairments were in the majority, the first issue we tackled was our right to accessible public transportation.

"We want to get on a bus! Aren't we part of the public?"

I'd never been on a bus. No matter how well I walked on prostheses, I still couldn't step up onto a bus. Though I was used to driving my car, riding on a bus had an egalitarian appeal. For those who couldn't drive or couldn't afford a car, access to public transportation was more crucial; it meant going places instead of being stuck at home.

Getting on a bus symbolized entering mainstream society, the beginning of an end to segregation. Riding public buses had been an important issue in the civil rights struggle. Rosa Parks had fought for her right to sit in the front of a bus. We couldn't get on a bus at all.

In June 1978, I went to the Clearwater Festival in Croton Point Park, on the Hudson River. DIA had formed a singing group, the DIA Singers, with support from Pete Seeger, the celebrated folk musician, and under the leadership of singer/songwriter Eric Levine, who had chronic kidney disease and was on dialysis. The group's songs reflected our struggle for equal rights. Frieda was in the group, though she'd be the first to admit she couldn't sing. Her life partner, Michael, on the other hand, had a baritone voice that could rival the very best. The DIA Singers were performing a song written by a member, Karen, who was blind.

> *Where, where, where have you left us,*
> *Right outside your door,*
> *We are your daughters and we are your sons*
> *And we won't be left out anymore...*

I was using my wheelchair. I planned to stay the whole day, and the park was huge, the various stages far from one another. There was a limit to how far I could walk; I still needed my wheelchair for distances. Frieda was using her Amigo scooter.

Around dinnertime, I sat with Frieda and Michael at one of the picnic tables and ate falafel and rice with lentils and onions, which Michael had bought at one of the food stands. Michael had dystonia, and though one side of his body was much weaker than the other, he walked quite well.

I told Frieda I'd applied for NYU housing in Washington Square Village. I knew there was a waiting list, but hoped I wouldn't have to wait too long.

"You want to move out of your little hole? I thought you loved it."

"I do love it. But Washington Square Village is much more accessible. The bathroom doors are wider. I'll be able to use my chair at home when not wearing my prostheses."

We had finished our dinner and decided we wanted ice cream. Michael went to get in line at the stand.

"Pistachio for me," I yelled.

All of a sudden, Frieda asked, "Are you happy you had the amputation?"

Was I happy? I hadn't thought about it. I'd been too busy showing others how well I was doing.

I looked at her, and couldn't answer. Then, without knowing what was happening to me, I started crying.

"What is it? Are you sorry you did it?" Frieda looked worried.

"Oh, no, I can walk a lot better and the legs look nice."

"Isn't that what you wanted?"

"I guess so," I replied, but I couldn't stop crying.

"Then what is it? Is it your father? Has he still not accepted it?"

"My father cannot look at me. He's afraid even to think of my not having legs. He wanted me to be cured. He'll never accept me as I am. It hurts like hell, but I have to accept my father the way he is."

Frieda nodded sympathetically. "What about boyfriends? Men?"

"Men?" I gave a sarcastic little laugh while still crying. "It was never easy with men when I had braces. Now they see nice legs, and then find out they're fake. I'm never eager to have sex, believe me. The moment of truth, when my legs come off, sure puts a damper on things."

Frieda's eyes rested on me, soothing and comforting.

I went on: "On top of it all, I'm having an identity crisis."

"What do you mean?"

"Though I hated the way they looked, I'd gotten used to my skinny legs and my braces. And I'd gotten used to having polio. All my life, that was my disability—polio. All of a sudden, I'm an amputee. I'm not sure how to answer when people ask about my disability. If I tell another polio survivor I had polio, I get a second look: 'How come your legs are not skinny like mine?' If I meet another amputee, I have to explain why I need crutches. If I sit in my wheelchair, wearing my prostheses, they think I'm spinal cord–injured."

Frieda just let me talk.

"When others are confused about me, I feel confused about myself.

At times I feel I betrayed myself and all my friends who had polio... and not just polio but other disabilities as well, like spina bifida... all my friends with skinny scarred legs, friends from long ago, even, friends long gone, whose legs looked just like mine—"

"You haven't betrayed anyone," Frieda said, interrupting me. "You know how it feels to have polio and now you also know how it feels to be an amputee. Instead of being confused, let your experience lead you to a better understanding of our differences and our commonalities."

I listened. She continued: "It's easy to bond with the people who are most similar to us. We must learn to connect with those whose disabilities are different, because we all have to deal with barriers, prejudice, and discrimination. We have to join together to fight for our rights: those of us with mobility impairments and those who are blind or deaf, and also those who have cognitive, intellectual, and psychiatric disabilities. We're all disabled. That's our common identity."

Once again, wise Frieda had spoken. Michael was back with the ice cream. I wiped my eyes and licked my pistachio cone.

A couple of weeks later, I joined Frieda and other DIA members in front of the United Nations. We blocked the entrance to the UN grounds, demanding wheelchair-accessible buses. In the following years, the battle would get increasingly fierce.

While fighting for disability rights, DIA also joined other groups in various battles for social justice. The DIA banner would be taken to peace demonstrations, women's rights rallies, gay pride marches. In September 1979, in the midst of the fight for accessible buses, we joined 200,000 people in a protest against nuclear power. The best thing about going to those other protests as a group was not getting patted on the head.

In 1980, a DIA member named Pat Figueroa, a handsome guy who had also started the first independent living center in New York, masterminded a 10-hour sit-in at the MTA—which I missed because I had to teach. A lawsuit was also filed against the Transit Authority. The next year, the first lift-equipped buses appeared on certain routes. But the bus drivers often told us they didn't have a key to operate the lift, or that the lift didn't work. We asked the drivers to call their supervisors and we got in front of the buses. One of our fiercest activists and the original cofounding member of DIA, Denise McQuade, threw herself out of her wheelchair and onto the bus steps and stayed there for hours, attracting lots of media attention.

I'd moved into an apartment in Washington Square Village, and walked around NYU all the time on my prostheses. But I used my wheelchair at demonstrations and protests. When it came to blocking buses, the wheelchair sure was useful. I learned to do a wheelie to jump a curb and park myself in front of a bus.

"If I can't get on, this bus is not moving!"

Delayed from their urgent affairs, many got furious.

"Don't they have ambulances for people like you?"

The battle for accessible buses continued well into the 1980s. At one of the demonstrations at the MTA, I watched Frieda, small and cute on her yellow scooter, with her bright, toothy smile and new short haircut. She was surrounded by big, tall cops.

"Who's in charge?" the cops had asked when they arrived, and we'd pointed to Frieda.

Now one of them wagged his index finger in Frieda's smiling face.

"You have to get these people away from here. You cannot block this entrance!"

Frieda didn't stop smiling.

"If you don't tell these people to move, we'll have to start making arrests."

Frieda shrugged: "You do what you have to do; I do what I have to do."

She kept calm, kept smiling, never argued with the police, and never budged. She did what she had to do. And so did we. There might have been disagreements and personality clashes in DIA, as in any organized group. But we knew how to act in unison, by watching Frieda and following her lead. That's when I realized how formidable she was, in her own unassuming way.

When the demonstration ended, I wheeled over to Frieda to tell her how formidable she was, how proud I was to be a DIA member and to have her as our president, and how proud I was to have her as my friend. But instead of saying those things, I threw my arms around her and gave her a big Italian hug. I'd wanted to do that since the first time I met her. I could feel the lordosis, the inward curve of her spine, which was much like my own spine, and like the spines of most of us who'd had polio. My scoliosis, the sideways curve, had been straightened when my spine was fused, but the lordosis couldn't be fixed. Even without my polio legs, my body was still similar to Frieda's.

I must have caught her by surprise. Her slender torso stiffened in my arms. Was I embarrassing her, or was she trying to keep her balance? Then I felt her relax, felt her arms tightening around me. She laughed.

"You crazy, passionate Italian, you!"

13

NOT A REAL CHEERY PICTURE

❀

I was trying to get to my 2:00 P.M. Advanced Composition class when a student, rushing past me in the crowded hallway, made me lose my balance. Down I went. Thank goodness these fake legs don't break like my real ones, I thought as two other students stopped, grabbed my arms, and stood me back up. Another student handed me my crutches.

I'd been falling more and more lately. I figured I was tired. After all, I'd been working full-time, even teaching summer courses, while being as active as I could in the disability movement, and managing to attend other demonstrations, as well. With my DIA friends, I went to a few disarmament protests in '82 and '83, carrying a sign that said BUILD RAMPS, NOT BOMBS! I'd also been in a relationship that ended leaving me sad and drained.

James, with whom I shared my life for a year and a half, was an artist. I saw his paintings lined up on the sidewalk at the Washington Square Art Show on Memorial Day in 1982, and fell in love—with the paintings first. With their long, heavy brushstrokes of brilliant colors on big canvases, the paintings possessed a strange spiritual, almost religious, quality.

I pointed to one. "How much do you want for that?"

"It's yours if you let me take it to your home and hang it."

Less than a month later, he moved in with his easels, canvases, brushes, and paints, and turned my apartment into an artist's studio. I didn't mind. I loved James. I wanted him to get me pregnant. My biological clock had started to tick. I wanted a baby with James's thick dark hair and penetrating eyes, his sensitivity and his artistic talent. He went along—counting days, taking my temperature, seizing the right moment... even getting up half-asleep to watch me fuss in the bathroom with an early-pregnancy test kit. Women were advised to use the first urine of the morning. He got excited with me, one month, when the color of the EPT vial seemed just right. And he comforted me two weeks later when I cried while fishing a big blood clot out of the toilet. If I didn't get pregnant, it wasn't James's fault. Nor could I blame him if he got tired of playing along. I came home from work one day, to find his easels, brushes, and almost all his paintings gone.

I was distraught. I decided I'd never again try to have a baby.

"You probably couldn't carry to term," my gynecologist said. "I've told you all along, it's best if you don't get pregnant."

Except for my gynecologist, I'd discussed my desire to have a baby only with my mother. If she told my father, he never let on. Both treated James like family whenever he accompanied me to Queens.

Right after he left me, I went to see my parents, and they had a big meal waiting—my favorite beef roll with pasta, good wine, cannoli for dessert, and even amaretto liqueur. The dining room table was set with the good china and silverware, as if it were a holiday. I couldn't tell whether my parents wanted to comfort me by feeding me, or if they thought my breakup with James was cause for celebration.

My mother took me aside. "I know how much you wanted a baby. But some things are not meant to be."

Now, I was having so much trouble, I couldn't imagine how I would have managed a pregnancy, or taking care of a baby. I was at the point where if I got through the day without falling, I considered myself lucky.

I need a vacation, I told myself. But when I went to Miami during the winter break of 1984–1985 to get away from the cold, which, unexplainably, was becoming intolerable for me, I came back more exhausted than ever.

I should have more protein in my diet, I told myself, and must remember to take my one-a-day vitamins. When my joints hurt, I decided I needed calcium.

"You need to stop walking and use your wheelchair," Frieda told me. "There's only so much you can ask of your body."

Stop walking? I'd gone as far as having my legs amputated in order to keep walking.

I started using my wheelchair when not at work. But I was afraid of going into a classroom in my wheelchair, afraid of not being able to write on the blackboard, and of what my students and colleagues would think.

NYU was such a hectic place. I was exerting all my energy moving around the crowded buildings, trying not to get trampled by the herds of hurrying students. I had loved NYU's fast-paced atmosphere. Now I found it nightmarish.

"What you're experiencing are symptoms of post-polio syndrome," another friend, Marilyn Saviola, told me.

Marilyn, too, was a polio survivor. Polio had left her quadriplegic and dependent on a ventilator to breathe. She used a power wheelchair, the ventilator attached to the back, an air tube snaking around to her mouth. She had been institutionalized as a girl but had succeeded in getting out, serving as an example to many others. She lived in an apartment in Brooklyn with around-the-clock assistance from personal-care attendants. I admired her competence and resourcefulness, and wondered how I would have fared had I been as disabled as she was. Just a few years older than I, she came from an Italian-American family. She had an ample, welcoming face crowned by dark curls, and exuded authority. I'd met her in the 70s, when she was president of Disabled In Action. Now she was executive director of the Center for Independence of the Disabled in New York (CIDNY)—having succeeded Pat Figueroa, who had moved upstate. Centers for Independent Living, CILs for short, modeled after the original CIL founded in Berkeley by Ed Roberts in 1972, had by now emerged in cities across the country.

I'd never heard of post-polio syndrome. "What the hell is that?"

"Doctors are still trying to figure it out."

She showed me a *Newsweek* article, "A New Scare for Polio Victims." Apparently, I wasn't the only one "suffering excruciating pain and muscle weakness." And "doctors [were] as baffled as the patients themselves."

In July 1985, another article appeared—this one in *The New York Times Magazine*. The title: "Polio's Painful Legacy."

"All over the country, survivors of polio are learning, to their dismay, that some of the symptoms of the disease they struggled so hard to overcome years ago are returning. Medical professionals have begun to refer to the condition as 'post-polio syndrome' or 'post-polio sequelae'; the symptoms are extreme fatigue, muscle weakness, debilitating joint pain, breathing difficulties and intolerance of cold."

I was experiencing all those symptoms, except for the breathing difficulties. I didn't have those—yet.

According to the article, symptoms appeared some thirty to thirty-five years after the original onset of polio. The numbers sure added up for me.

Those who had received the most aggressive intervention and rehabilitation were more greatly affected by the syndrome. Dr. Frederick Maynard was quoted: "What you gained during rehabilitation is what you're most likely to lose now. It's not a real cheery picture."

Another expert, Dr. Jacquelin Perry, said, "Polio survivors are over-achievers, they're out to prove they can do as well as those who didn't have polio. But now the strain has accumulated."

Was I an overachiever? Had I brought this upon myself?

That article scared the living daylights out of me.

Sensible Frieda tried to reassure me: "I'm sixteen years older than you and I'm managing, with the help of my scooter."

But I couldn't stop being afraid. And I wasn't just afraid; I felt deceived, betrayed—not only by the medical professionals who had pushed me to the limit but also by our movement. We'd been saying that our disabilities were _not_ the problem; our suffering was caused by an unjust and prejudiced society. Now my disability, polio, like an enraged monster, was turning on me. Was I being punished for having had my legs amputated? My thoughts were so incongruous, I was afraid of losing my mind.

In the past few years, I had seen young, healthy gay men suddenly get sick and die of a disease doctors were calling AIDS. I now identified with my gay friends, as I, too, lived in fear.

My condition worsened with the start of the new semester. I couldn't handle classes, let alone muster the energy to go to DIA, or visit my parents on weekends. When my mother called to tell me Nica had died, I was so overcome with grief and guilt, I couldn't get out of bed for days. That little dog had brought so much joy into my life, and now her life had ended without a final thank-you or a kiss good-bye.

The pain of missing James showed no sign of lessening. At work, I cried while writing verb tenses on the blackboard, my back to the class. At night, unable to sleep, I saw James's eyes, felt his paint-stained hands on my breasts. I blamed myself for driving him away.

I had no desire to be with another man. I tried to ignore a guy who kept crossing my path. When I first met him, I was in distress. Tired and sore after a day at work, I'd walked to my car, only to discover one of my tires was flat. He happened to be around and offered to change it. I was grateful. Another day, made clumsy by pain, I dropped the cup of coffee I'd just bought at the Waverly luncheonette, and there he was on his knees, wiping the floor with paper towels, then buying me another cup. The week after, I fell coming out of the Main Building, and who was lifting me off the ground? The same guy. He said he lived and worked nearby, and asked if he could take me out to dinner. I brushed him off with an excuse.

I should have been suspicious. I knew about men who pursued

disabled women because they got off on the disability and enjoyed the advantage their able bodies gave them. Stalking was one of the "games" some played. Other games could be humiliating and even dangerous. Audrey's cowardly boyfriend, Ray, always came to mind. I'd learned to recognize the type and stay away. Yet I fell into this guy's trap. He wasn't bad-looking, and he was polite, even charming. Having refused a few times, one Friday evening I accepted his invitation to dinner. I needed to relax. I had a first drink, which eased my pain, then another to try to make it go away completely, then one too many. I let him take me to his place, at the corner of Prince and Broadway, up two flights of stairs. He helped me up one flight, carried me up the other.

In spite of my inebriated state, I got suspicious when he became extremely aroused while watching me take off my prostheses. At the same time, I was grateful for the absence of anxiety and awkwardness that usually accompanied what I called "the moment of truth." I didn't need to wonder what he was thinking, or feel compelled to make bad jokes, such as "I'm the bionic woman."

My suspicion turned to alarm when the guy picked up my prostheses and crutches and put them out of my reach in a closet.

"You can't get away from me now," he said. But then he laughed and assured me he would get them when I needed them.

For a while, still drunk, I played along. I hoped he'd get tired of the game. I ended up being there for two days and two nights. The guy didn't hurt me. On the contrary, he carried me to the bathroom when I needed to go, fed me well, tried to keep me entertained. He had plenty of food in the fridge. In the bedroom were a TV and a stereo. Everything had been planned. Maybe he had brought other disabled women there before me.

"What can I do for you? Whatever you want."

"I just want to leave. Give me my prostheses and my crutches."

"Oh come on, aren't you comfortable here? What else can I do for you?"

The bedroom door was always shut. When he went out to the kitchen to get food, he closed it behind him. The phone never rang, so I figured he had disconnected it. The sex was never rough. He stopped when I fought back, and apologized; then he masturbated, while I tried to ignore him. Once, maybe twice, he promised to get my prostheses and crutches if only I'd let him do it, and I submitted. He never tied me up or beat me, but I was captive and helpless in his bed, the equivalent of a nondisabled woman in sexual bondage.

Neither one of us slept much. He slept even less than I. A couple of times when I dozed off, I awoke and found him watching me and playing with himself. Late Sunday night, I woke up after sleeping about an hour, and saw the bedroom door open. I could hear him in the bathroom. I leaned over until my hands touched the floor and lowered myself off the bed. Naked, I crawled on my stumps to the living room. I managed to reconnect the phone, which he had unplugged, back into the jack, and called the police. I thought he would get angry and hurt me when he came out of the bathroom and saw me crawling as fast as I could back into the bedroom.

He was angry, but he got my prostheses and crutches down and rushed me to get dressed. By the time two policemen arrived, he was helping me down the stairs.

"Just a misunderstanding!" he told them.

He walked me to my car while the policemen watched. I should have pressed charges, made sure he didn't do the same thing to another disabled woman. But I was too ashamed. I blamed myself for being naïve. I never saw the guy around NYU again. When I decided to look him up, there was no record of his having lived in the apartment where he'd taken me. I told no one about the experience. Some gay friends had confided they were swearing off sex for fear of AIDS. Shunning all advances seemed like a good idea for me, too.

Utterly dispirited, not only did I keep falling, I couldn't cope with the simplest daily routines. I had prided myself on never calling in sick. Now I did it every week. I decided I hated teaching, which I'd loved so much. I wrote a letter of resignation, but before I handed it in, I got notice that my contract would not be renewed. I was both defeated and relieved.

When a friend told me about a part-time position as junior producer at the Italian Radio and Television Network, it sounded like the change I needed. Being part-time, the job provided no health insurance. But I didn't think doctors could be of help to me. Besides, post-polio syndrome, being a preexisting condition, wouldn't have been covered by a new insurance policy. I resolved to use my wheelchair and see if that helped. I started working at the network in the summer of 1986.

When I stopped teaching, I was told I could remain in NYU housing until I found another accessible and affordable place. Rather than driving to my new job in midtown—fighting the traffic and worrying about finding a parking space—I decided to conserve energy by using the city buses, which we'd fought to make wheelchair-accessible.

Often, the driver, not wanting to bother getting me on, said he didn't have the key for the lift. But DIA had gotten keys from the MTA, and I always carried mine.

"Here's the key," I'd say with a forced smile.

The driver grumbled, and so did the passengers. But I got on.

Some people were outright nasty.

"Where are you getting off?" A guy angrily spat the question in my face as the driver was locking my wheelchair into place with the tie-down mechanism.

"Why do you need to know?"

"Because if you're getting off before me, you're going to make me late for work," he barked.

"I'm going to work, same as you."

The kindhearted observed how nice it was that "people like me" could get on the bus now. I explained how hard we'd had to fight for the right to ride a public bus. A few listened and nodded sympathetically. One might get teary-eyed and tell me how inspirational I was to be out and about.

The unpleasant incidents, forcing me to fight back, were ultimately empowering. And I enjoyed riding the bus in my wheelchair, with the air-conditioning chilling my neck and blending the diverse odors of the passengers—the nasty ones as well as the overly sympathetic—into an amalgamated, homogenized scent. I felt part of that idealized melting pot.

The work at the network was interesting enough. I produced mostly radio shows that aired locally for the NYC Italian-American community. After a few months, I managed to convince my boss to let me do a brief piece on the new disability rights movement in the United States, which I hoped could air in Italy.

Using my wheelchair helped a lot. The pain and fatigue diminished considerably. But I felt dissatisfied. This wasn't the kind of work I wanted to do.

Once a week I went to a post-polio support group that Marilyn led at CIDNY.

"We're not going to let the doctors scare us. We'll stop pushing ourselves, conserve energy, keep warm, but we'll go on living our lives," Marilyn repeated.

At one of those meetings—sitting in a circle with other polio survivors, some of us in wheelchairs, some sitting in regular chairs and wearing leg braces, their crutches lying on the floor—I admitted I missed teaching. Everyone encouraged me to get back to it.

Shortly after, the opportunity to teach at Fordham University, in the Bronx, came up. I was given a glowing recommendation from Professor DuBois. I went for an interview, not sure what I wanted or expected. As soon as I drove through the campus's gates, I was enchanted. Amid lush green lawns and century-old trees sat medieval-looking buildings, some covered in ivy. I hadn't seen anything like this since I'd left Italy. Later, I learned the architectural style was called "collegiate Gothic." I drove around, looking for the building where my interview was to take place. The atmosphere was peaceful; the students and the teachers looked relaxed. In spite of the steps I saw in front of some arched entrances, and the quaint cobblestone paths—bumpy when rolling in a wheelchair—Fordham seemed manageable to me, the opposite of NYU.

I rolled in for the interview in my wheelchair, then casually stood up on my crutches. At that time, employers could ask all the questions they wanted about those with disabilities. I told them I'd contracted polio as a child. I didn't mention post-polio syndrome or amputation.

When I was offered the position, I accepted it with apprehension but also with optimism. There was one problem with Fordham: I couldn't take a bus to the Bronx. The subway system was totally inaccessible. I had no choice but to drive there. Since I was given morning classes, I had to leave home practically at dawn. But I started to like practicing the old adage "early to bed, early to rise."

I decided to buy myself a new wheelchair when I started at Fordham—an ultralight, ultramaneuverable, bright red, beautiful little number. Manufactured by a company founded by a paraplegic woman, it had the evocative brand name Quickie. At first, I still walked into the classroom and stood throughout my lessons. Outside, around the picturesque campus, I used my new chair. Then, since the buildings where my classes were held had accessible entrances, I started going into the classroom in my chair and then got out of it to teach. I carried my crutches in the back, held by a bracket. The thrill of showing off my fake legs by wearing miniskirts and fishnet stockings had worn off quite a while back. I now wore pants over my prostheses—much more practical. Sometimes I stayed sitting in my chair for the whole class, but I couldn't do much writing on the blackboard. Frieda told me that in her math classes she used an overhead projector.

"Arrange to have one brought to your classrooms."

"And what do I do with it?"

"I'll teach you."

She drove to the Bronx, in big-sisterly fashion, brought me a box of transparencies, and taught me to use a projector.

Once I grew accustomed to using my wheelchair in the classroom, I realized all that mattered was my ability to teach.

NOT A REAL CHEERY PICTURE 🌸 165

I started going to demonstrations again. In response to the AIDS crisis, a direct-action group, ACT UP, had been formed to fight for health care and against stigma and discrimination. With gay friends, I went to an ACT UP demonstration and chanted, "Act up, fight back." We all needed to fight back.

My beautiful red Quickie wheelchair brought me enormous, unanticipated joy—such joy that I felt grateful to the effects of post-polio syndrome, which made using a wheelchair no longer just optional. The new wheelchair marked the start of a new phase in my life. So much that had happened in the last few years had made me feel weak, fearful, powerless. The Quickie helped me feel strong again, confident, even powerful. I loved the way I looked and felt in it. No longer in constant pain, I had energy for the things I wanted to do. And I loved being able to go faster than ever before.

"Can I help you cross the street?" people asked.

"No, thanks!" I gave my wheels a few strong turns, and left them all behind.

I'd been reading a recently published book by a polio survivor, Hugh Gallagher, titled *FDR's Splendid Deception*. The president with polio had fascinated me ever since, as a little girl, I'd listened to my father talk about him. Apparently, it wasn't just my father who thought FDR had been cured. The extent of FDR's paralysis was the best-kept secret of American politics. Though he needed a wheelchair, FDR was never seen in one in public. He always appeared to be standing and walking. The American people, who four times elected him president, never thought of him as disabled. FDR couldn't allow people to know of his condition, since being disabled was the antithesis of being a great world leader. Gallagher showed what a massive toll the deception took on FDR, who ignored what were now being recognized as the symptoms of post-polio syndrome in order to win a fourth term. At the end, his body could no longer withstand the strain.

The book was reviewed in *The Disability Rag,* an excellent, irreverent little paper that I read religiously, the voice of the national disability rights movement. The reviewer argued that, since he had hidden his disability, FDR could not be considered "a hero" for disabled people. A good point. Yet I felt for the man more than I ever could have for a hero. On a smaller scale, with much less at stake, I had put a terrible strain on myself while laboring to fit into the non-disabled world and achieve a modicum of success. I'd taken extreme measures, my poor body cut up, mutilated, forced to do more than was physically possible. In spite of priding myself on being part of the disability movement, I'd continued to take upon myself the burden of making the able-bodied feel comfortable, so they didn't even think of me as disabled.

Symbolically, my new wheelchair marked the end of the pretense. No more struggling to walk, no more dragging myself up steps. No more bending over backward to be accepted. Never again would I feel obligated to pursue the oppressive and absurd ideal of "normality."

Yet, my newfound liberation was left at the door whenever I entered my parents' house. There I felt I should walk as much as possible. I knew my father hated seeing me in a wheelchair. I also knew he never wanted to see me without my prostheses, and I made sure he didn't. My father's love was as important to me as the presidency was to FDR.

I missed many meetings of the post-polio support group when I started at Fordham. When I managed to get back, and announced I was teaching again, they all cheered. They complimented me on my new wheelchair. I told them how happy the Quickie made me. I had loved using a wheelchair since I first sat in one when I was thirteen, but I'd been made to feel I had to walk. We talked about how much agony we could have been spared.

"So many of us endured torture in order to be more normal…"

"Yet, all our experiences, good and bad, make us who we are," Marilyn said, sucking on her ventilator hose. "Let's be proud we got this far and not waste time with regrets."

Marilyn was right. I started spending more time with family and friends, being more active in DIA, attending demonstrations. Though still guarded, I was even more confident around men. The picture was again looking "cheery."

My parents, circa 1946.

My mother carries me, age 5 or 6, into the Church
of the Addolorata, Riposto, Sicily.

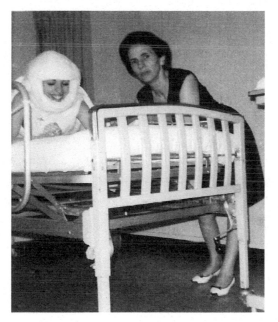

My mother is visiting me in the Hospital for Special Surgery, NYC,
after my body has been wrapped in plaster. The first step in the long process
of straightening my back, 1962.

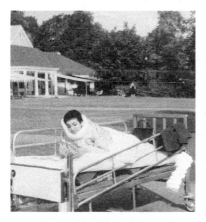

(*above*) At Blythedale, enjoying the
sunshine outside, in my bed, 1963.

(*right*) I'm getting ready to join a
demonstration, NYC, 1972.

PART III

Love and Activism

14

LOVE AND ACTIVISM ON TWO CONTINENTS

❋

About a week before Christmas in 1987, I received a phone call from one of the secretaries at the radio network. I hadn't been working there for months, so I couldn't imagine why she would call me.

"A man from Italy, who heard your show on disability, called because he'd like to meet you. Can I give him your home number?"

"Sure."

There had been no feedback about my piece on disability, which I'd heard was cut to five minutes when it aired in Italy. I was disappointed. I'd hoped not for recognition, but to reach disabled people in Italy. Now I wondered, Who is this man and why is he interested in me? Is he disabled?

He wasn't. His name was Maurizio. When we met in a coffee shop near Washington Square, I found him to be a pleasant man, "no longer very young"—as he described himself—but youthful-looking. I was thirty-nine and he was fifty-four. He told me he'd been listening to the radio by chance and found himself captivated by my words and "the passion in my voice."

Then he confided, "My mother, who's been dead for years, had a condition that caused her legs to be terribly swollen and made walking difficult. She was ashamed all her life. So hearing you talk so casually and publicly about your disability really affected me."

Maurizio lived in the small town of Bracciano, on the beautiful volcanic lake by the same name, only twenty miles from Rome. He was a widower and had a son who was in college. He taught high school, and loved to travel during holiday breaks and summer vacation. Since he'd been planning a trip to NYC, he thought he'd look me up.

A few days later, I had dinner with Maurizio in the restaurant of the hotel where he was staying. I drove up to Forty-eighth Street, not wanting to wait at a bus stop, since it was very cold. It had been snowing lightly all day. While we sipped pinot grigio and ate veal scallopini, the snow started falling heavily. We talked about teaching, families, art, books. Only when we were savoring our dessert of New York cheesecake did we start talking about disability.

"Is there anything in Italy similar to our disability rights movement?"

"I don't know, but I'll look into it when I get back."

When we finished our dinner and looked outside, we saw chains of white mountains along the street. I couldn't tell which car was mine. And it didn't look like the snow would stop falling. I don't want to make my way home in this blizzard, I thought. I like this smart, kind man, and there's no doubt he likes me.

As if reading my thoughts, he asked, "Can you stay with me tonight?"

"Promise you'll find out if there are groups fighting for disability rights in Italy, who the leaders are, where they are, and exactly what they're doing," I said rather solemnly.

"And if I don't promise, will you leave me right now?" Maurizio sounded amused. We were both nearly naked in each other's arms at this point.

I had taken off my prostheses. I felt much less anxiety and awkwardness now at "the moment of truth." I'd come to realize and learned to use the inherent sensuality in this strange kind of strip show.

That first night with Maurizio, I took off my prostheses in a slow, well-rehearsed but seemingly casual ritual I'd developed for such occasions. Not that such occasions presented themselves often, but when they did, being prepared helped.

I pulled up my long skirt, while still talking and without losing eye contact, gradually exposing the stockinged, shapely foam rubber. Pressing on the release valve, leisurely, I slipped one leg off, letting it fall at my side. Then I repeated the act, taking off the other leg. And all that time, I watched him, trying to guess what he was feeling.

Is he attracted or repulsed, shocked or aroused? I wondered.

Through my skirt at first, I gently massaged my stumps. Then, slowly pulling the skirt down over my hips and sliding out of it, I finally exposed my symmetric and almost perfectly conic thighs, which ended where the knees would be. I always massaged my stumps when I took off my prostheses to help the circulation, but this simple habit acquired an erotic aspect when done in the presence of a man.

It was quite obvious that Maurizio was aroused.

"If I don't promise, will you leave?" he repeated.

I glanced out the window of the hotel room at the steadily falling snow. I laughed.

"Yes, and I'll make you clear all the snow off my car. That'll cool you off!"

He was laughing, too, as he raised his right hand. "Well then, I have no choice but to promise."

In the next five years, I traveled to Italy to be with Maurizio every summer, and during Christmas vacations. I became a seasoned flier, staying in my chair until I checked it at the gate, and using my crutches to get to my seat. I learned to dry myself out by limiting fluid intake, so I never had any need for the impossibly minuscule airplane rest room. Maurizio traveled to New York every spring, over Easter vacation. Conveniently enough, our time off from teaching coincided.

The rest of the year, we made lots of overseas calls and wrote lots of letters. Maurizio sent me a postcard every day. I had a fabulous collection of photos of Rome and the Lazio region, and of other cities to which he'd traveled, as well as art reproductions from museums, churches, and galleries.

Maurizio made it possible for me to visit places I never could have visited on my own. With his help, I saw plenty of cathedrals and all the five thousand square feet of frescoes in the Sistine Chapel, got to touch the Colosseum and the Arch of Constantine, and hang out by the Trevi Fountain to my heart's content. I visited medieval castles and Etruscan ruins, palaces and mansions in the Lazio region as well as in Tuscany, Liguria, Lombardy, and the Veneto. I went to Venice, where Maurizio pulled me up and down the steps of the Rialto Bridge on the Canal Grande.

The one place we never traveled to in those five years was Sicily.

Whenever Maurizio came to New York, he would accompany me to visit my parents. They couldn't have been happier about my Italian boyfriend. They were pleased Maurizio was older and could take care of me.

"*Portala giù in Sicilia,*" my father inevitably said to him, urging him to take me to Sicily.

"What am I? A piece of luggage? I'll go to Sicily when I feel like it."

My parents didn't travel much anymore. My father, a heavy smoker, had had a bout with throat cancer. He was left with breathing problems, and a low, hoarse voice, which he tried to build back up by reciting Sicilian poetry into a tape recorder. My mother, too, had health issues— high blood pressure and cholesterol.

But in earlier years, my parents had gone to Sicily quite regularly. My father always invited me to go along and I always refused. I had stayed true to my resolve, made almost twenty years before, never to go back to Riposto.

Keeping his promise, Maurizio made it possible for me to connect with disabled people in Italy who were fighting for access and equal rights. I spoke at many meetings about the disability rights movement in the United States, the tactics we used, and which ones could work in Italy. I joined in if a battle was going on, and tried to incite more activism wherever I could.

Of all the disabled people I worked with and became close to, Gabriella stands out.

I first heard of Gabriella when Maurizio sent me a newspaper clipping about a group of disabled people who had taken over an abandoned children's camp on a beach in Marina di Grosseto, halfway between Florence and Rome. The headline read THE HANDICAPPED WANT A PLACE IN THE SUN.

But the paraplegic woman who was their leader—Gabriella—was quoted as saying, "This will be a place for independent living and for cultural exchange between disabled people from all Italian regions and from other countries as well."

"A place in the sun" indeed. I laughed at the stereotypical interpretation of the Italian reporter.

Maurizio managed to get a phone number for the camp, and I spoke with Gabriella briefly. "*Vieni, vieni!* Come, come!" she said.

The short trip seemed long, so impatient was I to get there. It was June and already quite hot. We got to the camp at sunset. The pine trees that stretched along the coast met with the whitest sand I'd ever seen. There were wheelchairs under the pine trees—a few empty ones, their owners lying nearby on the sand, others occupied by people busy working together, piles of papers on their laps. Waiting while Maurizio got my chair out of the trunk, I watched a nondisabled young man lift one of the people off the sand and onto a wheelchair with a flawless, well-learned technique.

The camp consisted of three small, low buildings. There were signs of ongoing construction, lumber lying on one side, a ladder leaning against a wall, pails and tools along the paths. Thanks to the fund-raising efforts of Gabriella and her husband, Beppe, the camp was being made more accessible. I hurried Maurizio, who was taking forever inserting the removable wheels into the hubs of my chair, then almost fell while transferring out of the car. I get clumsy when I'm excited.

I headed eagerly toward the buildings. Straight ahead, the sea merged with the sky in a fiery blaze. Suddenly, out of that blaze came a woman, maneuvering an old-fashioned hospital-type wheelchair, wearing a flowered sundress, her hair short and punk and as red as the setting sun, almond-shaped eyes drawing me to her like magnets. I knew immediately she was Gabriella. I gave my wheels a few strong pushes, and I was in front of her.

"*Sorella d'oltre oceano!*" she exclaimed. "Sister from across the ocean!" And she opened her arms wide.

Wheelchairs colliding, I let myself fall into those arms. I let Gabriella hold me tight against her soft, braless breasts and her round paraplegic belly, while my arms tightened around her. I felt I had forever wanted to embrace this disabled sister—my Italian disabled sister, who smelled of sea salt and perspiration and faintly of urine.

Gabriella excited everyone with the fire burning inside her. Colorful and dramatic, hot-tempered and incredibly loving, she was a poet, a true communist, an old hippie, the ultimate earth mother.

We'd talk and talk, Gabriella and I, during many a starry night with the moonlight making the white sand even whiter, while Maurizio and Beppe slept. She asked me what an orgasm felt like. Spinal cord injured at the age of thirteen, incontinent, and with no sensation below the waist, she told me she envied us "polios" who couldn't move but still could feel. In her most dramatic tone, she lamented the fate of her poor little clitoris, "*povero clitoridino!*" always wet and never knowing any pleasure.

"*Dimmi, dimmi, l'orgasmo,*" she repeated, "tell me, tell me."

I laughed as I hugged her. "Gabriella, you orgasm with each and every heartbeat."

Sometimes I fought with Gabriella. She called me a spoiled American capitalist when I ordered food from a nearby restaurant, instead of eating *panzanella,* the typical dish of the Tuscan proletariat, made with stale bread, which she got for free from the local bakery. She lovingly prepared *panzanella* every single day, until I had it coming out of my ears.

I would stay at the camp most of that summer and go back the next two.

I found out Gabriella enlisted and trained, as personal care attendants, conscientious objectors, who, in Italy, were given the option to do community work rather than military service. She was also good at recruiting students to volunteer as attendants. Since disabled people in Italy were commonly taken care of by family members and rarely left home unaccompanied, being away from home and getting assistance with activities of daily living from attendants was for most a new experience.

At the camp, I participated in discussion groups about personal attendant services. At one of those discussions, I was moved by the tears of a 45 year old man with CP whose mother had accompanied him to the camp, but surrendered to Gabriella's iron will and left after a few days. We assumed the man was crying because he missed his mother. Until we listened carefully to his impaired speech and understood what he was saying:

"I'm happy. For the first time in my life I'm free!"

I met the most exciting disabled people at the camp, as I organized demonstrations, gave lectures, conducted workshops. I became especially close to the women: like Mirna from Rome who had rheumatoid arthritis, hot little mama with a round face and a small round body, so savvy she had single-handedly succeeded in getting the media to point the finger of shame at the totally inaccessible Italian Railroad; Lorena from Pisa, long-haired siren, whose spinal cord was injured in a car accident at the age of 16; Irma from Treviso who was an amputee like me; and Filomena from Palermo, Sicily, like me a polio survivor.

I was proud of these disabled sisters, fighting for freedom and equal rights—in Italy, where people were ready to embrace you, but only to whisper "*pietà, pietà.*"

I talked of my childhood in Sicily, one warm moonless night, all of us disabled women sitting in a circle. "I'm still haunted by visions of Riposto. *Che peccato* I heard every day."

"*Pietismo*," my sisters murmured, pronouncing the word with great distaste. Commonly used in Italian as a derogatory term, I would translate it as a mixture of the English words pity and piety. We had all experienced *pietismo*, we had all been wounded and scarred by it.

"*Abbracciamoci*, let us embrace," Gabriella said, "*diamoci forza*, let's give each other strength."

And we opened our arms, those of us who could, and those who could stand stood and draped themselves over those who sat, as we formed a still-hurting but blissful mound of disabled female bodies.

I was happy those summers in Marina, working, sharing, and playing. On that resplendent beach, I felt comfortable taking my prostheses off and letting the still-hot late-afternoon sun redden my stumps. I lowered myself out of my chair, naughtily throwing handfuls of sand at Maurizio and screaming, feigning annoyance, as he kicked sand over me until I was almost all covered. I played the same game with others who joined me on that dazzling white sand, admiring the fascinating array of bodies, the scoliosed backs, the floppy atrophied limbs, the skinny legs covered with scars, like mine had been. I even let Maurizio carry me into the water. For the first time since my childhood, my body was immersed in the warm Mediterranean Sea. I trembled with delight and fear of drowning.

In the United States in the late 1980s, we'd been fighting for passage of the Americans with Disabilities Act (ADA).

At first, legislation of the scope of the ADA was nothing but a dream. If only we could have a law passed, stronger and more definitive than 504. A law that said we were equal citizens, and that the way we were treated was discriminatory. Our own Emancipation Proclamation. But the odds against it seemed insurmountable.

Ronald Reagan had been president since 1981. With deregulation, trickle-down economics, threats to women's reproductive rights, the days of civil rights legislation seemed long gone. Then, in February of 1988, the first version of the ADA was drafted by the members of the National Council on the Handicapped. They had all been appointed by Reagan, so I was skeptical. But they drafted a strong civil rights bill. It didn't go anywhere.

In 1989, George H. W. Bush took office, promising to make the United States "a kinder and gentler nation." A modified bill was introduced. Modified, of course, meant watered-down, but apparently, not enough for big business, which opposed the bill ferociously.

Disabled people across the country realized the ADA wouldn't be passed without a fierce battle. So for the first time ever, the national disability community came together. People of all different backgrounds, with all different types of disabilities, their families, friends, and allies, all joined in to fight for the ADA.

On Monday, March 12, 1990, having canceled my classes at Fordham for the day, I got on the train at the crack of dawn with some DIA friends, headed for Washington D.C.

A rally had been organized by a group called ADAPT. I'd been reading about ADAPT in my favorite paper, *The Disability Rag*. ADAPT was founded in 1983 in Denver, Colorado, though its roots went back to 1973, when nineteen young people with significant disabilities were freed from a nursing home, thanks to their activities director, a civil rights activist named Wade Blank. ADAPT stood for American Disabled for Accessible Public Transit, and before focusing on getting the ADA passed, they fought to get lifts on buses. DIA had fought the same battle, but we limited our efforts to NYC, while ADAPT, after succeeding in getting accessible buses in Denver, had been striving to accomplish the goal nationwide, disrupting conventions of the American Public Transit Association, wherever they were held, even in Montreal, Canada. ADAPT activists blocked doors, stopped traffic, chained their wheelchairs together, or threw themselves out of their wheelchairs, and always got arrested.

The rally that I and my friends were headed for was part of the 1990 ADAPT Spring Action. But many other organizations were also sponsoring it.

The weather was beautiful in D.C. It was a warm spring, and the cherry trees were in bloom. About 750 people were in front of the Capitol steps, a minuscule number by D.C. standards. But for disabled people, for whom traveling presented hardships, the number was impressive. The first speaker was Justin Dart, chair of the President's Committee on Employment of People with Disabilities. One of the main architects of the ADA, he had been traveling throughout the country, gathering support for the bill. He was a colorful figure, sitting in an old-fashioned wheelchair, with a cowboy hat and boots, and a Texas drawl. "Pioneer patriots of the twentieth century," he called the protesters. "We are Americans and we will struggle for however long it takes for the same rights other Americans have."

I later found out that Justin Dart fought to stop amendments to the ADA that would have excluded people with AIDS—proposed by some right-wing members of Congress, who apparently believed in the age-old connection of disability with sin, and agreed with televangelist Jerry Falwell in considering AIDS deserved punishment.

After a few other speakers, Mike Auberger, an ADAPT leader, rolled up to speak. He was quadriplegic, used a power chair, and wore his long hair in braids.

"The steps we sit before represent a long history of discrimination and indignities heaped upon disabled Americans."

As Auberger spoke, some thirty-five disabled activists got out of their wheelchairs and crawled up the Capitol steps. Photographers rushed to take pictures.

I stared at the spectacle of disabled bodies creeping their way up, paralyzed legs being dragged, bumping and banging over hard concrete, arms flailing and spasming, hips sliding sideways, hands slipping while grabbing the steps up ahead.

I was shocked. Why did ADAPT choose to show disabled people crawling? The image was one I associated with being pitiable.

But, on the train on the way home, I concluded that crawling accurately represented "the indignities heaped upon us." Literally, many of us had, on occasion, been forced to crawl. I had—in pain and in fear, and at times simply because of lack of accessibility. Figuratively, also, we were forced daily into humiliating situations.

The next day, back in New York, I called a friend who had stayed in D.C. She told me the ADAPT activists had filled the Capitol rotunda, chanting loudly and refusing to leave. Over one hundred of them had been arrested. I decided I'd do whatever I had to in order to get to the next ADAPT action.

On May 22, the House passed the ADA. The Senate had passed it the year before. Not surprisingly, it had been watered down a lot more. Compliance dates were extended way into the future, and an "undue hardship" loophole was included to protect businesses. It was a law with no teeth—no strong enforcement mechanism, and largely unfunded.

I feared that after waiting for years, we'd need lawyers to represent us, only to have a judge rule our rights were too costly.

I also feared that since the ADA was sold to Republicans as a law that would save government money by making it possible for more disabled people to work, social programs that some relied on might be eliminated or severely cut. I was aware of being privileged. Many disabled people had never worked, had not received adequate education, couldn't make a living, let alone go flying back and forth on jet planes like I did.

I wasn't as optimistic about our new law as some of my friends. Yet I recognized that the ADA, in spite of its extensive limitations, did something extraordinary: It validated our struggle for equal rights. Congress had put its stamp of approval on what we'd been saying for twenty years: The way we're treated is wrong because it's discrimination.

I decided not to wait around for the signing of the law by Bush. From

Italy, Gabriella had sent an SOS. The city's newly elected conservative administration was threatening to shut the center down. I was needed more there.

Maurizio picked me up at the airport in Rome and drove straight to the camp. There were red triangular signs with an exclamation point—meaning danger—and police tape around the buildings.

"The fascists want us out so they can build a luxury hotel here. They'll make billions, trillions, those capitalist pigs!" The fury in Gabriella's almond-shaped eyes made them even more magnetic.

The camp had been slapped with all kinds of violations, mainly because of the work done to render it more accessible. And the city administration claimed disabled people's lives were being endangered, since the camp was not a medical facility.

Gabriella had planned a conference for the end of June. People were expected to come from all over Italy. I was to speak, and I had invited a friend and colleague from Fordham, Louise Duval, an anthropology professor who had multiple sclerosis and taught a course on "disability as a social construct." Such courses were starting to sprout up in different universities.

The situation became thornier as the date of the conference approached. We had frequent visits from city officials. Gabriella chased them away, yelling, "Fascists!" and "Capitalist pigs!"

Then she came up with a brilliant idea. Since the camp was supposedly "unsafe," we would hold our conference in the town square. It would be both a conference and a demonstration. We made signs protesting lack of services and of access, prejudice, discrimination, unequal treatment under the law, and fascism.

I never thought we'd attract so much attention. The townspeople came to check us out, reporters from both local papers were there with their notebooks, photographers were snapping pictures, and the camera from the lone TV station rolled.

My colleague and I spoke about the fight in the United States for the ADA.

"The real significance of the ADA," Louise explained, "is that it's a civil rights law."

"In Italy, our needs are never seen as rights" was the response in the audience. "Whatever we get is out of a sense of duty to help the less fortunate."

"In the United States," I said, "we had the example of the civil rights movement of the fifties and sixties, which spurred other minorities to fight for their rights. We were latecomers. Most Americans don't consider ours a civil rights struggle. We hope the ADA will help change that."

"Are the health-care needs of disabled people addressed in the ADA?" someone asked.

"No," Louise replied. "There's nothing about health care in the ADA."

"Why not? Isn't health care a right in America?"

Louise and I looked at each other. "Good question."

That got us talking about the differences between the health-care system in Italy and that in the United States. Gabriella complained about the inadequate care provided by the Servizio Sanitario, the Italian national health-care system. Louise and I remarked that, in spite of its limitations, the Italian system was more equitable than the segmented and mostly profit-driven U.S. system. We talked about private insurance, which most people got through their employers; about waiting periods for preexisting conditions, which affected those of us with disabilities; and about the prohibitive cost of paying for one's own insurance when unable to access it through an employer, which left many Americans uninsured.

"There are also some government programs that cover different groups," Louise added. "Veterans with service-connected disabilities are covered by the Veterans Administration, seniors and those ruled disabled by Social Security, because unable to be gainfully employed, have Medicare, and then there's Medicaid for certain groups of poor people, including poor disabled people."

"*Che casino!* What a mess!" quite a few Italian friends exclaimed. All agreed the U.S. health system was not only unfair but absurd. Still, most remained convinced higher-quality care was available in the United States.

"I'm sure the American doctors are the best," someone said, echoing words I'd heard throughout my childhood.

On July 26, 1990, when George H. W. Bush signed the ADA into law, instead of celebrating with Frieda and my American friends on the White House lawn, I was with Gabriella and my Italian comrades at the camp, surrounded by police tape and red danger signs.

At the end of August, I hugged Gabriella good-bye, encouraging her to keep fighting.

She did. When the township turned off the water and electricity, she refused to leave, even in winter, when Beppe had to go back to work in Florence. She fought back like the tigress she was, but in the end, the capitalists won.

The camp was demolished and a hotel erected on that idyllic spot. Rich vacationers would be lying under those pine trees and on that white sand. But the work done in those years wasn't lost. The camp would be held up as an experiment in independent living and a model to follow.

On February 5, 1992, the "*Legge Quadro* for the assistance, the social integration, and the rights of disabled people" would be passed. It wouldn't be the strong law Italian activists wanted, but it was a victory nevertheless, and a first step in the ongoing struggle for disability rights in Italy.

15

FREE OUR PEOPLE

❁

ADAPT actions took place in different cities twice a year, in spring and fall. The 1990 fall action was in Atlanta in the beginning of October, too far and at a time when I couldn't take off from work. But I did manage to go to the following one, at the end of April 1991, in Baltimore, conveniently close.

About three hundred disabled activists were at the action. We stayed in a motel. I looked around me as rolled-up banners and cases of beer were brought in from parked vans. There were disabled people of all ages, some with gray hair, some my students' age, and there were children, too. I saw many more people of color than at DIA meetings, a larger percentage of quadriplegics, and a greater variety of disabilities, though people with mobility impairments were still in the majority. Some were well educated, engaged in serious conversations; others appeared coarse and scruffy, loudly cracking crude jokes. But the ones talking seriously laughed at jokes the others made, and scruffy characters joined in conversations with appropriate remarks. A few were obviously quite drunk. Somebody handed me a bottle of beer. I took a sip, not to seem unfriendly, and gave it back.

There was a festival-like atmosphere. T-shirts were being sold, and I bought one with ADAPT's new logo, a stick figure in a wheelchair, raised arms breaking chains, and the words FREE OUR PEOPLE, ADAPT's new slogan. Now that passage of the ADA had been achieved, ADAPT's focus had shifted to freeing people from institutions. ADAPT now stood for American Disabled for Attendant Programs Today. Specifically, arguing that no matter how disabled, we could live in our own homes, usually at a much lower cost to the state, ADAPT was demanding that a portion of the Medicaid dollars going to nursing homes be used instead to provide home-based personal-attendant services.

Some disabled people spent their whole lives in nursing homes, "serving life sentences for the crime of having a disability," I'd learned from the *Rag*. Antiquated federal policy mandated Medicaid dollars be spent for institutional care but only made it optional for states to provide care in one's own home. Apparently, New York did provide home care, but many states didn't. ADAPT's immediate goal was to fix the inequity in the Medicaid law.

I needed no help with my personal care. And I had never been in a nursing home—at least not a real nursing home, only in Blythedale. As pleasant as my Blythedale memories were, I wouldn't have wanted to spend my whole life there.

Only recently had I been learning about Medicaid. DIA, wishing to treat disability as a social rather than medical problem, focused mostly on access issues. But the Independent Living Centers were good sources of info on programs and services. I found out that many disabled people were on Medicaid. To qualify for Medicaid, you had to be poor, and many disabled people were poor. What I found interesting was that most of those who needed help getting themselves in and out of bed, washing and dressing, and going to the bathroom were on Medicaid. Such care, whether provided in a nursing home or in your own home, was considered long-term care and was not covered by private insurance, or by Medicare, the program for seniors and those receiving Social Security disability benefits. Only Medicaid covered it, once you had impoverished yourself enough to qualify. In other words, people were being forced to be poor and stay poor because of their need for personal care.

I'd come to the conclusion that the ultimate solution was a national health-care program similar to the Italian one, funded by taxes, covering everyone from birth to death, providing the best available care, including long-term care—in your own home rather than in institutions. But I wasn't so naïve as to think change of that magnitude could be brought about easily. Therefore, I applauded ADAPT's efforts to focus on the most urgent need: freeing people and allowing them to have a life.

That day in Baltimore, I sat with my issue of the *Rag* open on my lap, checking photos of the previous action and looking around me. I recognized Wade Blank, Bob Kafka with his full beard, Stephanie Thomas with her mass of wild reddish hair... More activists arrived; some were in groups, their travel expenses paid for by Independent Living Centers and other organizations. Suddenly, there she was. There could be no mistaking the slight, delicate woman in the power chair, with the long skirt, the long light brown hair, the glasses, the sculptured face with high cheekbones. She was an ADAPT leader, a powerful activist and a lawyer.

"Diane!"

I didn't realize I'd called her name out loud, as if she were an old friend I was happy to run into. She was looking at me, probably wondering whether I was someone whose name she'd forgotten.

"We've never met, but I recognized you from the pictures in the *Rag*." I held the paper up.

"Is this your first action?" Her voice was as sweet as her smile.

"Yes, and I'm so excited!"

She came closer, our wheelchairs almost touching. "I'm Diane Coleman, from Nashville."

Oh no, what was the matter with me? I now introduced myself, apologizing for not having done so immediately. My right hand was ready to shake hers.

Instead of taking my hand, Diane opened her arms. "Welcome, welcome to ADAPT."

I hugged her carefully, as if handling something extremely precious. The moment her thin arms tightened around me, I knew I would be her friend, fight alongside her and get arrested with her.

I went to a workshop where they taught us the basics of civil disobedience, and then to a bigger meeting where we were all crowded in a room like sardines and did a lot of yelling and chanting.

Later that evening, I saw Diane talking with a group of women and I rolled toward them. A bit shy about being a newcomer, I stopped at the edge of the circle of wheelchairs.

A woman in a power chair, who apparently had spent many years in a nursing home, was talking about the horrors she'd experienced—being left for hours lying in her own urine and feces, or in the shower, naked and cold, getting a pressure sore that became infected and almost killed her, being raped… The woman's speech was hard to understand. She appeared to have CP. Did she say she was raped by an aide? Hospital memories, long buried in the dark chambers of my mind, suddenly resurfaced. My breasts fondled by an orderly in the middle of the night, the X-ray technician's hand between my thighs, the intern in my bed.

"Do you have a good life now?" someone in the group asked.

"I don't have an easy life. It's hard dealing with attendants. But no one tells me when to go to bed, when to eat, when to go to the bathroom. I can make decisions about my life. I want to go to school now. I want an education. They never thought I was worth educating."

"And I bet you're saving the state a lot of money," someone else said. "Why are we having such a hard time making people understand?"

I'd wanted to ask that question myself. ADAPT's demand seemed reasonable, not that big a deal to me, not when I'd been envisioning an overhaul of our whole health-care system. I moved a few inches closer and listened. "The nursing home industry is greedy and powerful…" "They have money to lobby and we don't…" "The politicians have been bought off…" "People have no idea what goes on in nursing homes…"

"Yeah, they think they're good places, where they take care of poor cripples like us!" Everyone was talking.

"In general, people are uncomfortable around us. They'd rather not have to look at us, because when they see us, they see their worst fears. And, of course, they'd rather not have the trouble and the expense of accommodating us, dealing with our needs…" Diane was talking now and everyone else was listening. "Warehousing us in nursing homes is a convenient way of getting us out of their hair."

"That's what my parents did," the woman who'd been in a nursing home agreed. "When they realized I couldn't be cured, and would always need a lot of help, they shipped me off."

The word *cure* brought me to the past, to my father's wish and promise. My parents would never have "shipped me off" to a nursing home, I thought. But I was lucky to be able to attend to my own personal care. What if I were as disabled as this woman?

"Yes, the cure. Everybody is waiting for the day when doctors will find a cure for everything and there will be no disabled people left. They give money, so the CEOs of corrupt charities can ride in Cadillacs. They listen in tears to Jerry Lewis using us as objects of pity."

A young woman with short brown hair in a power chair was talking. She spoke forcefully, but her voice was soft. "Our families want us to be cured because they love us. If they really love us, they should accept us, instead of making us feel we're not okay the way we are, that we're not and never will be the sons and daughters they want."

Diane was nodding in agreement. "You're so right, Laura."

I should have recognized her. The young woman was Laura Hershey. She had muscular dystrophy and, having been a poster child for the Jerry Lewis telethon, was now fiercely against it. She wrote beautiful poetry, too. I felt proud to be inside the circle, to be surrounded, enveloped by these beautiful disabled women who were so eloquently expressing my own thoughts and feelings.

Diane kept talking: "People think being disabled is a fate worse than death. Some say they would kill themselves rather than be like us. Others won't say it outright; they'll cover up their contempt with compassion and admiration. They'll say, 'You're so brave. I don't know how you can go on.'"

Suddenly, I felt a lacerating pain deep in the pit of my stomach.

Everyone was nodding. A nervous giggle came from a pretty blond woman in a manual chair. Diane went on: "The Nazis found a less costly, final solution for the incurables, the useless eaters who were such a burden on society. Euthanasia." She enunciated each syllable.

She was obviously referring to Hitler's T4 Program. Over a quarter of a million disabled people were killed in Nazi Germany, before the better-known Holocaust. I started shivering.

"I almost committed suicide," the pretty blonde said, interrupting Diane. "I would have had I not met other disabled people who showed me I could still have a good life."

"You're one of the lucky ones," Diane told her. "The support of our disabled sisters and brothers is crucial. A disabled person's wish to die is often seen as reasonable. So we don't get the suicide prevention we need."

Now I was shaking. Diane was right in front of me, talking, but I couldn't see her face. The face in front of me was Audrey's.

I pulled back on my wheels, bumping against someone's power chair. Trembling, my vision blurred by the tears I was trying to hold back by keeping my eyes wide open, I made my way to the elevator through corridors crowded with disabled people talking, laughing, hugging.

Audrey. By the time I found my room, I was sobbing loudly. I managed to get the key in the keyhole after a few frantic tries, then slammed the door behind me. I threw myself from my chair onto the bed, facedown. Audrey. I called out her name, clutching the blanket and burying my face to muffle my cries, my body shaking violently. The bed squeaked painfully, as if it, too, were crying. My lost sister. My beautiful crippled sister. Audrey.

It was astounding that my pain could feel so fresh after twenty-one years.

Audrey didn't get appropriate treatment, despite suicide attempt after suicide attempt. Her family, her nondisabled friends, even the psychiatrist she saw every week, all thought it was understandable that she wanted to die.

Audrey killed herself, but I didn't. Was it because I was chicken? Or was it strength that kept me alive? The same strength with which, as a child, I'd struggled to free myself from Sister Angelica's ominous embrace.

Why didn't I give Audrey some of my strength? The guilt hit me anew, an unbearable weight crushing my body against the mattress.

But I couldn't have saved Audrey. Twenty-one years ago, I didn't have the words and the ideas of the disability movement to expose the better-off-dead mentality for what it was: a lie, a lethal lie.

Like the blond paraplegic woman, I was one of the lucky ones. I might never have climbed out of the deep depression Audrey's suicide threw me into if I hadn't met strong disabled people who were fighting back, working together to change the world. When Audrey died in 1970, the new movement of disabled people was starting to bud, from coast to coast. If only Audrey had held on a bit longer, she, too, might have been saved.

I sat up on the bed, slowly peeling away the damp strands of hair stuck to my red, sore face. It was too late for Audrey. But others needed my help. I had to do everything in my power to silence the lethal lies and spread the lifesaving truths. I had to work my ass off to make this a better world in every way for all my disabled sisters and brothers.

From now on, I vowed, I would put activism ahead of everything—absolutely everything, including teaching.

I couldn't wait for the action to start. I couldn't wait to be on the front lines and get arrested with Diane, and Laura, and the woman who had been in the nursing home, and the blond paraplegic woman...

But I didn't get arrested on that first action.

Monday morning, we marched, one closely following the next, to the Social Security complex. ADAPT's demand: a meeting with the secretary of Health and Human Services, who was then Louis Sullivan. I kept turning around to admire the endless single file. Three hundred of us of every shade, shape, and size, tiny bodies and huge ones, some utterly still, some wildly spastic, some with missing parts, with all kinds of appliances, in all kinds of chairs, scooters, and gurneys, one behind the next.

The complex was vast, yet we managed to shut down all entrances. The single file broke into separate lines, with different groups going to the front, the sides, the back...

"Block the doors! Block the doors!" the leaders yelled.

We did, chanting furiously, "Free our people! Now!"

It looked like chaos, but I could tell the moves had been carefully orchestrated. The rain that started falling couldn't dampen my enthusiasm. In the afternoon, we moved away from the doors. With amazing speed and precision, some of us were led to the right, others to the left, and, unbelievably, we blocked a big intersection. The police rerouted traffic but didn't arrest us.

In the rain, we chanted, "Down with nursing homes!"

The next day, we went back to the same complex but targeted one building. More and more police arrived. My heart beat faster when I saw the blue latex gloves and the plastic handcuffs. Some people got out of their wheelchairs and lay on the ground.

"You are ordered to disperse or be placed under arrest!" The cop spoke into a bullhorn.

"That's only the first warning. We get three warnings before being arrested," the quadriplegic guy next to me explained.

Then the anticlimax: The police walked away. According to the ADAPT leaders, they weren't prepared to deal with so many of us. Though disappointed, I was also relieved.

The last day closed with a party. I almost decided to skip it. I wanted to catch an early train home in the morning. I felt drained both physically and emotionally. Then I heard the rock-and-roll music and peeked into the room where everyone was dancing. Before I knew it, I was twirling in my wheelchair, being grabbed and spun around, clutching on to someone's power chair and letting him or her pull me in a zigzag across the room, being hugged by and hugging back the scruffiest characters, taking big gulps of someone's Heineken, forgetting how much I hated beer, and drags from hand-rolled cigarettes, forgetting I didn't smoke. I danced with everyone in that room and kept dancing well into the night, with such gusto as I had not experienced since the hospital parties at HSS.

16

NO NEED TO SETTLE

❋

I was never "madly in love" with Maurizio, but I did love him. He was a kind, thoughtful, sweet man. He had brought up marriage a few times. I knew my parents would have given us their blessing. But I wasn't ready to consider the subject seriously, especially with an ocean between us. Which one of us would move to the other side?

I also had doubts about our compatibility. When we were apart, I missed him. I anxiously waited for his letters, postcards, phone calls. When we were together, especially for a long, hot Italian summer, the differences between us surfaced.

Mostly, Maurizio and I fought because I hated the way he made me feel dependent. Family members, relatives, and nondisabled friends didn't understand. How could I complain about the help Maurizio gave me so lovingly?

My parents were happy a nice Italian man wanted to take care of me. My relatives in Italy were always reminding me how lucky I was to have found someone so willing to help me. I did feel lucky to be traveling around Italy, connecting with the most remarkable disabled people, doing important disability rights work. I was grateful to Maurizio for making it all possible. But I hated when people made me feel like his help was some form of charity. They seemed to forget or purposely ignore that, after all, he was getting something out of this relationship, too. At times, I didn't think they even saw him as my boyfriend, just as my helper.

Once, at a dinner at my aunt's house, I must have been in a particularly bad mood when someone made the usual comments about Maurizio's generosity. I replied, "*Mi aiuta solo perché gli piace scopare.* He only helps me because he likes to fuck me." My aunt's jaw dropped. Everyone around the table sat still and silent. My youngest cousin, though, couldn't suppress a giggle.

Maurizio's face was beet red. Was he embarrassed, or angry?

I wanted to take back my words. At the same time, I felt great pleasure in having said them. After all, we weren't hiding our relationship. If instead of seeing us as two consenting adults, they preferred to see us as a noble man helping a poor cripple; if they chose to assume that, because of my disability, our relationship was platonic, or if it wasn't, I should be grateful and discreet about it; if they were uncomfortable with disabled people having sex—well, whatever the case, it was about time they were confronted with the reality.

What bothered me more than people's assumptions was Maurizio's apparent enjoyment of my need for his help. Wherever we went in Italy, he always picked a place to spend the night that was horribly inaccessible. Usually it was a *pensione,* with lots of stairs and never an elevator. If I complained, he laughed. "I'm carrying you and I'm not complaining!" Seldom was there a bathroom I could use on my own. He had to carry me in, sit me on the toilet. He found it sexy; I found it demeaning.

Once, in Milan, I'd been waiting in his car while he went to inquire about vacancies at a *pensione,* and when he came back all smiles to tell me they had a room on the third floor, I exploded.

"I'm not staying here!" I'd had enough of being schlepped up and down flights of stairs. I could see a Hilton just down the block. I pointed to it. "I'm staying at the Hilton."

"Do you know how expensive that is?" He sounded exasperatingly cool and collected.

"What do I care? It's accessible!" And I started pulling my wheelchair out of his car.

With a smile, Maurizio got the chair out and held it in place while I got into it. I grabbed my handbag, which held my American passport and my wallet with my American Express card. That's all I needed. I thought of Gabriella calling me a capitalist and laughed in spite of my anger. All I wanted was to spend at least one night in a nice accessible place. I figured I'd wear the same clothes the next day, wash my under-wear in the hotel sink. But Maurizio was holding on to the handles of my chair, trying to push me toward the *pensione*.

"It'd be better if we left the chair in the car. I don't want to carry it up the stairs." He didn't realize how infuriating he was.

"Don't you understand? I'm staying at the Hilton. You stay in the *pensione*!" But he wouldn't let go until I hollered, "*Aiuto! Quest'uomo mi vuol far male!* Help! This man is trying to hurt me!"

Lucky for me, the street went downhill, so when he let go of the push handles, I took off. There was a driveway leading to the hotel, also going downhill. My Quickie was flying. I went right through the door, which was being held open by a uniformed doorman, and up to the front desk. Speaking in English, my passport and American Express card in hand, I asked if there was a wheelchair-accessible room available.

"Yes, madam."

I beamed, anticipating the luxury of grab bars in the bathroom and a raised toilet seat, maybe even a roll-in shower. Just the sight of the elevator gave me immense joy. But the man at the front desk was looking past me.

"Is the room for two?"

I turned around, to see Maurizio's smiling face. I should have known he would follow me. I grabbed the key the man was handing me and, trying to sound calm, still speaking in English, said, "No! I'm alone." Then I quickly headed for the elevator and the coveted wheelchair-accessible room.

The next morning, Maurizio was waiting in the lobby.

"Good morning, rich American lady," he said. I didn't complain about his sarcasm. I didn't ask if he had spent the night at the *pensione*. I just wanted to get to the conference—with the promising title of *"Inclusione Sociale delle Persone con Disabilità"*—which was the reason we were in Milan. Whenever he visited me in New York, Maurizio didn't seem happy to see me driving my car with hand controls, using my special permit to park where no one else could, or getting on and off lift-equipped buses, going up and down ramps... I suspected he hated not being needed.

Yet I was sure Maurizio was not a "devotee." That's what those who were turned on by disability called themselves. The ones I'd met were pretty unsavory, even dangerous. But many others were totally harmless. Some disabled women were happy to marry them. The argument went: "Some men are turned on by big boobs, or big butts, or little feet, and some are turned on by the absence of limbs, by paralysis, etc."

Great, if ever we'd succeed in changing our society, if disabled bodies were appreciated for their unique beauty, and our sexuality affirmed and applauded. But as things were, I suspected attraction to disability was complicated by the guilty thrill of violating taboo and the imposed need for secrecy. The very use of the religious term *devotee* played into our society's view of the sexual partner of a disabled person as either saintly or perverted.

Particularly unsettling were the "wannabes," nondisabled people who pretended to be disabled.

Before Maurizio, I had met by chance on the street a man who wore braces and walked with crutches. He stopped me with a friendly greeting and we started talking about our disabilities. He told me he'd had polio.

We had a few encounters, but always in public places. Mostly, we chatted on the phone. Without my realizing it, our conversations became longer and more intimate. I started thinking of him as "my disabled lover."

Not counting the hospital boyfriends I had as a girl—and the playful experimentation that never went past heavy petting—I'd never had a disabled lover. Why not? Were the disabled men I met not attractive enough to me? Or were they all looking for nondisabled women?

My high school crush, Frankie, had put it plainly back then. "We're both good-looking enough to attract normal boyfriends and girlfriends. We don't have to settle for each other."

Audrey had been of the same opinion. "If you have a disabled boyfriend, people see you as even more disabled."

During a particularly intimate conversation with "my disabled lover," I suggested we meet either at my place or his.

"Yes... it would be wonderful... But I have a secret I have to reveal to you before..."

A secret? I couldn't imagine what it could be. And he couldn't bring himself to tell me on the phone.

Finally, I said, "Let's meet and you'll tell me in person."

After much hesitation, he gave me his address. He didn't live far.

"I can come over right now."

"Get ready to be shocked," he warned me.

When the door of his apartment opened, I was more disoriented than shocked. The man standing in front of me was not on crutches, not wearing braces, not disabled.

The secret was revealed: He was a "wannabe." He started explaining his irrepressible need to appear, and indeed to be, disabled. Had he been honest from the beginning, I might have listened, asked questions. But, having been fooled, I was too angry for any curiosity, let alone compassion. I just wanted to get the hell out.

Driving home, I told myself: If I got so excited believing this guy was disabled, I need to find a disabled lover. But soon after, I met Maurizio.

To some degree, all my past relationships had been plagued by problems related to disability, or, to be more exact, disability prejudice, or *ableism*—a term we were starting to use. I thought of James as the exception. I attributed our breakup to my obsession with getting pregnant. But had there been no prejudice against a disabled woman getting pregnant, I might not have been so obsessed with proving I could. Come to think of it, my gynecologist might have done more to help me, and my own mother might have been more supportive.

These thoughts and the increasing problems with Maurizio made the idea of a disabled lover ever more appealing. Wouldn't it be nice if we both knew where the other was coming from? If no explanations were necessary, no walls needed to be broken down?

Yet, when I finally decided to take the plunge, it wasn't because of disappointments with nondisabled partners, or problems with Maurizio. The decision had more to do with my sense of pride in being disabled.

Disability pride was a concept slowly taking root in our community. Having come together to fight for our rights, we were succeeding not only in making some remarkable changes in this world but also in forging a common identity. Realizing there was nothing "wrong" with being disabled, we were redefining disability as a natural part of the human experience. Rejecting stereotypes, we were starting to celebrate our newfound selves and our community.

I'd been learning to be proud of who I was from other disabled women.

Gradually, I'd stopped comparing myself to nondisabled women and started noticing how beautiful my disabled sisters were. Not beautiful by dominant standards, but in a different way, one that challenged those tired ideals, so oppressive for nondisabled women, as well. Beautiful, not in spite of the disability, but in spite of the prejudice, of being made to believe we could not and did not have a right to feel beautiful.

It was disabled sisters like Frieda and Gabriella who taught me by example that I didn't need to hide or compensate for my disability, who showed me how to be casually, unflinchingly, nonapologetically, defiantly disabled.

Disability pride was difficult to explain to others. So we discussed it only among ourselves. Not all of us felt it. Those of us who did had trouble explaining it to those who didn't. We pointed to our movement's accomplishments, and to the bonds that united us. Or tried to draw parallels with black pride and gay pride.

"Disability pride is the pride of the oppressed" was my take. "It's the pride of all those who've been made to feel ashamed of who they are, the pride of all who have to fight for their place in this world."

But such reasoning was hard to encompass, since our oppressors were usually not openly hostile; on the contrary, they might have had the best of intentions, might even have been acting out of love for us. "The oppression is ingrained in our society," I argued, remembering the question my father had asked: "Who are the bad guys? Are your mother and I bad guys?"

My own coming into pride had not been easy. On the contrary, it was a long and tortuous process, with a lot of ups and downs, falling back and having to start over...

I couldn't be sure I was there yet. Deep down inside me was a vulnerable place. Whenever I got sucked back into the past, even if just for a moment, it still hurt like hell.

That's why I needed to hug my disabled sisters. When I hugged them, I was also hugging myself, trying to heal from all the hurt of the past. My sisters' beauty made me feel beautiful; their strength made me feel strong; their pride made me feel proud.

Now I wanted a disabled man with whom I could feel proud; a disabled man proud of himself and of me, proud of our common identity as disabled people.

I tried to explain my feelings to Maurizio but could not make myself understood.

I met Luke through a DIA member, Irene, who lived in the same government-subsidized housing he did, near the South Street Seaport. Eight years younger than I, Luke had broken his neck when diving into a swimming pool five years before, and was still struggling to adapt. Irene asked me to try to bring him out of the lingering depression that was keeping him from moving on.

204 LOVE AND ACTIVISM

So on a beautiful fall day in September 1991, I drove down to Fulton Street and fell in love—with the view of the East River, the bridges and the Brooklyn Navy Yard, the boats docked at the pier, the cafés by the water, and with the good-looking, melancholic young man whose life had changed suddenly and drastically.

Luke had personal-care attendants around the clock, paid for by Medicaid. New York City was one of the few places where, thanks to the work of strong activists like my friend Marilyn, assistance was available 24/7—at home, rather than in a nursing home. Luke told me he was eligible for Medicaid because his income consisted only of his Social Security disability benefit. His disability and his low income also qualified him to live in subsidized housing. His apartment, for which he paid a ridiculously low rent, had windows facing the East River and was totally wheelchair-accessible.

"What if you wanted to go back to your job?" I once asked. He had worked for an accounting firm before his accident. "You can request reasonable accommodations under the ADA. But would you risk losing your Medicaid and this beautiful apartment?"

"I'm not gonna try to find out. It's obviously better if I don't work."

I visited Luke regularly on weekends.

"Stay with me tonight," he said after I'd been going to see him for about a month.

Luke's night attendant was a nice Haitian woman. After she got him settled in bed, Luke told her to go home. She was happy for the break. I was grateful for the privacy.

Luke couldn't do much for himself. So I gave him water when he got thirsty, scratched him when he got an itch, arranged the bedcovers over him or pulled them off of him. Always having been on the receiving end, I enjoyed doing things for someone more disabled than I was. And when it came to lovemaking, I discovered I enjoyed being on top and in control. Afterward, we'd have a midnight snack—crackers and cheese, or cookies. I fed him as I fed myself.

But it soon became obvious that Luke was not the proud disabled man I longed for. He could not accept what had happened to him. I hoped that would change with time and my help. But I found myself trying so hard to convince him he could still have a good life that I could hardly enjoy being with him.

When I went to Italy during Christmas vacation, I told Maurizio about Luke. He refused to take my news seriously. He thought my wanting to be with a disabled man was a whim, a phase that would soon pass.

"Get it out of your system," he told me. "I love you and I can be patient."

17

THE HANDSOME NEW GUY

❊

"Inominate Danny and Nadina." Marilyn sucked on her ventilator hose as she pronounced the last vowel of my name. She was presiding over this meeting, round face crowned by short curls, sitting majestically in her massive power chair, with the ventilator humming.

She had nominated me and Danny, a relatively new DIA member, to chair the steering committee for the second annual Disability Independence Day March, an event in celebration of the signing of the ADA.

In July of that year, 1992, the first march had taken place. To attend it, I limited my time in Italy to the month of August. I visited with Gabriella, still grieving over the loss of the center, and discussed the new disability law. Then I insisted on seeing as many friends as possible, making Maurizio drive from city to city, which proved exhausting for us both and caused us to argue more than usual. Whenever I was angry at Maurizio, I brought up my relationship with Luke. He still didn't take me seriously.

The first march, though small, kindled feelings of disability pride. Wanting to make the following year's event larger and better, we were starting to plan for it ten months ahead, in October.

I was too stunned to say "I accept" or "I decline"—stunned not by the nomination, but by the sound of my name paired with Danny's. Marilyn had pronounced our names in one breath, not bothering with last names. Danny and Nadina. I was shocked by how good our names sounded one after the other, as if they belonged together.

Danny, sitting up straight and tall in his power chair on the other side of the room, was smiling at me, but only with his maddeningly sexy eyes, while the well-defined features of his handsome face remained appropriately solemn. With his right hand, he pushed his dark hair back, his arm spasming before resting on the armrest. He'd apparently already accepted the nomination, and everyone seemed to think I had, too, though I hadn't said a word.

Now Gerry Nuzzi, who with Kipp Watson, a lawyer who'd had polio, had organized the first march, was expounding on disability pride in his musical CP drawl, skillfully extracting from the group a nomination for himself. "We're going to have three co-chairs," Marilyn announced, "for the '93 Disability Independence Day March." It was too late to decline.

I was happy Gerry had jumped on board. Gerry and I went back a long way. I called him "little brother" and he called me "big sis." I wasn't sure how that started; maybe we meant it as an acknowledgment of our similar Italian family backgrounds. I was only a year older.

Actually, it was Gerry's wife, Ellen, I'd known forever. Ellen and I had been in the same "handicapped homeroom" at Grover Cleveland High School, in Brooklyn. I'd met Gerry when, after one of my periods of absence, I went back to DIA. I had not kept in touch with Ellen. She told me she worked as a counselor at Long Island University. Then she introduced me to her husband, who worked for a nonprofit.

"What a nice couple you make!" I said.

Ellen had dystonia, which affects the body similarly to CP. Both Gerry and Ellen used scooters. Both could stand and charmingly wobble about. Ellen's speech was not quite as slurred as Gerry's. I observed their similarities with a kind of fascination.

I hardly knew Danny. But I knew that some strange magnetic force got activated whenever we were within rolling distance of each other. From opposite sides of the room, if our eyes met, the urge to move toward each other seemed irresistible. But neither of us was willing to yield to the mysterious pull.

I'd met him that past January—January 27, 1992. The day before, Title III of the ADA, which calls for the accessibility of places of public accommodation, had gone into effect. Without an enforcement mechanism in the law, businesses weren't going to become accessible unless we forced them. The "burden of proof," our lawyers explained, was on us. We needed to file lawsuits. Disabled In Action decided to file the first ADA lawsuit in the country—against Helmsley Spear, owners of the Empire State Building.

We chose the Empire State Building for its symbolic value. We also figured such a lawsuit would draw media attention. And it sure did. The cameras were waiting as we rolled into the lobby for our press conference and demonstration.

I'd seen Danny talking to Frieda, and decided to go ask her who he was. But when I got close enough to whisper, "Who's the handsome new guy?" Frieda was about to speak to reporters. I felt Danny's gaze on me throughout the press conference. He had intense, insistent eyes, but the kind that rest on you softly, gently caressing without being invasive.

We all went up in the elevator to the eighty-sixth floor, which was as high as wheelchair users could get. The only way to the observation deck was via a flight of stairs.

"We'd like to enjoy the view of the city like everyone else," I was telling the reporter from *Newsday,* when I was again distracted by those caressing eyes.

We never spoke that day. I left the Empire State Building without knowing the handsome guy's name.

When I got a call a few days later from someone named Danny, who wanted to send me a tape of the TV coverage of the demonstration, I wasn't sure who he was.

"Am I in it?" I'd gotten home too late to watch the news.

"Oh yes, you look so beautiful and sound so eloquent!"

My heart beat faster as I realized the man's voice had the same caressing quality as the eyes that had so insistently yet so gently sought mine out at the Empire State Building.

Danny started attending DIA meetings, becoming increasingly active. Frieda, great at spotting potential and making sure it got used to advance our cause, was always recruiting him to help organize demonstrations, write press releases or articles for our newsletter. Everyone seemed impressed with Danny's talents, and his ability to get whatever we wished for: sound equipment for our rallies, a ramped platform to use as a stage, banners of all sizes. He had worked as a propman and set decorator in the film and TV industry, until multiple sclerosis forced him to stop.

"Getting whatever the director wanted was my job," he said.

The Empire State Building lawsuit was settled out of court, and the observation deck was soon to be made accessible. DIA had a few other good demonstrations that year, the last one against the Labor Day Muscular Dystrophy Telethon.

Two years before, on September 2, 1990, five weeks after the ADA became law, Jerry Lewis, the telethon's host and hero, had written a cover story, for *Parade* magazine—a national Sunday newspaper insert—titled "If I Had Muscular Dystrophy." He had put himself in a wheelchair, to him a "steel imprisonment," and concluded, "My life is half. So I must learn to do things halfway... to be good at being half a person."

"This is most outrageous and patronizing," said Mike Ervin, from Chicago, whom I'd met the year before at the ADAPT action. He and his sister had MD and were former poster children. They founded a national antitelethon organization, Jerry's Orphans, so named as a rebuke to Lewis's habit of calling all people with MD his "kids," no matter what their age.

People with all disabilities, not just MD, were harmed by that image of "half a person." We all shared the outrage, especially when we had fought to get a law passed that declared us "equal citizens." Having always hated telethons, I was almost grateful to Lewis for forcing our community to spring into action. Since 1990, demonstrations against the MDA telethon had been, and would continue to be, held across the country. It would take many years for the telethon to begin to clean up its act.

In 1992, DIA organized a great protest in front of the hotel where the NYC phone bank accepting contributions for the telethon was set up. We were in the papers and on TV, holding signs that said RIGHTS NOT PITY. Always one to reuse signs, I held one I had made in 1990, during the buildup phase of the Gulf War. It read LET THE MILITARY HOLD A TELETHON TO PAY FOR WAR.

"In a rich country like ours, where there's always plenty of money for war," I explained to a reporter, "there should be enough to conduct medical research and cover everyone's health-care needs, without making children beg on TV."

"But when government fails us, shouldn't we be grateful for any help charities can give?" the reporter responded, egging me on.

"Do you think disabled people—children or adults—are benefiting from this or any telethon?" I angrily rebutted. "I'll tell you who's benefiting: the charities' CEOs, who are paying themselves six figure salaries; the businesses that send a rep with a check and get tax write-offs and free TV airtime; the have-been and would-be stars, and the viewers, feeling 'superior to the unfortunate' and 'noble' when they pledge ten bucks, figuring they can continue discriminating against us..." I have trouble stopping once I get started.

The reporter chose not to quote me.

A lot of the credit for organizing that demonstration and especially for getting the word out to the media went to Danny.

I knew Danny had a girlfriend, Martha. She was attractive in an inconspicuous way, with her short brown hair and large, sad eyes. She came with Danny to DIA but didn't say much. Like Danny, Martha had multiple sclerosis. Unlike my colleague from Fordham, Louise, who lost function during an exacerbation and then regained it, Danny and Martha had the kind of MS that doesn't go into remission. Martha's MS seemed less advanced than Danny's. She used a scooter, which required better balance than a wheelchair, and, unlike Danny, who had no function in his legs and somewhat limited function in his arms, she could still stand, albeit unsteadily.

I had a chance to talk with Martha on the Fourth of July, on a boat ride chartered by Mayor Dinkins. Frieda and Michael and other DIA members were also on the boat. Longtime DIA activist Anne Emerman, then director of the Mayor's Office for People with Disabilities, got us invited. Danny was in the hospital at the time, because of a pressure sore, but had encouraged Martha to go with her twelve-year-old son, who, she said, loved fireworks. I told Martha what I loved was being on the water. We chatted as the long summer twilight turned into darkness, enjoying the delicate breeze rising from the gently rolling polluted waters of the East River. Martha told me she had met Danny at an MS support group. She had been married for fifteen years. Her husband had taken off when her MS advanced. Danny's marriage also had ended when he became disabled.

"How wonderful," I said, "that the two of you have so much in common."

I wasn't looking for a boyfriend. I was already "attached" or "involved," or whatever the word. Doubly so, since I was seeing Luke while still in a relationship with Maurizio.

"We want this to be a disability pride march, like the gay pride march," Gerry said.

We had always felt a particular affinity with the gay rights movement, and some of our members were active in it.

"Of course we do," I replied, though I couldn't imagine our community pulling off an event resembling in magnitude and spectacle the annual pride parade. "But we'll need to work on getting the disability community together. We're too splintered. We need unity."

Uniting our community had recently become a favorite crusade of mine. When I'd discovered our movement some twenty years before, I sought those who were most like me. It had taken years before I became troubled by the lack of diversity. Frieda had begun earlier to reach out to those with different disabilities, and to people of color and other minorities.

"Unity. That's a good word. Write it down," Danny said. I was the one writing things down, because my hands worked best out of the three of us.

We were working on the platform for the march, sitting at a table in a room at the International Center on Disability. Danny and I were next to each other, wheelchairs touching. Gerry sat across from us.

"I can't get close enough to you," Danny whispered.

I noticed Gerry's smirk. I felt foolish. I leaned toward Danny, pushing my notebook where he could see what I was writing. Our arms barely touching was enough to make my heart beat faster.

I tried to focus on the task at hand. "Empowerment is also what we're about. The ADA empowers us."

"Unity! Empowerment! Pride!" Danny intoned those three words with such enthusiasm. I loved his voice, both when it resonated so clear and strong and when it was a soft, intimate whisper. "Can't you see it? 'Unity, Empowerment, Pride,' on a huge banner." His arm shook as he drew a wide arc in the air.

Danny was so ardent about his role in our movement that I was surprised to learn he was relatively new to disability. He had been diagnosed less than five years before, in 1988, and had continued to work, until his symptoms became so pronounced that he retired on disability. He started using a manual chair in 1990, and went to a power chair the year after. That's how quickly he was losing function. I felt admiration for Danny, and, at the same time, suspicion. Was the guy still in denial? I wondered. Had he so passionately plunged into our movement in order not to deal with what was happening to his body and his life?

Since I'd always been disabled, my experience had been one of "difference" rather than "loss." Only when my legs were amputated had I felt the need to mourn. I had at times compared notes with friends who'd become disabled later in life. Naturally, it took some longer than others to accept the changes brought on by disability, depending on personality and past experience.

I couldn't help comparing Danny with Luke, who was making no progress adjusting. Since I felt the disability movement had saved my life, I tried to draw Luke in. I'd hoped I could be his lifeline. But he showed no interest in our movement or in being saved. I thought a relevant factor was the difference between Luke's background and Danny's. Luke came from a conservative family. He had studied business administration, and he'd never been to a demonstration in his life. Danny's parents were Jewish atheists and old-time Communists. His father had also been a set decorator, his mother a teacher. I'd met them a few times when they joined our demonstrations. Danny had studied liberal arts; he was, like me, a hippie, demonstrated against the war in Vietnam, worshipped Martin Luther King, cried when he sang "We Shall Overcome."

When, by chance, Danny met one of our DIA members on the street and she encouraged him to take a bus, telling him how we'd fought to get wheelchair lifts, he was immediately curious and excited. That's all it took, he told me, for him to want to join our movement.

"Did you know any disabled people before?" I asked.

"Only one, Leslie, a friend's girlfriend. She's young, walks with a cane. I think she has CP."

I was curious about this young woman. Had knowing her made Danny's transition into the disabled world smoother?

"Why don't you ask her to come to DIA? I'd like to meet her."

"She wouldn't be interested. She only hangs out with able-bodied friends."

I'd once surrounded myself with nondisabled people, too, trying hard to be accepted, to fit in. Was it that long ago?

Danny and I saw each other only at meetings. But we talked on the phone, usually at night or early in the morning. We always started with the organizing work at hand, and ended up talking about ourselves. I learned he was barely a year older than I was. He had a sister who had gone to San Francisco with flowers in her hair in '67, and there she still was, making a living as an acupuncturist. He had been married not once but twice. He had left his first wife for his second one, who, in turn, had left him when he became disabled. He had a total of four children, one from the first marriage, three from the second. They lived with their mothers, the eldest in South Carolina, the others in Minnesota.

"Because of my children, I was able to qualify for Medicaid, which pays for my attendants."

I was puzzled. "How's that?"

"Most of my Social Security goes to child support."

I found it hard to believe he was able to claim poverty, especially when I learned he'd been so successful as a set decorator that he was nominated for an Oscar—for a Woody Allen movie, *Interiors,* which I'd never seen.

Danny talked of actors and directors casually. It sounded like name-dropping, but he had worked on a daily basis with those people who for the rest of us existed only on movie and TV screens. To me his pre-disability life seemed enviable. Not true, he told me. He had abused alcohol and drugs, and becoming disabled forced him to address the problem. He also felt disability freed him to do things he'd always wanted to be involved in: activism and acting. He auditioned for parts in plays and was often an extra in movies and TV shows, having no trouble getting calls, since he was well known to directors. We talked about how being seen in a wheelchair on the screen, even for a fleeting moment, could help change perceptions. Disabled people were mostly absent from film and TV; when they made an appearance, they were portrayed in the most stereotypical ways, as villains, victims, or heroic overcomers. Therefore, his acting, I told Danny, could be a form of activism.

Sometimes when I talked with Danny on the phone, I could tell Martha was there. Sometimes I called him right after hanging up with Maurizio. Or I'd call from Luke's apartment early in the morning, while Luke was still sleeping. I felt guilty, and I could tell Danny did, too. But why feel guilty when all we were doing was talking?

At the beginning of the holiday season, Danny and Martha threw a party. It was in Martha's apartment, a few blocks from where Danny lived. The apartment was a nice size and the furniture had been pushed against the walls; but it was so packed with people, quite a few of us in wheelchairs, Danny and I couldn't get anywhere near each other. Good thing. The caress of his eyes was enough to make my skin tingle. He looked more handsome than ever, because he had grown a beard. He wanted to audition for the part of Uncle Vanya, he explained, for a small acting company. He said he'd shave it off afterward.

"Don't shave it off. I like it," I told him from across the room.

"Okay, I'll keep it, just for you."

At that party, I met Leslie, the young woman Danny had mentioned. She had the type of cerebral palsy that affects one side of the body more than the other; one of her arms was weaker than the other, and she used a cane for balance. She was pretty and petite. I could tell she was uncomfortable being in that living room with so many disabled people. She'd been trying to pass as nondisabled, I deduced.

Leslie was starved for contact. I sensed it by the uneasy yearning in her voice; by the way, once we started talking about disability, she clung to my words. I suspected she was at a crossroads, ready to accept that part of herself she'd been trying to suppress. I wanted to open my arms and welcome her home. I asked her to come to our next meeting. "Maybe I will," she said. But she didn't.

The next meeting was the last before the holidays. Danny read the platform and the ADA preamble, which we had included in it. The pre-amble consists of the findings of Congress, the reasons why the law was necessary. I could tell Danny had rehearsed this reading. He used his best actor's voice. But I could hear the genuine emotion in every word.

Individuals with disabilities are a discrete and insular minority who have been faced with restrictions and limitations, subjected to a history of purposeful unequal treatment, and relegated to a position of political powerlessness in our society, based on characteristics that are beyond the control of such individuals and resulting from stereotypic assumptions not truly indicative of the individual ability of such individuals to par-ticipate in, and contribute to, society. The Nation's proper goals regarding individuals with disabilities are to assure equality of opportunity, full participation, independent living, and economic self-sufficiency.

Everyone applauded.

Then I talked about the need to unite the different segments of our community. We had to commit to doing some serious outreach, I said.

"Who will volunteer to outreach to the Deaf community? To psychi-atric survivors? To people with cognitive disabilities? With intellectual disabilities? To people living with AIDS? And what about outreaching to disabled people of color? Ethnic minorities?"

As people volunteered, I wrote down their names. Howie Geld, better known as "Howie the Harp," had surprised us by showing up for the meeting, and now he promised to bring in psychiatric survivors. I couldn't believe our luck; the guy was a legend, one of the founders of that movement. How about cognitive disabilities? A young man, who had come regularly to meetings and had no visible disability, stood and with a certain pride identified himself as autistic. Pat Walls, from the Harlem Independent Living Center, committed to doing outreach to the African-American community. Rafaela Puerto wanted not only to do outreach but to translate material into Spanish. We were rolling.

After the meeting, I wheeled out of the room, right behind Danny.

The crowd moved at a snail's pace toward the elevator. Suddenly, Danny broke away from the others and headed toward an open door. Without thinking, I followed him into a dark room. Our wheelchairs nearly collided as we gravitated toward each other. I couldn't see him, but I felt his spasming arms closing around me, surprisingly strong. I was locked inside those arms. When our mouths found each other's, transported by passion, I lost my awareness of time and space.

"Big sis, where did you go?" Gerry's voice brought me back.

Oh no! Did they see us going into this dark room? What about Martha? She was at the meeting. Did she suspect?

Danny wheeled out nonchalantly. I followed him nervously.

"What are the two of you up to?" Gerry asked, and winked. Ellen gave me a sly smile.

No sign of Martha. Frieda and Michael were getting into the elevator. A few others were waiting with Gerry and Ellen. Marilyn was still there. I grabbed the bar on the back of her power chair and rested my arm on the vibrating, humming ventilator box, warm to the touch. I felt like I was hugging Marilyn, though I was hugging her chair. Its solid mass steadied me.

I'd never been able to give Marilyn one of my Italian hugs. With the ventilator on the back, the tray mounted on the armrests in front of her, the hose snaking around to her mouth, I would have needed arms like Stretch, the comic book rubber man, to hug her the way I wanted.

"It was a great meeting." Marilyn's head turned toward me, while the rest of her body remained motionless. With her eyes, she embraced me. "You're doing wonderful work; I'm proud of you."

"Let's wait and see the end result."

Her brown eyes twinkled as they looked right into mine. "You and Danny work well together."

"You really think so?" It's your fault, Marilyn, I wanted to tell her; you had to go and nominate us.

I kept leaning on her chair until everyone, including Danny, was gone. Then we went down in the elevator together.

18

DEAD OF WINTER

❀

As the fall '92 semester drew to an end, Maurizio tried to convince me to go to Italy during the winter break as I'd done other years, but I was firm. Impossible, I told him; I was too involved in organizing an important event for my community.

On Christmas Day, he called.

"I can get a flight on standby at a reasonable price and be with you for New Year's."

I said I'd rather he didn't. I'd promised Luke I would spend New Year's Eve with him. There would be fireworks at the South Street Seaport. From Luke's apartment, we'd have a great view.

"Maybe I can join you. You can tell your disabled boyfriend I'm your Italian uncle."

I don't know what got into me. No doubt I was irritated by Maurizio's refusal to take my desire to be with a disabled man seriously. Had I been seeing a nondisabled man, he would not have been so magnanimous and cavalier. Maybe I also felt the need to confess. I started talking about Danny. Nothing much had happened, I told Maurizio, but I felt an irresistible attraction to this disabled man. I went on to

describe our meetings, our phone conversations, our wheelchairs touching, the dark room...

"I think Danny's the disabled lover I've been looking for."

When Maurizio didn't respond, I thought the line had been
disconnected.

"*Ci sei ancora?* Are you still there?"

His voice was low and serious. "*Sì.*"

"Then say something, please!"

"Would it help if I jumped in front of a truck? Then I'd be disabled,
too." There was laughter in his voice, but I could tell Maurizio was
taking me seriously this time.

"*Mi dispiace tanto,* I'm so sorry," I murmured.

"*Buon Natale,* Merry Christmas," he said, and hung up.

Immediately after, I felt terribly guilty. I could have picked a better
time and a more considerate way to break up with Maurizio—if that's
what I wanted to do. He'd been so good to me, enabling me to do
things I never could have done on my own. His biggest fault was being
too helpful.

And why did I say Danny was the disabled lover I'd been waiting
for? I'd already acted on my wish to be with a disabled man. At least
consciously, I hadn't given any thought to whether Danny would be a
better choice than Luke. The only comparison I'd made was Luke's
failure to adapt to disability versus Danny's admirable ease. But MS
was progressive; would Danny keep adjusting so admirably as he lost
more function? And if we were to have a relationship, which at this
point I had not considered, how well would I adjust? Wouldn't someone
with a stable condition, preferably someone who'd been disabled all
his life, be a more appropriate partner for me? Wasn't Danny better
off with Martha, who, like him, had MS? To further weight the scale
against Danny, in addition to Martha were the two ex-wives and the
four children. In the past, I'd made a point of staying away from men
whose lives were too entangled.

As the weeks passed and Maurizio didn't call, when his letters and postcards stopped, I felt more and more dejected. The days so dark and the temperature dropping added to the gloom that now enveloped me. My heart was freezing along with the puddles in front of every curb cut. Never had the idiom "dead of winter" rung more true to me.

Right on cue, my symptoms of post-polio grew severe—as severe as they had been when I first become aware of the syndrome and was still forcing myself to walk. In previous years, symptoms had been manageable. Now, the cold was insufferable, the pain in my joints unbearable; all my vibrancy turned to lethargy.

Luckily, we had fewer meetings in the winter. Nonetheless, I found myself calling Gerry several times to tell him I couldn't attend. Other nights, after pushing myself to appear energetic in the classroom during the day, I dragged myself to a meeting but let Danny or Gerry run the show. When Danny and I saw each other, the attraction was still there, but for me now, it was buried under layers of guilt, weariness, and physical pain. Our phone conversations were shorter and less frequent.

I went to see Luke only sporadically, and then told him I was too tired to make love. While at first I'd enjoyed being in control, now I wished I could lie docile on my back and let Maurizio take over. As much as I'd resented Maurizio's help, now I longingly remembered how he'd carry me into a bathroom, place me into a tub full of warm sudsy water, and get in it with me. I started many letters. I picked up the phone, ready to dial. But I kept postponing the call, until it was his birthday in February.

"*Tanti auguri,* many wishes," I said. He thanked me, inquired about my heath, told me he missed me and loved me. I kept repeating "*Tanti auguri*" instead of telling him I missed him and loved him, too. The phone call left me feeling even worse.

I thought diving into the pages of the *Rag,* when it arrived at the end of the month, would help. But the first article announced the death of nondisabled ADAPT leader Wade Blank. While on a family vacation, he'd drowned, along with his young son. I was utterly shattered by the news. My reaction was extreme, undoubtedly because of my already-miserable state of mind. I'd met Wade at the ADAPT action but had hardly talked to him. I remembered that he'd said to me when I was leaving, "Come back, you hear?" He probably said that to everyone; still, I felt I'd betrayed him by not going back.

The action following the one I'd previously attended was in Orlando, Florida. Over seventy disabled activists were arrested and kept in jail for three days and three nights. When I read about it, I felt both guilty and happy I wasn't there. In 1992, ADAPT had gone to Chicago in the spring, then to San Francisco in the fall. I didn't go to either because of the distance, and because I was busy demonstrating at home. We didn't get arrested in New York City. The NYPD didn't want the trouble of dealing with our access needs. If hard-pressed, they gave us summonses. When rounded up together with nondisabled activists at mass protests, we were hastily released, while the others were held in custody. I now vowed to go get arrested at the next ADAPT action—though given the way I felt at the moment, I couldn't imagine going through the ordeal.

It took all my strength to get to work and teach my classes. Though I didn't leave home at the crack of dawn anymore—with the ADA came the courage to ask for later classes—driving back and forth to the Bronx was becoming unendurable. I was still living in NYU housing and, at this point, feeling pressured to leave. In the fall, when I still had the energy, I had been looking near Fordham for an apartment to rent. Even when the building had a level entrance and an elevator, the bathroom was too small, the doors too narrow. I envied Luke his accessible apartment.

"If I were poor, could I get a place like yours?" I asked half-jokingly.

I was thinking the only solution was to buy an apartment. Then I'd be able to make the accessibility modifications I needed. But could I afford it? Once, I shared my thoughts with some DIA friends and got shocked looks.

"You're thinking of buying an apartment? Are you that rich?"

I was neither poor nor rich enough. But I was plenty unsatisfied and indecisive. I was having doubts about teaching Italian. I wanted to teach disability studies, a new academic field, an offshoot of the disability rights movement, comparable to women's studies and ethnic studies. To me, it was crucial to teach about disability in this new way. My teaching Italian felt unnecessary. There were plenty of Italian courses taught by teachers as good as or better than I was. I wanted to bring to a classroom the perspective I'd developed over a lifetime of struggle. But disability studies courses were taught by those with degrees in sociology or anthropology. I didn't think that academically I had a chance.

No matter how I tried, I couldn't shake off the gloom. Everyday annoyances, which I'd learned to ignore, became hard to deal with: the man who insisted on helping me cross the street, grabbing my wheelchair despite my protestations; the complete stranger who stopped me on the sidewalk to ask if I would ever get cured and exhorted me to pray; the one who tried to give me a quarter, assuming I was a beggar, though I was dressed for work, in casual chic; the woman who kept repeating what an inspiration I was when she saw me shopping in a store instead of, I assumed, at home wallowing in my gloom.

The refrain I'd heard since early childhood, "What a shame," which had become background noise in my life, was again painful to hear.

We were planning an event to express our pride in ourselves and our community, but the rest of the world insisted on seeing us as pitiable. It didn't matter what we said; it was Jerry Lewis people listened to.

On one of my days off, when the temperature for the first time in months reached forty degrees, feeling less despondent, I met a friend for lunch at Bruno Bakery on LaGuardia Place. The owner had been my student at NYU, and the waitresses knew me; all asked where I'd been hiding. I felt welcomed, the opposite from the way I'd feel in a new restaurant, where the waiters might address my lunch companion, assuming my wheelchair made me unable to decide what I wanted to eat.

I was rolling back home in an almost cheery mood when a man going in the opposite direction on the sidewalk looked straight into my eyes and, as he passed me, crossed himself. Yes, crossed himself; I couldn't be mistaken.

Was he praying for my sins to be forgiven and for me to be cured? Or was he thanking the Lord that I was the one in the wheelchair, not him? Was he asking for protection against life's perils, accidents, illnesses, which could result in his becoming disabled? With the sign of the cross was he warding off "the evil of disability"? The evil of disability that I personified for him? I couldn't get rid of the image of that man's hand quickly drawing a cross from forehead to chest and from shoulder to shoulder. Damn. Just when I was coming up for air, that fleeting encounter pushed me back into the pit.

I wished I'd gone to Italy during winter break. Danny and Gerry could have carried on the organizing in my absence. I didn't miss just Maurizio; I missed my disabled Italian friends, and I missed the work we did together. I was overcome with sadness at the thought of not being able to travel to Italy without Maurizio's help. I called Gabriella. "*Quando vieni?* When are you coming?" she asked. I couldn't answer her. "*Ti abbraccio.*" She used the customary Italian good-bye—"I embrace you"—among close friends, and I longed for her arms around me; I wished I could let myself fall against her soft breasts and paraplegic belly.

My parents, upset that I wasn't visiting them, came to see me a couple of times. They brought savory Sicilian care packages. Knowing how much my seventy-five-year-old father hated driving into Manhattan made me feel even more grateful.

On one such visit, my father asked, "Is Maurizio coming for Easter?"

I'd told my mother there were problems with Maurizio, but with my father I'd avoided the subject. I mumbled something about the event I was helping to organize.

My father wasn't giving up. "So are you going to Italy in the summer after this disability thing?"

There was no point in lying to my parents. I told them Maurizio and I had broken up.

My eyes filled with tears. My mother hugged me. My father nodded sadly.

I appreciated not being asked questions. I wanted to tell the truth but didn't know where to start. I didn't want my parents to blame Maurizio. All they'd heard about Luke was that I was helping him adjust to his disability. I'd never mentioned Danny.

Now, heavyhearted, my father said, "*Peccato,* what a shame that you and Maurizio never made it down to Sicily."

I felt remorseful for not having followed my father's wish. I hadn't been ready for a trip back to my painful childhood. But maybe that was what I needed to do: confront and exorcise the haunting memories. My reaction to the recent encounter with the man who'd crossed himself seemed to confirm the stronghold my childhood experiences still had on me.

Suddenly, a big smile brightened my father's face. "Maybe the three of us will go!" he exclaimed, putting his arms around my mother and me.

My father's smile was contagious. Soon my mother and I were also smiling. But I knew we weren't about to go.

How my father missed his homeland! No matter how backward it was, how harsh the poverty, how ruthless the Mafia, how corrupt the government, how ignorant the people... In spite or even because of all that, my father loved his Sicily. He had only left it because he loved me more. With Maurizio, I had traveled in northern Italy, where discrimination against Sicilians was most rampant. The Sicilian accent of the "*terroni*" was ridiculed. I now remembered comments northerners made when I mentioned I was born in Sicily. "Really, I never would have known! You speak Italian so beautifully." I didn't react, didn't get angry at the prejudice behind the praise, which my father would have. Which I would have if anyone now said to me, "You're not like those other cripples."

I wished the pain of my Sicilian childhood didn't prevent me from sharing my father's pride in being Sicilian. And I wished his pain over my not being cured wouldn't keep him from trying to understand my disability pride.

As soon as my parents left, I decided I would reconcile with Maurizio. I would call him and ask him to come visit me during Easter break. Then right after the March, I would go to Italy, see my friends, visit with my *sorella d'oltre oceano,* Gabriella. And this time, I would ask Maurizio to travel with me down to Sicily, to Riposto.

19

DANNY

✿

The days were growing longer, the sunshine getting brighter and warmer. Spring was around the corner. As soon as the first shy violets appeared, the pain in my joints subsided. I called Maurizio one morning, but he didn't answer.

That evening, we had a meeting, and I realized the magnetic force between Danny and me was mysteriously being reactivated.

That meeting was exciting in many ways.

We had in attendance some "single payer" advocates. I'd joined the movement for a single payer national health-care system a while back, after comparing our unfair, mostly profit-driven, and messy patchwork of a system to the simple Italian Servizio Sanitario. Now our new president, Bill Clinton, was holding up to the nation the promise of health-care reform. If there was to be reform, we wanted true reform.

The advocates at the meeting argued that universal health care, and specifically "single payer," should be included as a theme at our event. We had already chosen one theme—telecommunications. That year, title IV of the ADA would go into effect mandating relay service, enabling hearing and speech impaired phone users to communicate to users of standard voice phones. Having telecommunications as a theme would bring in the Deaf community.

I saw nothing wrong with adding single payer. The issue of health care couldn't be more timely, and its inclusion in our platform would call attention to and partly compensate for its exclusion from the ADA. Others were strongly opposed. They felt it was right for the ADA not to include health care, since we didn't want to be seen as "sick." Focusing on health care, they said, fed into the "medical model."

We used the term *medical model* with reference to the custom of seeing disability exclusively as a medical problem, not a social one, and of seeing disabled people as in need of treatments and cures rather than accommodations, equal rights, and opportunities.

I'd rejected the so-called medical model as stalwartly as anyone, objected vehemently when treated as an invalid, and chanted "We're disabled, not sick," and "We're people, not patients" at the top of my lungs countless times. But remembering my Italian friends' question, "Isn't health care a right in America?" I'd been wondering if we weren't hurting ourselves by being too rigid. I argued that under a national health-care system we'd be truly equal.

Danny backed me up by quoting Martin Luther King: "Of all the forms of inequality, injustice in health care is the most shocking and inhumane."

I said I also felt our rigidity was hurting people. Was it right to make those who were not only disabled but also sick feel excluded?

One of our strongest activists, a gay man named Harry, with achondroplasia, a common form of dwarfism, had brought to the meeting a few friends from ACT UP. They took my last question as a cue, and requested that we include fighting for a cure for AIDS as another theme. Someone else observed that conditions other than AIDS also needed cures. That remark was met with a chorus of objections. Of course, I, too, cringed at the word *cure*. But I argued that, as strongly as we felt we didn't need to be cured to have a good life, we couldn't be against all cures, or reject all those who sought cures.

Danny cut in. "I must say I was put off when I realized *cure* was a four-letter word in our movement."

I avoided looking at him, but there was no denying the effect his voice had on my heartbeat.

"This is supposed to be a pride march. *Pride* and *cure* just don't mix." That pronouncement came from Gerry.

"Really? You don't say!" one of the ACT UP activists sneered.

The arguing back and forth continued.

Eventually, we decided to make universal health care the other theme of our march. As for cure, for the rest of the evening, we carefully avoided the word.

Every morning, I woke up thinking I should call Maurizio. "April is almost here." But April arrived and I still hadn't called.

The first Saturday in April, Gerry, Danny, and I went to Madison Square Park. We already had a route for our march—down Madison Avenue to the park. We were now trying to decide where to hold the rally.

"The lawn!" Danny exclaimed.

"It's hard to maneuver on grass with wheelchairs, especially manual wheelchairs." I objected.

"The space on the street at the east side of the park might work," Gerry suggested.

"Yeah! At the mouth of Madison! We can have our stage at the south end and everyone will be sitting over here!" Danny sounded more enthusiastic than ever.

I was worried there was no shade in that area. Our march would take place on July 25, the closest Sunday to the actual anniversary of the signing of the ADA, July 26. No doubt it would be very hot, and the rally would be long—at least in my opinion. My idea had been to invite only Judy Heumann and local speakers. Judy was an important lady now. Clinton had appointed her assistant secretary of Special Education and Rehabilitative Services. She was back on the East Coast, in D.C., having left Berkeley, where for years she had worked with Ed Roberts. But then Danny insisted on inviting Justin Dart, and others all had their favorites. We ended up inviting too many.

"If people can't take the sun, they'll go under the trees," Danny said. "I'll have the best sound system, trust me; they'll be able to hear the speeches throughout the park."

Gerry and I didn't doubt Danny could get the best equipment. We declared our mission accomplished, and Gerry left us to take the express bus back to his home in Brooklyn.

Danny headed west on Twenty-third Street.

"Wanna come with me?" he asked.

With the winter behind me, I felt lighthearted, even light-headed. Maybe the best way to deal with the attraction is to stop fighting it, I thought. Maybe it will burn itself out. I grabbed hold of the bar on the back of Danny's power chair and let him pull me. I'll follow you to the moon.

I knew he lived on Ninth Avenue and Twenty-sixth Street. Was he taking me to his place? But we passed Ninth Avenue and kept heading west. Then we passed Tenth Avenue.

"Where are you going?" I was not at all familiar with this part of town. I felt giddy, intoxicated with the warm sunshine. Okay, I'll follow you anywhere.

But the area was starting to look nasty. The sidewalks were a mess, full of cracks and potholes. Danny stayed on the street, and I kept holding on to the back of his chair. Luckily, there wasn't much traffic. We passed workers unloading a truck. I let Danny pull me, but now I wasn't so sure I wanted to follow him. There were barrels and plastic boxes lined up against a wall. Then I knew where we were. On a pier. He had taken me to the Hudson River.

Had I told Danny how much I loved the water? That I got carried back to the sea of my childhood by bodies of water—the ocean, a lake, a pond, a river. There was no better place he could have taken me. There was nothing I could love more than the constant movement of this blue-green water. We stopped at the end of the pier. The water shimmered in the sunlight. The Hudson was so much wider than the East River.

On the other side was New Jersey. On this side, there was no one but the two of us.

Our wheelchairs instinctively assumed the best position for our bodies to get as close as possible. With my eyes closed, as our mouths found each other, I saw dancing sparkles of green light. Danny's hands trembled—was it MS spasticity?

"Help me," he said as he tried to get under my clothes.

I took off my denim jacket, and the spring air felt cool on my arms. I shivered. Was it the chill or the excitement? With overwhelming urgency, I grabbed and guided Danny's hands.

"Let me see you," he whispered, and I opened my top to expose my eager breasts to the breeze, which carried the musty smell of the river. Every inch of my goose-bumped skin, every cell of my crippled body hungered for the touch of those spastic hands.

I didn't call Maurizio. He called me on Easter Sunday. We exchanged the most sad-sounding good wishes. He asked no questions; I offered no explanations. After I hung up, I cried. I felt a mixture of remorse, regret, and relief.

The word that came to my mind now whenever I was with Danny or thought of Danny was one I hated when I was growing up: *destiny*. That word had been used against me in Sicily. It was my destiny to be a cripple, to suffer, never to be loved, never to be happy.

As a girl in the hospital, I'd listened with Audrey to Paul Anka singing, "You are my destiny." My English was still too poor to explain to her why I hated that word. Suddenly, the word sounded right.

I tried to pull back on the reins as I reminded myself of my belief that we make our own destiny. This is my choice, mine alone. Again, I went over the reasons why Danny was not the ideal partner for me. But after I listed all our differences, there he'd be, singing a song I loved, or quoting Dr. King.

We started talking on the phone again, early in the morning, late in the evening... I told him about my dissatisfactions, doubts, wishes.

He told me about his worries, his fears. "My biggest fear is ending up in a nursing home; that's where most people with my kind of MS end up, unless they meet up with Dr. Kevorkian." I had been wrong to suspect he was in denial. "You should go to an ADAPT action," I told him. "ADAPT fights to keep people out of nursing homes." He already knew all about ADAPT. He read the *Rag* from cover to cover, just as I did. "I'm not sure I'd have the stamina to do what those guys do."

The next ADAPT action was in D.C. It would start with a big march and rally on Sunday, May 9, Mother's Day. A few friends were planning to go just for the day. I wanted to go and get arrested. I now had a concrete reason for wanting to get arrested. I had to make sure Danny never ended up in a nursing home.

But on Mother's Day, I felt I should be with my mother, like a good daughter. And there was another reason I wanted to visit my parents that weekend. I planned to tell them about Danny. They were blaming Maurizio for leaving me brokenhearted.

Danny's parents already knew he was in love with me. They seemed happy about it. His mother was a sweetheart. His dad was a big flirt, constantly complimenting me and asking me to teach him Italian.

Right after our romantic interlude at the pier, Danny had broken up with Martha. I'd felt compelled to call her, imagining how hurt she must be.

"I don't want any bitterness between us," I told her.

"Sure," she said sullenly.

Had she been a nondisabled woman, I might not have felt as guilty; the bond of sisterhood wouldn't have been as strong.

I hadn't seen Luke much. I was trying to gather the courage for a heart-to-heart talk. I kept stalling, not wanting to hurt him. I decided to talk to my parents first.

So on Mother's Day, at the dining table, the customary place for revelations in my family, I broke the big news: I was madly in love with a disabled man, and he with me.

My parents stared in disbelief. I knew what they were thinking. That I'd been so distraught over the breakup with Maurizio, I'd turned to the first man who happened to be at hand. I couldn't possibly have left Maurizio for a disabled man. I set them straight.

"I ended the relationship with Maurizio when I started falling in love with Danny. For months, Danny and I tried to stop ourselves, but we couldn't. We love each other."

They kept staring in disbelief.

"Can't you tell me you're happy for me?"

"We're happy if you're happy," my father said finally, and gave me his big smile.

My mother stood up and came around the table to hug me.

Monday morning, I got up at the crack of dawn, made some espresso, and got ready, putting on the ADAPT shirt I'd bought in 1991. I went out the door, got to Penn Station, and boarded the next train to D.C. On automatic pilot, I hadn't packed a change of underwear, but I had slipped the last issue of the *Rag* into my bag. It had the name of the hotel where ADAPT was staying.

But by the time I got there, it was almost noon. I figured they couldn't still be in the hotel. They would be blocking the doors of some government building, for sure, or stopping traffic at a major intersection. How was I going to find them?

Surprise. They were all in the hotel. A meeting was going on with a small woman who must have been important, by the looks on everyone's faces. I asked a guy in a power chair who she was. The guy had CP and his speech was impaired. He said something that sounded like "Sha-Na-Na" or "Tra-La-La." He kept repeating it, trying to make me understand, annoying the people around us, who were muttering, "Shh! Shh!" I felt embarrassed and guilty for not understanding the guy with CP, for arriving late, for not recognizing the small woman, for causing a commotion.

Then I noticed Diane Coleman, who was going all the way around the back of the room. I sensed, rather than saw, her approaching behind me and stopping her chair alongside mine.

"Welcome back," she whispered, and suddenly I felt ecstatic. She told me the little lady was Donna Shalala, Clinton's secretary of Health and Human Services. She had come to meet with ADAPT, exhibiting the goodwill of the new administration, and figuring it was preferable to having her office doors blocked. When Shalala left, a mixture of optimism and skepticism filled the room.

After a typical ADAPT lunch of McDonald's hamburgers, we lined up outside the hotel. Then we marched in single file to the Capitol. We entered the building and kept moving in. "Go, go, go! Move, move, move!" The leaders were not yelling, but the urgency in their voices made it seem as if they were. There must have been five hundred of us. We filled an entire wing of the ground floor, spilling out into the rotunda. Since I was toward the end of the procession, I found myself in the rotunda. A pleasant woman with graying hair in a power chair came around, announcing that ADAPT was there to meet with the congressional leadership. I strongly doubted the Republican majority leaders in the House and the Senate would agree to meet with ADAPT.

"But the congressional leadership is busy at the moment and we will have to wait," she added, emphasizing the word *wait* as she moved around, making sure everyone heard.

I took her words literally. "How long do we wait?" I asked the guy next to me, a paraplegic with massive shoulders and arms. "As long as it takes," he replied as he slid out of his chair, sat on the floor, and put his head on my lap, looking up at me with a smile. Others were getting on the floor. "Might as well make ourselves comfortable." I understood. We weren't waiting for a meeting. This was a sit-in—a huge sit-in.

At a certain point, we heard chanting coming from farther inside the building. I couldn't see what was happening, but I caught the words of the chant: "I'd rather go to jail…"

Diane was coming. "Those who are not willing should move to the other side," she repeated sweetly a few times, making sure we all heard, like the gray-haired lady had done before.

"Not willing to do what?" I asked the paraplegic guy still sitting on the floor next to me, his head no longer on my lap.

"To go all the way, baby!" He winked.

Was he coming on to me, or was he talking in code?

Then I saw the cops moving closer. Two of them got a guy off the floor, one cop grabbing him under the shoulders, the other holding his legs, and carried him away.

"Weren't they supposed to give us three warnings?" I asked the paraplegic guy, remembering what I'd learned at my first action.

"They did. You didn't hear them."

Quite a few people were moving in the direction we had come in from, and I understood they were leaving to avoid getting arrested.

I recognized one of the women I'd met at my first action, the one who had been in a nursing home. Her power chair was being pushed from the back by a policeman while a policewoman pulled the front. She had plastic handcuffs on her wrists, and I worried her spastic movements would cause the plastic to cut her skin.

A handcuffed man who didn't look disabled was being dragged away, his belly on the floor. I wondered where the arrestees were being taken.

"I'd rather go to jail than die in a nursing home," everyone was chanting. Did I really want to go to jail? What if they kept us for three days and three nights, as they had done in Orlando? Or longer? I had a pile of still-ungraded finals on my desk, and didn't have a change of underwear.

I watched a blind man with a long beard being handcuffed and led away, a cop carrying his white cane. When I turned, the paraplegic guy was gone. So was his wheelchair.

Now a cop was in front of me. "Do you want to be arrested?" I couldn't believe my ears. Was he polite by nature, or did I look chicken to him? Maybe it was okay to chicken out, slip away, and head for Union Station. Danny was in no danger of going into a nursing home—not yet.

At that moment, I saw Diane smiling at me as she held up her hands and let a policewoman handcuff her.

I looked up at the cop, held up my hands as I'd seen Diane do, and, being as polite as he had been to me, replied, "Yes, Officer, I want to be arrested."

We were all taken to a nasty place that smelled like a garage. Maybe it was a garage. They cut the handcuffs off. There were four card tables lined up side by side, with a cop sitting behind each. Four at a time, we went up to the tables. When my turn came, after a good half hour, I was asked for ID. I took out my driver's license. I was told I could pay a fifty-dollar fine in cash and be released. I had about $150 in my wallet. I saw Diane looking at me and shaking her head. I remembered what I'd learned at the workshop in '91. "We get arrested together, we get released together." Many of the people there probably didn't have fifty dollars; some might not even have had five dollars. I politely refused the offer. The policeman emptied out my purse and listed the contents on an official sheet of paper: the cash to the penny, my credit cards, my Fordham faculty ID, a small bottle of Motrin with ten pills in it, a tiny tin box of pure Italian licorice, which he suspiciously inspected and sniffed, my red pen... Another cop took the bag from the back of my chair and shook everything out of it. I remembered having been told at the workshop, "Carry as little as possible if you're planning to be arrested." But I hadn't checked into the hotel. Out of the bag came my denim jacket, which I'd worn when I left New York, since it was chilly in the morning, my leftover breakfast, bought at the station—half a bottle of Poland Spring, a half-eaten croissant wrapped in cellophane, and a banana—and my copy of the *Rag*. I was now glad I'd forgotten the underwear. Everything was thrown into a black plastic bag, and I was given a number: 84.

When the last of us had been processed, that person held up her number: 114. That's how many had been arrested. A few were not disabled, at least not visibly. Some might have been attendants. An attractive woman, who saw me watching her reposition a quadriplegic man in a power chair, introduced herself as Carolyn and told me she was available should I need anything. I thanked her.

Next, one at a time, we had our pictures taken with a Polaroid; then they started fingerprinting. Photographing someone wildly spasming, then getting prints from fingers permanently contracted into a fist was challenging for the police, and horrific, I imagined, for the arrestees. There was a guy with no arms. After conferring and deliberating, a white-shirted cop waved him away. The whole process took many hours. We had nothing to eat. When many complained of being thirsty, we were given water. I refused the water because I didn't want to have to pee—not after hearing the police had to accompany us to the bathroom. When a few insisted they needed their meds, a medic was called to check their medicine bottles and administer the prescribed dosages.

While waiting, I sat next to Diane and told her I'd wanted to be arrested for Danny. I told her what he'd said about people with MS ending up in nursing homes, unless they found Kevorkian.

"Yes, quite a few of the people Kevorkian has, quote, unquote, assisted had MS or other nonterminal conditions. Instead of getting help dealing with their fears and depressions, they were offered a lethal injection."

Her words sent chills down my spine.

During those long hours in that nasty place, I spoke to each and every one of my strong comrades; we exchanged phone numbers and promises to stay in touch, shared stories of struggle and hopes for a better world. The bond I developed with each one would last a lifetime.

I took the train home the next day, having slept a few hours in my clothes in one of the ADAPT rooms with three other women, the best accommodation Diane could arrange for me after we got released late at night. I was sorry to miss the party but eager to get back to Danny.

When I told Danny I had gotten arrested because I never wanted him to be in a nursing home, his eyes misted. He thanked me. He had been worried when he couldn't reach me on the phone. "I thought you went back to your boyfriend in Italy, or to the one at the Seaport."

"I have no other boyfriends," I said.

I decided it was time to tell Luke the truth.

I went down to the Seaport. We sat by the East River, our chairs side by side, as we had many times. I looked at the water, so I didn't have to see Luke's face. He'd been expecting this talk. My growing discomfort had made him suspicious. He listened in silence.

"I feel that I've failed you, Luke." I started crying. I had indeed failed. I'd entered the relationship hoping to help him accept his disability, and I was leaving it without accomplishing my goal.

"You're a great guy, Luke; other women will fall in love with you. Please believe me, you can have a good life." I was still trying desperately to throw him that lifeline. I turned to look at him. His face was expressionless.

"Stop crying," he said.

But I couldn't.

Danny and I acted like teenagers, laughing for the silliest reasons and laughing at our silliness. We explored different regions of each other's bodies at different times, remaining in our chairs, though once or twice I managed, without my prostheses, to get out of mine and sit on Danny's lap. We put our crippled bodies to the test, playing all the erotic games we could think of, either on the then-deserted Twenty-third Street pier, with the Hudson River serving as backdrop, or in the more prosaic but comfortable setting of Danny's apartment after a take-out Chinese dinner.

Danny lived in a co-op in Chelsea, in a one-bedroom apartment that had belonged to his parents. He moved there after his divorce. The building was accessible enough, but his apartment presented the usual problems. The bathroom door had been removed and replaced by a curtain to allow entrance in a wheelchair, but the hallway to the bedroom was impossible to navigate. Danny was waiting for permission to renovate from the co-op board. In the meantime, instead of using his bedroom, he slept in a hospital bed placed against a wall in his living room.

On another wall were shelves with hundreds of vinyl records—33s and long-obsolete 45s. He had all the silly love songs from the fifties and sixties that I'd listened to with Audrey so many years before. He played them on his turntable after our take-out dinner, and we shimmied and bopped until our wheelchairs collided and, overcome with passion, we found ourselves in each other's arms.

He knew the words to hundreds of songs and he sang them to me. I loved his singing voice. He sang as we sat in his apartment, or rolled down the street, or waited for an elevator after a meeting.

Sometimes, following a meeting, we'd get into some heavy petting right on a busy sidewalk.

"We're doing it to educate those who think crips are asexual," I said to Gerry and other friends who loved to tease us. Indeed, it was quite amusing to see the looks of patronizing benevolence on people's faces turn to shocked horror when confronted with the unabashed expression of our lust.

We usually saw each other in the daytime. Danny told me his attendant situation made it difficult for him to be out late at night. I hadn't met Danny's attendant. He never accompanied him. And whenever I went to Danny's apartment, the attendant was always on an errand or on a break. I knew that Danny, unlike Luke, didn't get round-the-clock services; Medicaid paid for only twelve hours, he told me. He had to figure out the best way for us to be together at night.

Then, at the end of May, Danny had to be hospitalized. He had not followed his doctors' orders to stay off his butt, and the sore he'd had for over a year had gotten larger and become infected. Even in the hospital, he worked on organizing, making call after call from his bed, running up a huge phone bill.

"I'll do the wheel work," I told him.

Since I was off for the summer, I had more time to devote to organizing, and I went to various groups to get them to commit to bringing
their members to our march. I also had more time to look at apartments
for sale.

Danny was discharged from the hospital at the end of June. The
infection was gone but the sore not quite healed. He was told he should
be up for only a few hours, lie in bed as much as possible, preferably on
his stomach. But, with the day of our March approaching, I knew it
would be harder than ever for him to follow doctors' orders.

Less than a week after Danny's discharge from the hospital, I put in
an offer to buy a studio apartment, and it was accepted. The studio was
on Fifteenth Street, close to Fifth Avenue. If I was going to put all my
savings in an apartment, it had to be where I wanted to live. I had
decided not to stay at Fordham and was already looking for a position
in the city.

The studio was no larger than four hundred square feet. Some work
was needed to make the bathroom accessible. But it was in a lovely
building with a lovely ramp. The moment I saw that ramp, I decided I
was going to buy the apartment. To a wheelchair user, a ramp says
"Welcome"; it says "The people living here want you, and probably
other wheelchair users live here."

The location was ideal—close enough to Washington Square Park
that I could still feel "at home," and close enough to Danny's apartment
in Chelsea. It was also practically next door to the New School for Social
Research, an alternative, very progressive university. I'll take my curriculum vitae to the New School, I thought. Maybe they will even let me
teach a disability studies course.

I hesitated about sharing the news with DIA friends. Being a home-
owner made me more aware of being privileged. Stronger than ever was
the discomfort I felt knowing so many disabled people were poor. Of
course, strangers seeing me wheeling on a busy sidewalk had no inkling
of any difference between me and the poorest disabled people. Some
still saw us all as beggars. "I just bought an apartment," I told a man

who tried to hand me a dollar bill just a few days after my offer was accepted. But he didn't understand. He looked offended as he put the dollar back in his pocket.

On July 8, after so many obstacles and postponements, Danny and I got to spend our first whole night together, and celebrate his being home from the hospital, my buying an apartment, the fast approaching day of the march, and our growing love for each other.

When I got to his apartment, Danny's attendant, whom he introduced as Martin, was still there. Danny was already lying in his hospital bed in the living room. For the first time, I noticed how narrow that bed was. How were we both going to fit? The side rail was down and Danny was covered with a sheet. I knew that under the sheet he was naked. Of course, it was for practical reasons. Danny wouldn't have been able to get in bed or undress himself. So Martin had done all he needed.

"Anything else? Is that all?" Martin asked.

The presence of a stranger at our long-awaited rendezvous was making me feel uncomfortable. Martin was a tall, dark, handsome man. Somehow, the thought of his handling Danny, taking off his clothes, positioning his naked body, made me feel jealous in a weird way.

I'd never been bothered by Luke's attendants handling him. The nice Haitian woman used to undress Luke while I busied myself with other matters, or got myself ready in the bathroom. One would think I'd be more jealous of a woman.

"Anything else? Is that all?"

I was so glad when Martin finally walked out the door and Danny and I were left idyllically alone.

But now what? Why was Danny's naked body under the sheet making me feel uneasy? Paintings of reclining nudes by European masters came to my mind; in all of them, it was the woman who was naked—from Giorgione's and Titian's paintings of Venus to Goya's *Naked Maja*.

"What do you think of the food?"

I'd glanced at the spread on the table across from the bed but had not paid the deserved attention to all my favorite Italian delicacies—prosciutto, mozzarella, dried sausage, olives, artichoke hearts—and a nice crusty loaf of bread. Nor had I shown my appreciation for the tiger lilies in the vase or the bottle of Moscato wine. I smiled as another famous painting flashed through my mind, Manet's *Déjeneur sur l'Herbe*.

"I see you went overboard at Manganaro, but why did you get wine? You can't drink wine."

"I can taste it on your lips. We have to toast to your new apartment."

Thinking that wine would help me relax, I picked up the bottle. But I was never good with corkscrews; my hand kept slipping.

"I should have had Martin open it," Danny said.

"Oh, I can do it," I insisted. But the corkscrew refused to cooperate.

The wine can wait, I decided. And so can the food. It was the inequality between us that bothered me; I didn't want to be fully dressed in my chair while Danny lay naked under the sheet.

"You look comfortable in bed. I think I should make myself comfortable, too."

I slipped off my prostheses and set them on the couch. I easily slid out of my long Indian skirt and let it fall to the floor. I left my black tank top on, as well as my black underpants. I was ready to get in Danny's bed, when I noticed how high it was. Then suddenly, as if by magic, it lowered itself. Of course, that's one of the advantages of hospital beds: They go up and down. Danny was smiling, the control in his hand.

I could climb on the bed now, lifting myself out of the chair with my arms, the absence of legs below my knees facilitating the maneuver. Above the bed was a trapeze bar to aid with positioning, and I grabbed the triangle with my left hand as I climbed right on Danny's supine body, straddling him. I pulled my tank top off, sliding it over my head. Danny's hands pulled at my underpants and I lifted just enough to allow him to slide them off over my stumps. He grabbed my stumps and pulled me closer toward his flushed face, toward his scratchy beard, toward his avid open mouth, toward heaven on earth.

I slept that night on top of Danny. That solved the problem of the narrow hospital bed. As I drifted off, he softly sang the old Carol King song made famous by the Shirelles: "Tonight you're mine, completely..."

No possessive pronouns, please. I only said it in my mind. My breasts against his hairy chest, my head nestled in the hollow between his shoulder and his face, I drifted languidly in and out of slumber.

Danny sang, "Will you still love me tomorrow?"

Oh yes, I will, and the day after, and the day after that... But I couldn't speak, because I was already asleep.

The food was still fresh and tasty in the morning, thanks to the air-conditioning. Naked in bed, we had prosciutto and mozzarella for breakfast.

20

CRIPS ARE BEAUTIFUL

❖

The big day for our march arrived, and I surprised myself by not feeling nervous when I woke up. I wanted to call Danny but decided not to. His oldest boy was visiting from South Carolina. They were leaving early to go to the rally site, where Danny's buddies from the film industry would be putting together our stage.

I'd talked to Maurizio briefly a few days before. I told him I missed him and all my Italian friends and would visit but didn't know when. I told him I wanted to go to Sicily someday, too.

The last few weeks, still waiting to close on my new apartment, I'd been thinking about decorating—what furniture to take, what new pieces to buy. The day before, on impulse, I'd bought a full-length mirror at the Houston Street flea market. I'd never owned one before. This wasn't the flimsy frameless kind you hang on a door, but one with a heavy silver frame studded with colorful stones of various shapes and sizes. I knew just where I would hang it near the entrance of my new apartment. But at the moment, it was leaning against the wall facing my bed, where my neighbor, who had graciously carried it for me, placed it.

Sitting up in bed now, I looked admiringly at my new purchase, and couldn't help but see my reflection. I slipped off the T-shirt I'd slept in and was amazed. My naked, legless, curved and scarred body looked and felt so right, so perfect, so complete. As my fingertips traced the scars on my stumps, I tried to remember what my polio legs had looked like. So ugly, those legs, that Audrey and I had only looked at ourselves in the mirror from the waist up. Suddenly, the strange thought came to me that if I still had my legs, my body would feel just as right. I realized that my feelings had nothing to do with the way my body actually looked, but with how far I'd come in being able to accept it and embrace it. I claimed the disabled body in the mirror, which once I'd felt didn't belong to me, which once I'd allowed to be tortured and abused. I claimed its pain and its beauty.

I took the bus to Thirty-fourth Street, then wheeled up to Madison and Thirty-eighth, our assembly point. It was not quite eleven yet, but already people were being dropped off by Access-A-Ride, the NYC door-to-door paratransit service—needed when use of accessible mass transit is problematic because of significant disability or particularly difficult routes.

The day was promising to be very hot, but at least not humid. I wore a T-shirt designed for us by quadriplegic cartoonist John Callahan, imprinted with marching disabled caricatures of all types and stripes. There was already quite a crowd on Madison. And throngs were arriving from all directions. Some were wheeling and some were walking—on crutches, with canes, with guide dogs.

The first face I noticed was Martha's. I maneuvered hesitantly through the crowd toward her. I wanted to give her a hug but was afraid she wouldn't want to be hugged by me. She smiled. Had she forgiven us?

A familiar voice was calling my name. My old friend Susie! I hadn't seen her in ages. She'd moved way out on Long Island after she got married about ten years before. Her husband was pushing her in a wheelchair. She, too, had stopped walking because of post-polio syndrome. And was that her little girl? I couldn't believe how tall she was. Why, of course, she must be seven or eight now. I hugged Susie and her daughter again and again. I made her promise to come back to the city soon, so that we could catch up.

Now a new friend was walking toward me. Hope. We'd met at a disabled women's conference and bonded in the ladies' room. In a clairvoyant instant, as she'd handed me a paper towel from a dispenser too high on the wall, I saw us being the closest of friends in the future. Small and slender, looking sixteen, though she was a year or two older than I, Hope walked fast, zigzagging and swaying from side to side. A pediatric nurse, she had cerebral palsy. She bent down to hug me.

More and more people were arriving. Many wore the Callahan T-shirt. Signs were hanging from wheelchairs; posters and banners were held by hands, some of which shook and spasmed: ADA IS HERE TO STAY; DISABLED AND PROUD; CRIPS ARE BEAUTIFUL.

The term *crip* was becoming widely used in the disability community. In the past years, there had been much arguing about language. "Put the person first!" said those sold on the somewhat awkward but official-sounding "person with disability" and "people with disabilities." "We like putting the disability first," the "disabled and proud" among us countered. I was even in favor of capitalizing the *D,* following the example of "Deaf" people. Lately, we had also been inundated with euphemisms such as "physically challenged" and "differently abled," dreamed up mostly by ableist people who were uncomfortable with the word *disabled.* We reacted by trying to reclaim the utmost negative word, *cripple.* "Let's turn the insult on its head," the *Rag* proposed. I loved it. But for some, *cripple* just didn't apply, or had too painful connotations. The shortened version, *crip,* snappy and hip, caught on. For that day, we had even made CRIPS ARE BEAUTIFUL buttons.

Friends and acquaintances were waving to me enthusiastically; I didn't know which way to go. Nearby I saw Paula, a legally blind wheelchair user, who had taken over Frieda's role as president of Disabled in Action. "It's Nadina," I said as I hugged her. Next to Paula was a lesbian couple from Connecticut I'd met at ADAPT, Elaine and Patty, both on scooters. Elaine, a talented singer/songwriter, had her guitar case tied to the back of her scooter. She grabbed me, leaning off her seat, while I still had my arms around Paula. Patty jumped in and the four of us held one another, laughing.

I moved through the crowd, bumping into other wheelchairs, trying not to run over standing people's toes. Phyllis, a veteran of our movement, who taught at the CUNY School of Social Work, looked smashing on her scooter in her PISS ON PITY T-shirt and wide-brimmed straw hat. She was talking to a small woman with a head of blond curls who was sitting in a wheelchair, Carr, another longtime activist. I hugged one, then the other.

Jackie yelled out my name. I turned around and there she was, all blond ebullience and sprightliness. She was jumping up and down, her wheelchair jumping right along with her. A dancer, she could maneuver that chair like magic. We threw our arms around each other and rocked back and forth with great relish. Her silky blond hair smelled like almonds.

It was her hair against my face, its almond smell that made me suddenly miss Audrey. How I wish I could hug you, blood sister! I spoke to her as I hadn't done in years. But not like we used to hug when we were girls unhappy with our lives and ashamed of who we were. I wish I could hug you, Audrey, like I'm hugging my disabled sisters today, happy and proud to be like them, happy and proud to be who I am.

"What a wonderful manifestation of pride!" Anne Emerman, looking elegant and sounding aristocratic, pulled me out of my reverie. Before I put my arms around her, I took my wheeling gloves off, not wanting to get dirt on her clothes.

But where was Judy Heumann? And our other guests? And was Danny still down by Twenty-third Street? I hoped there were no problems with our stage. I found Gerry talking to the handsome executive director of the Harlem Independent Living Center, James Billy, who wore a hook prosthesis.

"I haven't seen Danny," Gerry told me. "Judy and the others are having coffee at the luncheonette at the corner."

Pat Walls and her husband, Phil, were unfolding the Harlem Center's banner. Pat's hair was elaborately braided, with rows leading toward the top of her head, where a mass of shiny curls sat like a crown. I wheeled up behind her wheelchair and leaned forward, throwing my arms around her shoulders. "You look like a beautiful queen," I said as she tilted her head back so I could kiss her creamy cheek.

Down the block, on the shady side of the street, next to the CIDNY banner, was Marilyn. I couldn't get close to her. I blew her kisses. I aimed some kisses toward Eileen Healy, DIA's treasurer and CIDNY's board president. Slightly built, she looked almost waiflike in her chair next to Marilyn's substantial and solid form. Frieda and Michael were on the other side of the street with the DIA banner. I blew them kisses, too.

The various segments of our community were well represented. A group was feeding in from Thirty-seventh Street with a banner that said WE'RE PEOPLE FIRST. I'd worked especially hard to reach out to those with intellectual disabilities. At times, they'd been shunned by those of us with physical disabilities, because of the importance we were conditioned to place on our brains, especially since our bodies were considered defective.

I watched another group signing to one another, and I raised my right hand—thumb, index, and little finger extended—to flash the love sign their way. Those who identified as Deaf, with a capital "D," didn't consider themselves disabled, but simply members of a linguistic minority, sign language users. Getting them to join us had been an accomplishment. Frank Bowe, longtime activist, professor, author, and one of our guest speakers, broke away from the group and moved toward me.

"You did a good job, Nadina," he said. He read lips and spoke with a delicious "Deaf accent." He bent his lanky frame down and kissed my cheek. I let my right hand flutter in front of my chest to sign *happy*.

At the corner, Howie the Harp was talking with a sassy Italian-American woman, a psychiatric survivor named Rosary. I recognized many faces in that group from demonstrations I had attended to protest against electric shock and forced drugging. Having intimate knowledge of depression, though I'd been lucky enough to avoid stigmatizing psychiatric labels and harmful interventions, I felt I belonged with them.

I was starting to worry about Danny. We'd have to get marching soon. Our Disability Independence Day float, an open truck bedecked with red-white-and-blue bunting and flowing banners that read DISABILITY INDEPENDENCE DAY and UNITY, EMPOWERMENT, PRIDE, was slowly coming up Madison. Everyone was cheering.

Then, alongside the float, I saw Danny, sitting in his manual chair in his Callahan T-shirt, being pushed by his son. I quickly wheeled toward them.

"My power chair wouldn't start this morning," Danny said, shaking his head from side to side, his jaw clenched.

Ah, the drawbacks of our dependence on technology. You could count on being let down when most in need. The night before, I had printed the little speech I was to give at the end of the rally, for fear my spiteful printer would decide to go on strike in the morning.

"Lucky your son is here." I smiled cheerfully to calm Danny down. I hoped the power chair wouldn't need major work. It was traumatic to have a mobility device taken away for repairs. You never knew how long you'd be stuck without it. Danny could use the manual chair at home, but his arms were too weak to push himself outdoors.

The float made a U-turn, amid loud cheers. I noticed Danny's parents were sitting on the truck. After it came to a stop, they got off.

"Stay on, so you don't get tired," Danny told them.

"No. We want to march," his mother insisted.

I wished my parents were there. I wanted my father to see us all together, so many of us, all happy and proud. But I knew my parents weren't coming.

Gerry was now bringing our invited guests to the front. I took my place between him and Danny. Alongside us were Judy Heumann, madam secretary, rebel turned presidential appointee; Justin Dart, still chair of the Committee on Employment of People with Disabilities; Marca Bristo, a radiant paraplegic woman, founder of the Chicago CIL and newly appointed chairperson of the National Council on Disability; and Paul Miller, an attorney and person of short stature, Bill Clinton's disability adviser. Though I liked and admired them all, and sincerely hoped they could work from within the system, the revolutionary in me felt a bit uneasy next to these crips who were government emissaries. I was glad that radical ADAPT activist Eric Von Schmetterling was there from Philly, and that Johnny Crescendo, British activist and singer/ songwriter, would be singing his rebellion songs.

Promptly at noon, we started moving behind our huge banner. I was glad it was a short route. There wasn't much shade on Madison, and I worried about Danny and all those who couldn't tolerate the heat. But Danny seemed fine. I hoped the sore on his butt wasn't getting worse. I kept turning to look behind me at the flowing multitude of beautiful disabled people. There were over two thousand of us. It was the largest disability event we had ever had in New York City. And I'd done my part to make it happen.

Today's celebration would not magically change the way the ableist world saw us. Many would continue to think of us as pitiable, or at best as inspirational. After today, we would still have to fight discrimination, struggle to break down barriers. We had a long way to go, but today the seeds of pride were being sown. Those of us taking part in the event, as well as all who would learn about it and in the future organize similar ones, would nurture those seeds, make the pride grow and spread like wildflowers.

As the march reached the rally point, the area quickly filled, an overflowing mass of diversity and joyfulness. Danny's buddies had put together an impressive stage. Really a flatbed truck, made wheelchair-accessible by an electric forklift, it was festooned with bunting, backed with banners, and looked festively perfect.

Leslie limped past me toward her partner and the other nondisabled guys in work clothes still applying the finishing touches. She tentatively smiled at me. I was proud of her for marching. I wanted to reassure her, be her guide, her mentor.

Now Judy was approaching the stage, staring at the forklift. "Is this how we get up there?"

"It's safe," Danny said.

She raised her eyebrows. "Not exactly ADA-compliant." Then she laughed. "I guess it'll do the job."

The rally, as I'd feared, proved too long. People wandered off into the park, looking for shade. But we had the best sound system, so the speeches and songs could be heard throughout the area.

I couldn't listen to the speeches. I sat behind the stage as John Hockenberry, our emcee, introduced one speaker after another. I stared at the program in my hand. I worried that everyone would leave before all our guests had spoken, and those scheduled to speak toward the end would get angry; and I worried we had not hired enough sign language interpreters. I only picked up bits and pieces of speeches—Judy exclaiming, "It's good to be back home!" and Justin Dart proclaiming in his Texas drawl, "I'm a human being; the ADA says so! Hallelujah!"

Then, out of the corner of my eye, I saw Luke, sitting apart from the crowd in a shady spot near one of the park entrances. Had he marched? I wheeled over to him.

"What do you think of this?"

"I'm finding it very"—he was searching for the right word—"validating."

I almost started crying. I touched his hand. "I'm so glad you're here."

By the time our last guest spoke, many had left, but quite a few remained. It was our turn to get on the stage. Gerry went up first. Danny had his son push him onto the forklift, then waved him away. He pushed himself to the middle of the stage. I went up and got between my two co-chairs.

"It wasn't just the three of us who made this event happen," Gerry said. "A lot of people worked on organizing it. So all of you, come on up!"

Ellen was already on the forklift. She rolled next to her husband.

Frieda and Michael followed, and Marilyn. One by one, others joined us, until there was hardly space left on the flatbed.

Danny started singing "We Shall Overcome." In spite of the heat, his voice sounded strong. We all joined in. I tried to fight the tears that civil rights anthem inevitably brought to my eyes. I took Danny's hand. It was exhilarating to be on this stage with the man I loved, and to be surrounded by my sisters and brothers in the disability movement. It was as if all my life I'd been waiting for and working toward this moment.

When the song was over, I took the mike. The word *overcome* was often used to mean rising above what the ableist world considered "our misfortunes." We felt we needed to make sure there was no misunderstanding. I unfolded the page with the brief speech I'd prepared. My hand shook but my voice came out surprisingly clear.

> We just want to make sure
> everyone understands
> that, when we sing "We Shall Overcome,"
> we are not saying:
> we shall overcome our disabilities.
>
> For too long,
> we were made to believe
> that we had to get over all the obstacles
> that were put in our way
> with our willpower.
> If we couldn't be cured,
> we had to make our disabilities
> as inconsequential as possible
> in order to fit in.
> That was called "overcoming."
> No more of that!
>
> We do not overcome our disabilities,

we just live with them.
Some of us not only accept our disabilities
but we embrace them,
because we know,
even if they cause us pain,
our disabilities
are a very important part of who we are.
We are no longer willing to minimize, camouflage,
suppress that important part of ourselves.

We will no longer try to change
to fit the mold.
Instead, we will destroy the mold
and change the world
to make it a just,
welcoming, and comfortable place
for everyone.

So when we sing "We Shall Overcome,"
what we are saying is:
we shall overcome prejudice,
we shall overcome ignorance,
we shall overcome discrimination,
we shall overcome injustice,
we shall overcome fear.

We shall overcome the fear
that makes those who are not disabled
stay away from of us
because they don't want to be reminded
that we are all
human and vulnerable.

And we shall overcome the fear
that keeps us, people with all disabilities,
from being ourselves,
and being proud of ourselves;
the fear that keeps us from shining
and showing the world
how beautiful we really are!

But today we are proud,
we are proud of ourselves,
we are proud of each other.
Today we are shining bright!
Let us stay proud!
Let us keep shining!
We are all so beautiful!

PART IV

Come Sono Contenta:
How Happy I Am

21

VADO VIA CONTENTO:
I'M GOING AWAY HAPPY

❁

My cousin Victor went to open the front door and let the nurse in. I was sitting with my mother and Victor's wife, Josie, at the kitchen table in my parents' house in Queens. We were not eating, as many times we had done around that table, nor talking, just sitting. In the bedroom, across from the kitchen, my father slept. Or at least he appeared to be sleeping. His eyes had been closed for the past two days. The bedroom door wide open, we listened to his labored breathing.

Nicky, the black-and-white mutt that my parents got after Nica died, had been lying on the floor beside the bed, only coming out to drink water from his bowl and go to the backyard to relieve himself. In his other bowl, the food that my mother kept replacing remained untouched.

It had been only a week since I'd driven my father to the hospital to have fluid removed from his lungs—a painful procedure he'd already undergone three times in the past six weeks. And it had been four months since we'd gotten the verdict: lung cancer. A large tumor with deep roots, spreading into both lungs—inoperable.

"The best we can do is radiation, to slow down the growth and gain a little time," the pulmonologist had said.

My father had shrugged his shoulders. "Gain time for what? *A che fare?*" And he'd looked at me, half a smile on his face. My father had never done anything halfway. His smile had always been big and bright.

Cancer was not new to my father. Twenty years before, he'd had a good part of his voice box removed. But he'd never for a moment looked defeated. Because his voice, once thunderous, was low and hoarse, his friends called him *il Padrino*, the Godfather. He looked annoyed, but I suspected he was also flattered.

After the cancer surgery, he quit smoking. But in the last few years, he'd started sneaking a cigarette when my mother wasn't looking. She smelled the smoke on his breath and got furious. Once, when I was visiting, she'd found a pack of Parliament Lights he had forgotten to take out of his shirt pocket and hide in the glove compartment when he got out of his car. Without saying a word, but with a look of pained determination, she went into the bathroom, leaving the door wide open, and one by one, she took the cigarettes out of the pack, broke them in half, and flushed them down the toilet.

"But can't you see those are not real cigarettes? *Non sono vere!*" My father, who had smoked filterless Chesterfields when he couldn't find the strong Italian or French cigarettes he liked, stood by the bathroom door, looking more amused than guilty. He winked at me.

I knew my mother expected me to intervene. So, I reminded my father of the close call and how grateful we were that the cancer was gone, what a risk he was taking every time he lit up. My father nodded.

"*Hai ragione!* You're right! *Non fumo piu!* I won't smoke anymore!" But I knew he didn't mean it.

The radiation didn't slow down the growth of the tumor. Twice a week, for eight weeks, I drove out to Queens to take my father to the hospital. Because of his illness, I missed an ADAPT action. I'd been going to actions and getting arrested regularly in the past few years. I had more freedom to cancel and reschedule classes, since I was now teaching at the New School, as had been my wish. I had classes only three days a week. On the days when I didn't teach, I took my father for the radiation treatments. I sat with a magazine on my lap for half an hour, until he came out of the room at the end of the hall, looking weak and pale—weaker and paler after each treatment.

Soon after the radiation cycle ended, fluid started accumulating in his lungs. When breathing became too difficult, I'd drive him to the hospital so he could have it drawn out. Always with a magazine on my lap, I waited in my wheelchair for him to come out of the treatment room. He'd be white as a ghost, hardly able to walk, his once-powerful shoulders looking frail and stooped.

On those shoulders I had sat as a little girl, trying to keep my balance.

"*Non aver paura!* Don't be afraid! I won't let you fall!"

But on my father's shoulders, I wasn't afraid of anything. No longer the poor little cripple, I was the fairy tale princess being carried by her knight in shining armor.

When I last drove him to the hospital, my father kept his eyes closed most of the way there. He opened them while I was parking in the space with the wheelchair-access sign.

"Turn the wheel to the left a bit more," he whispered, as if I still needed instructions on how to park after driving for nearly thirty years.

He watched me pull my wheelchair out of the car, a look of deep sadness in his eyes. Of course he's sad, I thought, tears blurring my vision; my father is dying. Yet, I thought I recognized an old, familiar look. Was my father still unhappy because I'd never been cured?

Maybe he could tell I was having a harder time lifting the wheelchair in and out of the car as I got older and the post-polio symptoms progressed, and wished he could do it for me, the way he used to. So strong, my father could lift my chair with one hand. But he always grabbed it in such an angry way, as if he would have liked to smash it on the ground.

As we made our way to the elevator, a nurse recognized us. She asked my father how he was feeling and, seeing how weak he was, offered to get him a wheelchair. My father shook his head. Smiling the half smile

I had now grown accustomed to, he pointed to me rolling alongside him, and said to the nurse, "One is enough."

Then he came behind me and grabbed the push handles of my chair. I let him set the pace as we made our way to the elevator, my father holding on, using my wheelchair like a walker to keep his balance.

But his legs were steady and his back was straight when he walked into the treatment room. I felt proud of him.

I didn't see the doctor come out of the room and walk toward me. I must have been staring into space; I certainly wasn't reading the magazine open on my lap. His voice startled me.

"Ms. LaSpina!"

My eyes had trouble focusing on the somber but benign-looking face.

"Can you come with me?"

Maybe my father is so weak after the procedure that he needs to hold on to my chair to walk out of the room, I thought. But I looked at my watch and realized he had been in there only ten minutes. He couldn't have had the fluid drawn out of his lungs yet.

In silence, I followed the doctor into the room. My father was sitting on the examining table, his shirt still on, his legs dangling, his hands holding on to the edge and his arms straight back, elbows locked, trying to keep his shoulders from stooping. He smiled at me as I rolled in—his old big bright smile.

"Your father has decided not to have the fluid drawn out of his lungs." I looked at the doctor's somber face, not sure what I was hearing. "We have to respect his wishes. The procedure is painful and will have to be repeated more and more often, and before long we wouldn't be able to do it anyway."

"What will happen?" I asked, though I knew the answer to that question. I knew exactly what would happen. My father would die very soon. I didn't want to ask the doctor how soon. I shook my head.

"We have to respect your father's wishes," the doctor repeated as I kept shaking my head. "Your father wants to be home. We'll have hospice in place immediately. He will be kept comfortable."

I couldn't speak. I was afraid I would burst into tears. I turned to look at my father. He was still sitting in the same position, forcing himself to hold his shoulders straight. He smiled his big smile again and nodded.

We made our way out of the hospital slowly, in pained silence. When we finally sat in the car, side by side, and my chair sat folded in the back, I put the key in the ignition, but instead of starting the engine, I rested my arm on the steering wheel, lowered my head on it, and cried.

"*Non piangere.* Don't cry," my father said, trying to comfort me. "*Vado via contento,* I'm going away happy. I know I don't have to worry about you, because you have a good life. I'm proud of all you've accomplished."

I sobbed, my head still on the steering wheel. Even though I didn't get cured? After all the years, I still wondered. But I was crying too hard to talk.

He let me cry for a few minutes; then he put his hand on my back. "*Dai, smettila, gioia!* Come on, stop it!" He spoke in the same tone of voice he'd used with me when I was a child.

I leaned to the right, toward him, and let his arm encircle me until my head was on his shoulder.

"*Papà,*" I cried as my father held me, "*Papà.*"

I wanted to make myself real small in his arms, become that little girl who thought her father was the strongest, smartest, handsomest man in the world. I wished we could go back, back through the years, back to Riposto, together. Don't leave me, *Papà.*

"*Vado via contento.*"

I decided to stay at my parents' house. It was June and I was off for the summer. I called Danny to tell him not to expect me. I lived with Danny pretty much full-time now. I should have known when I bought my apartment on Fifteenth Street that I wouldn't really be living there. I used it mainly as an office.

"Take good care of Pico," I told Danny. Pico was our cat.

"Pico'll be fine, but he'll miss you, and so will I."

"It's just for a few days, to get the hospice set up."

"I could go out there with Access-A-Ride if you need me to bring you anything."

I didn't. I always kept clothes and other necessities at my parents' house. I also kept my crutches in the closet of what used to be my room. My parents' house was the only place where I would still, at times, struggle to walk.

After my father's decision to stop treatments, I made a great effort to walk with my crutches around the house as much as I could. I wanted to please him in his last days. I wanted his last image of me to be standing upright, even if not on the legs I'd been born with.

At the same time as I was putting on this last performance for my father, a controversy was taking place over the FDR Memorial, presently under construction in D.C. The Memorial Commission had decided not to show FDR's disability, out of respect for his having painstakingly hidden it, always showing himself standing and walking, during the twelve years of his presidency.

"They're trying to take our hero from us," said Hugh Gallagher, author of *FDR's Splendid Deception*.

Even those in our movement who didn't consider FDR "our hero" wanted him to be shown as disabled. FDR hid his disability because society could not accept a person with a disability as a world leader. Faking being cured was a performance he had to put on for the American people at the time. Today, we needed to show America and the world that a person with a disability could achieve greatness. We needed to show that being cured was not necessary to lead a country, or a meaningful life. A statue of FDR in his wheelchair would tell America and the world that disability was no longer something to be hidden or to be ashamed of. Indeed, for some of us it was something of which we were proud.

These thoughts filled my mind as I pulled myself upright, ignoring my pain and fatigue, and walked while my father lay dying.

Hospice had started right after my father and I returned from the hospital the week before. My father gave the first nurse who came to our house a big welcoming smile; then he let me answer all her questions. She filled out the necessary forms. The next day, they brought the oxygen and started the morphine.

"Why morphine? He's not complaining of pain."

"It will help him breathe more easily."

I knew the nurse meant it would help him die more easily.

The hospice nurse whom my cousin let in that evening was new. She was dark and exotic-looking, Indian maybe, with deep brown eyes and a gentle smile. She introduced herself, but I didn't quite catch her name. I didn't want to make her repeat it. I now grabbed the edge of the table to get myself up, and reached for my crutches. I followed her slowly into the bedroom and watched as she took my father's blood pressure, checked his vital signs. My father's eyes stayed closed; he didn't stir, but his breathing was irregular and loud. The nurse moved away from the bed, turning toward me. Her face was beautiful and serious.

"Your father may not make it through the night."

I heard my cousins in the kitchen, saying good night to my mother. They stopped at the bedroom door, and I walked over to say good-bye to them.

"How is he doing?" Josie asked.

"The same," I replied.

The nurse just looked at us, serious and gentle.

I went into my room and closed the door. I sat on the bed and called Danny on the phone.

"Sing to me," I whispered.

And he sang, as he did every night, "Lullaby and goodnight…"

But I knew I wasn't going to sleep.

After I hung up, I unzipped my pants and slid them down under me. Then I reached inside the pants' legs to push on the valves and release the suction that kept my prostheses on. I wiggled out of both the pants and the prostheses, pushing myself farther back on the bed and leaving them sitting on their own.

I massaged my naked, smooth white stumps. Danny thought they were beautiful. When he ran his tongue along the scars, he drove me wild with passion. My father had never seen them. Maybe if he had, he would have realized they were not as scary as he imagined.

I got into my wheelchair, wearing only a T-shirt and underpants; I opened the door and wheeled out of my room. My father's breathing sounded louder. Was it because the house was so quiet? I could see my mother lying on the couch in the living room. I doubted that she was sleeping, though she didn't seem to see or hear me. I wheeled into the bedroom. Only the light on the night table was on. Nicky was in his spot; he raised his head for a moment, then put it back down between his outstretched front paws. The nurse looked at me and seemed surprised. Maybe she hadn't realized I'd been wearing prostheses earlier.

I went to the bed, where my father lay with his eyes closed. His breathing didn't seem as loud now.

"*Guardami, Papà*," I whispered. "Look at me."

I'm not so scary, am I? And though I didn't get cured the way you wanted me to, I am fine! Just the way I am! Why couldn't I make you understand that? Why did I always feel I had to act as nondisabled as possible to spare you pain, to make you happy?

"*Guardami, Papà!*"

I thought he opened his eyes, but I probably imagined it, the room was so dimly lit. Did I imagine he was smiling at me, his big bright smile?

I sat in my wheelchair at the side of the bed. The nurse sat in the armchair at its foot. Once in a while, she got up and checked my father's pulse. I sat caressing my exposed stumps.

Suddenly, my mother was standing behind me. I felt her hands on my shoulders.

"*Tuo padre ci lascia*," she said. "Your father is leaving us."

There was so much sorrow in her voice. I tilted my head back and let it rest against her body.

Then she said, and her voice now sounded surprisingly matter-of-fact, "We should call the priest."

I was jarred by her request. I hadn't thought of calling a priest. My father was not a religious man. But if my mother wanted a priest, I had to get a priest. I wasn't sure how. I grabbed the Yellow Pages. I wondered if there was a listing under *P* for priests. The thought made me want to laugh.

Luckily for me, my mother seemed to know what to do. "Look up the Church of Mary Immaculate; that's only a few blocks away."

I did and called the number listed. I was surprised when I got an answer. It was about 3:00 A.M. I was even more surprised when less than fifteen minutes later, the doorbell rang. My mother handed me what looked like a folded bedsheet. I was puzzled. I didn't know what I was supposed to do with it.

"Cover yourself; the priest is here."

I realized I was still wheeling around with my stumps exposed.

My mother cried softly as the priest administered Last Rites to my father, and I cried softly along with her. Nicky didn't move from his spot. The priest was elderly and plump; he hugged my mother and me as he left, as if he'd known us forever. We thanked him profusely.

When the priest was gone, my mother sat on the bed, tenderly stroking my father's arms, which lay motionless on the neatly tucked-in sheet. His breathing was much quieter now. As a matter of fact, he seemed to be sleeping very peacefully. Maybe he's not dying after all, at least not yet, I thought. The nurse kept checking his pulse. My mother and I sat silently, she on the bed, I in my chair on the side of the bed. My father's breathing got quieter and quieter, until it was perfectly soundless. The nurse nodded.

My mother bent down and kissed my father on the mouth. She kept crying softly. She stretched out her arm and let it encircle me, gently pulling me down. I kissed my father on the forehead.

It was 4:30 A.M. on June 20, 1996.

22

COME SONO CONTENTA:
HOW HAPPY I AM

❋

"*Come sono contenta!* How happy I am!"

My mother helped me hang my skirts in the closet, made room in her drawers for my underwear, watched me set up my computer. "It's like I'm dreaming! I'm so happy you've come home!" Her eyes sparkling, her face glowing with excitement, my mother looked young.

"*Come sono contenta!*" She kept saying it, and my heart ached each time she said it. I couldn't tell her I was happy to be home. I'd moved in to take care of her because she was dying. She had inoperable pancreatic cancer.

She seemed so genuinely happy, I couldn't help wondering whether she had fully understood what the gastroenterologist had told us.

We'd sat side by side in the doctor's office after the results of her tests came in. In the thirty-five years she'd been in this country, my mother never learned English well enough to carry on a long conversation, but I knew she had no trouble understanding what was said.

The doctor used plain words. What could be plainer than the word *cancer*? And the word *nothing*, as in "nothing to do"?

I'd wanted to put my hands over my mother's ears to block out those words, drown them out with my own fast talking, to confuse her, shield her. But she heard, and she understood.

I was sure my mother knew she had cancer long before she had the tests. She'd been covering up the symptoms, had not told me about the vomiting, constipation, pain. She'd hidden her weight loss and her swollen abdomen with loose clothes and shoulder pads, her paleness with blush-on.

When I insisted she have the tests, she shrugged. "*Tuo padre mi vuole,* that's all." Your father wants me, that's all.

She said "that's all" in English. There were some English expressions my mother was particularly fond of. Like many immigrants, she spoke a hybrid language. Hers was a mixture of the standard Italian she kept from forgetting by reading novels and magazines and watching the Italian TV channel, her native Sicilian dialect, imports from other southern Italian dialects her friends spoke, and certain English words and expressions.

"That's all" was one of my mother's favorite English expressions. So curt and final. "That's all" meant there was nothing else to do and nothing else to say, no arguments allowed. And what arguments could I have? Always the good Sicilian wife, my mother never went against my father's wishes. What did it matter that my father had been dead for almost a year? Thirty-five years ago, she had left her family, her friends, her town, to follow him to a faraway land. She was now ready to follow him again.

I argued with her the best I could and managed to convince her to go see her doctor, then the gastroenterologist he recommended. I had to beg her to have the GI series and the MRIs. "Just do it for me," I said.

The day we went to the gastroenterologist's office to talk about the results, my mother got dressed up—a loose pink sweater with shoulder pads, and matching pink lipstick.

"I don't want the doctor to think I'm afraid," she said when I told her how pretty she looked.

"Afraid of what?"

"Of dying."

On the way home, after we got the news, I suggested we get a second opinion.

"I don't want to talk about that."

I was too stunned and grieved to talk anyway. I kept my eyes on the road.

"Your father wants me with him, that's all!"

Three months, at the most, had been the gastroenterologist's verdict. And that was in April. A month had already passed.

"I'll move in with my mother," I told the doctor. "I'll take care of her."

He gave me a look. Obviously, he didn't think I was the ideal caregiver.

"We can set up hospice, but you'll need more help than hospice can give you."

"I'll hire an attendant," I said. Then realizing *attendant* might not be the word the doctor would use, I corrected myself. "I mean an aide."

But I couldn't move to Queens in April. I'd skipped the ADAPT action, but I couldn't skip my classes. The past year, in addition to teaching Italian, I'd fulfilled my dream of teaching a disability studies course, which I created.

Throughout April, I felt as if I were in a race with my mother's cancer. Danny tried his best to be supportive, helping me prepare for the move, buying me things I needed—new underwear, toiletries, laxative herbs. I knew he was sad and anxious about being left alone.

Now my mother was saying, "This is the greatest Mother's Day present. *Come sono contenta!*"

Bending down, she put her arms around me, hugging the back of my wheelchair, as well. I hugged her and all I felt was bones. Nicky raised himself up off the kitchen floor and came to put his front paws on my lap. When there were hugs going around, Nicky demanded his share.

"It feels like you never left," my mother said.

And I remembered her crying when I'd moved out twenty-some years before. "*Come sono contenta!*" she'd exclaimed, smiling through the tears.

When my mother undressed that night, I saw how much more weight she'd lost since the last time I'd seen her without clothes, at the doctor's office. She was a skeleton, my mother, who. though always slim, even at seventy-eight, had been quite shapely. She wore a padded bra to hide the emptied-out skin sacks that had once been beautiful full breasts. Her belly was that of a woman ready to deliver. Its size made her every movement difficult. Her bony legs trembled as she struggled to keep her balance.

I remembered my mother's supple young body, the body I'd been so close to when I was a little girl in Riposto. I remembered my mother's strong arms holding me, carrying me; the softness of her breasts, her sweet lavender smell. The feelings those memories evoked were over-whelming. I wanted to close my eyes, not have to look at her; at the same time, I wanted to hug her. I was filled with tenderness. She quickly put on her nightgown, sensing my discomfort.

In the morning, she stood, wobbly, at the stove to make espresso. It was a beautiful day, so we decided to drink it out in the backyard. I carried the hot pot in one hand and wheeled my chair with the other, carefully. She brought out two dainty gold-rimmed cups. We sat in the sun sipping coffee. The garden was a bit of a jungle, since she hadn't been able to tend it lately. I couldn't help much with gardening, but I managed to unwind the hose and water her rosebushes.

"Be gentle," she cautioned me; "don't let the water hit too hard."

My mother did all she could to show me how happy she was to have me there. We celebrated Mother's Day with veal parmigiana delivered from the Italian restaurant on Bell Boulevard, and she kept repeating "*Che buona,* how good it is," while delicately spitting into a paper napkin. I made believe I didn't notice. But Nicky let her know by whining that it would be less wasteful to let him have what she was spitting out.

We looked through the Italian magazines I'd bought for her, and I read aloud while she sat holding her belly, trying to hide her pain. We watched *Cinema Paradiso* on video in four or five sittings, since she couldn't sit through a whole movie.

"I'm okay," she reassured me when I heard her crying in the bathroom and looked in on her. And when at night I got up because I heard her moaning, she apologized for waking me. "I forgot you were here, *come sono contenta!*"

When the hospice nurse came, I was surprised to hear my mother communicate in flawless English.

"I feel better because my daughter is here."

The nurse's name was Ellen. She was my age, maybe a little younger. She told me she needed to look at me when I spoke, because she was hard of hearing. That's when I noticed she was wearing hearing aids. I liked her. I felt we had a bond, the three of us, my mother with her cancer, me with my wheelchair, this nurse with her hearing aids.

Ellen went over my mother's medications. She said to increase the Colace, when we told her about the bathroom problems. She explained to me that my mother had refused stronger pain medication because she didn't like to feel drowsy. She could have it, though, whenever she was ready. Ellen said she would be coming more often as my mother got sicker, and we could also have a home health aide when it became necessary. I was less anxious. Ellen was the right person to see us through this.

May 16, my birthday, was coming up. My mother decided she was going to make my favorite Sicilian meal, *falsomagro*. The word means "fake lean," since the slender-looking beef roll is stuffed with fattening delicacies. The day before my birthday, she made a list of all I needed to buy at the Italian store on Francis Lewis Boulevard: prosciutto di Parma, Parmigiano-Reggiano, soppressata... For the large thin slice of beef, she sent me to the meat shop on Bell Boulevard. "Your father never bought meat at the supermarket."

We didn't have a very good night. We made repeated unsuccessful trips to the bathroom. Bent over in pain, she held on to my wheelchair, using it as a walker. I wheeled slowly, carefully maneuvering around furniture and through doors. All the time, we talked, mostly about her beloved hometown of Riposto—old neighbors I'd long forgotten, the nuns remembered only in dreams, events and places that now seemed surreal to me... To my mother, the past was close and palpable. I pretended I remembered more than I did.

Between heart-wrenching moans and toilet attempts, we kept talking, both of us acting as if we were truly enjoying this nighttime reminiscing. As if she wouldn't rather be sleeping—free of pain. As if I wouldn't rather be sleeping—at home in bed with Danny and our pussycat, Pico. Both of us acting as if we didn't mind at all that she was dying.

"I wish we had gone back to Riposto." Her voice was now a whisper. "Like your father wanted to. Maybe you'll go back."

"Maybe I will."

In the morning, we started preparing the *falsomagro*. We sat at the kitchen table, side by side. She had me beat the beef down, so it would get thinner and more tender, while she peeled and quartered three hard-boiled eggs. We moistened the beef with olive oil, then sprinkled bread crumbs and grated Parmesan cheese on it. A few sprigs of parsley, a layer of prosciutto, then she placed the quartered eggs and sliced cheese along the middle, together with lots of broken-up sausage. Nicky sat at attention between my mother and me, waiting patiently for bits of cheese and sausage. My mother did the rolling, because I was too clumsy. Even with her hands shaking, she could do it better. She tied white string all around the *falsomagro* so it wouldn't come apart while cooking. When it was all done, we sat back and admired it.

"*Che bello!* How beautiful!" my mother said with pride.

But we had a hard time browning it in the frying pan. My mother couldn't stand at the stove for long. It was too painful. In my chair, I was too low to do a good job. Then I remembered my crutches were stored in the closet in my old room. The last time I'd used them was when my father was dying. I went to get them, and I stood, very precariously.

"*Attenta!* Careful!" my mother kept saying as I stepped, holding on to the crutches for dear life. When I was in front of the stove, standing with my legs apart for maximum balance, my crutches securely under my arms, I bravely let go of one, so I'd have use of that hand. My mother sat in my wheelchair and positioned herself right behind me. I felt her trembling hand on my back as she tried to balance me. "Put the brakes on," I told her.

Feeling safe and steady now, I lit the burner and started turning the *falsomagro* with my free hand. From behind, my mother gave me instructions. When the beef roll was all browned, she told me to lift it out of the pan and put it in the big pot where the tomato sauce was cooking.

That's when I ran into trouble. It was so long that if I stuck the fork in the middle of it and tried to lift it with one hand, I was sure to break it. But I was afraid to let go of the crutch with my other hand. Then my mother, still sitting in my wheelchair, put both her hands around my waist to steady me. Carefully, with my left hand, I slid the spatula under the beef roll while I stuck the fork in it with my right. I was able to lift the *falsomagro* out of the pan and place it, not as gently as she would have liked, but all in one piece, into the pot with the sauce.

While the *falsomagro* cooked in the sauce, we could both relax. I got back in my chair; my mother lay down on her bed.

"Check to make sure it's not sticking to the bottom of the pot," she said from time to time. I obediently went to the stove and, not seeing what I was doing from my chair, gave the *falsomagro* a push with the long wooden spoon.

"It moves, so it's not sticking," I reported.

Then it was time to cook the pasta. My mother made her way to the stove, holding on to the walls. We chose *rotelle* from the rich variety of pastas in her cabinet. While from my chair I stirred the *rotelle,* she got a serving plate out of the china closet.

"We have to get the *falsomagro* out of the pot," she said. And this time, I was the one to position myself behind her and put my hands on the small of her back to steady her. She put the *falsomagro* on the plate and we looked at each other. Who was going to carry it? I picked up the heavy plate and held it with both hands while she slowly pushed me to the dining room. She sat down at the table and sliced the *falsomagro* with surgical precision, in spite of her shaky hands.

Finally, proud of our joint accomplishment, we were ready to enjoy my birthday meal. My mother had put out her prettiest dishes, with the blue trellis border, her crystal glasses, and her best silverware. She had insisted on an embroidered tablecloth and embroidered napkins.

I poured myself a glass of pinot grigio; she poured herself some San Pellegrino water. The meal was pure perfection. The pasta was exactly al dente; the sauce was sweet and tangy. I took a slice of *falsomagro* and ate it together with my pasta. I just couldn't wait and follow the Italian etiquette of eating the *primo piatto* before starting on the *secondo*. The *falsomagro* was the best I'd ever tasted. It was so good, I wanted to remember the taste forever. I knew my mother would never make it for me again. I doubted I would ever be able to make it for myself.

My mother couldn't eat. She faked it. She chewed and spit in her napkin, trying to do it without my noticing. Or dropped piece after piece on the floor for Nicky to eat.

"*Ti piace?* Do you like it?" she kept asking me.

I wished I had the words to tell her just how much I liked it, how much I appreciated the effort she'd put into making it, and how much I wished she could make it for me again on my next birthday.

I ate so much *falsomagro*, I was too full for my birthday dessert. I could only manage to eat half a *cannolo*. It was delicious, the shell so light and crisp and cinnamony, the ricotta cream so smooth. Bits of candied fruit gave the cream a fresh taste.

"The Italian pastry shop on Francis Lewis is better than any in Little Italy," I told my mother. She smiled as she picked up the other half of the *cannolo* and ate it. She really ate it. I waited for her to spit it out, but she didn't. She swallowed it effortlessly.

"*Che buono!* How good it is!" She closed her eyes to enjoy the taste without distractions.

When she opened her eyes again, I was surprised to see a look I hadn't seen on her face for a while. A look of mischief.

"We need some amaretto to get this down."

"We sure do," I laughingly agreed as I went to get the bottle and two long-stemmed cordial glasses from her china closet. I filled the glasses.

She raised hers. "*Buon compleanno*, happy birthday," she said to me.

Her eyes sparkling, her face glowing with excitement, my mother looked young. She looked as beautiful to me as she had forty-some years ago, when she carried me in her arms and her face, smooth and always a little flushed, was only a kiss away. We clinked glasses.

"*Grazie, Mamma,* this is the best birthday I've ever had."

She laughed as she sipped her amaretto. "*Come sono contenta!*"

My mother died on July 23, 1997.

23

THANK YOU, LIFE

"I'd like the class to know that after trying to get pregnant for a long time, I have finally succeeded."

What a way to find that out! Leslie had posted the happy news on the New School website of my online crip culture course.

Couldn't she have called me before posting? Leslie wasn't just a student. I'd helped her "come home" to disability, welcomed her into my disabled women's group, took her to conferences and ADAPT actions. I'd mentored her. She was like a younger sister to me, almost a daughter.

I knew how hard she'd been trying to get pregnant. Not merely taking her temperature and picking the right time of month but trying hormone therapy, in vitro fertilization...

I couldn't have been happier for her. I must have screamed. Danny rolled out of the bedroom and approached the desk, a concerned look on his face.

"Another computer crisis?"

Since I'd started teaching online, my screams were usually in reaction to the disappearance of my work into cyberspace due to a wrong mouse click. I was no techie. I'd decided to teach online, not knowing what I was getting into. I had to learn to make my lessons into Web pages, present material interesting both in content and form, and accessible for students with various disabilities. Images, for instance, necessitated detailed descriptions for blind students.

There were advantages, such as not having to worry about the weather, about what to wear, or about how I looked. I sat at the computer in a comfortable old sweatshirt, and without prostheses. I didn't wear them at home unless I wanted to stand or take a few steps holding on to Danny's power chair for exercise.

Originally, the Languages Department had me trained to teach Italian online. But those courses never materialized.

Sondra Farganis, head of the Social Sciences Department, suggested I put a disability course online. I was so grateful to Sondra for letting me teach disability studies despite my lack of a degree in sociology or anthropology. I'd first met her at a faculty party in 1996. I'd cornered her, literally. I parked my chair in front of her, blocking her into a corner with a glass of wine in her hand. I started talking about disability studies.

"That's a relatively new field of inquiry, isn't it?"

"Yes," I replied, and explained that the field of disability studies was having trouble finding its place in the curriculum because it was assumed disability belonged in applied fields such as rehab, social work, special ed. "Like the rest of the world, the university thinks the only ways to deal with disability are treatment, care, and cure."

Sondra appeared interested. So I kept talking: "Disability studies examines and theorizes the social, political, cultural, and economic factors that define disability. It is comparable to women studies." I'd read her book *Situating Feminism* and made a reference to it.

She sipped her wine and nodded. "Write me up a course proposal."

I couldn't believe my ears. I was thrilled to be given the opportunity, but also to have found someone who seemed to "get it." More than once at the New School I'd been bitterly disillusioned when a colleague I admired showed little understanding of disability. The most enlightened seemed to think it all boiled down to the need for accessibility.

The next day, in one sitting, I wrote a proposal for a course titled "Deconstructing Disability." When Sondra accepted it, I was afraid I wouldn't get the required number of students, so I recruited people I knew. Leslie was one of my recruits. She took that first course and wanted more.

For a while, I taught out of two departments—Languages and Social Sciences. Then I stopped teaching Italian to devote more time to my disability studies courses in the classroom and later online. My life now revolved around disability. Danny and I were the NYC ADAPT organizers. Together, we also served on the board of CIDNY, and I was president of DIA, a role I'd let Frieda talk me into. Danny was DIA's corresponding secretary. I had to laugh, thinking how I'd once resolved never to make disability a profession.

The courses I taught, both in the classroom and online, attracted mainly disabled students—not the case at most other universities, where such courses were attended by nondisabled students pursuing degrees in applied fields. Especially in the online courses, I got students eager to connect, even "come out," and "come home" to disability.

Teaching disability courses was different from teaching Italian. As the "Italian teacher," I had a well-defined role, which made me feel covered, shielded. When discussing disability, there was no way to be objective, no matter how much theory I brought in. In these classes, I couldn't hide inside a role. Often I felt naked and vulnerable. The experience could be frightening or exhilarating, or both, but it was always immensely rewarding.

The official title of this fall 2000 online course was "Celebrating Differences: Disability Culture." We relished the creative voices of disabled people, read stories that crushed stereotypes and told the truth about our lives, read plays, watched films, and explored art that honestly gave expression to the disability experience.

"Did something happen with the computer?" Danny still wanted to know.

"Everything is okay with the computer. It's Leslie. She finally did it."

"Did what?"

"She got pregnant."

"Wow!"

I could tell by his smile that he was as happy as I was about the news.

Would Leslie be able to devote as much time to my course now that she was pregnant? Instinctively, I caressed my flat menopausal belly, imagining Leslie sitting at the computer, the baby she had longed for curled up warm and comfy in her swelling womb. But the baby was still only a mass of cells, resembling a fish more than a human being. I hoped with all my heart everything would go well with her pregnancy and that she'd give birth to a healthy baby. I laughed as I formulated that ableist thought, and even completed it with the cliché that in the crip community we liked to ridicule, "a healthy baby with all its fingers and toes."

As I stared at the monitor, I could see congratulatory postings appearing in response to Leslie's news. I started my own post: "No student ever made such a momentous announcement in any of my classes before."

But communicating with Leslie online felt odd. I wanted to hug her; I wanted to touch her belly. At the very least, I wanted to hear her voice.

"Wanna call her?" Danny must have been reading my mind.

I dialed the number and turned on the speaker. In the seven years we'd been together, Danny's MS had progressed. He'd been hospitalized and undergone surgery a few times. Because I made sure he stayed off his butt, he had fewer problems with pressure sores. But he had lost a kidney to a bad infection and had acquired a colostomy. His muscles had weakened considerably. Since he could no longer hold the receiver, he needed the speakerphone. I liked the convenience of us both talking at the same time.

Leslie answered on the second ring.

"Congratulations, mom," Danny said.

"Thank you. I still can't believe it's true!"

I shrieked.

Danny translated my shriek. "We're both so happy for you."

We made a date to meet the next week so I could hug her and the baby in her belly.

Leslie had posted the happy news quite appropriately in the item "The Disabled Body." "Items" was what the school called my web pages, each representing a lesson with a discussion following. This particular one dealt with how the disabled body, which had been devalued, seen as defective, broken, asexual, ugly, was today being "reclaimed" through the arts.

My students read essays, excerpts from memoirs and short stories, but we relied heavily on images—examples of disability culture art depicting the disabled body, as well as photos and video clips of performers with visible disabilities flaunting their differences.

I tried to show how through art we could learn to appreciate the beauty of disabled bodies, find the frailty of atrophied limbs as interesting as the frailty of a Giacometti sculpture, the curvature of scoliosis as fluid as a Matisse cutout, see the classic timelessness of the Venus de Milo in a body with missing limbs, see the wild grace and sensuality in spastic, uncontrolled movements, be filled with wonder before the variety of shapes and sizes our bodies come in, and the different ways our bodies move or don't move, function or don't function, and even of the different devices and types of equipment we use to help us move and function.

I used the visuals to spark stimulating discussions: Was there a difference between the flaunting by disabled artists and performers and the exhibitions in circuses, in "freak shows"? Was it a reaction to the exhibitions of our disabled bodies in medical settings? Or to the everyday staring of strangers? Or was this our way of expressing pride, the same kind of pride that made African-Americans in the sixties stop straightening their hair and grow beautiful huge Afros, and made the drag queens come out and parade?

This semester, I had the incredible good luck of having as a student a wonderful artist, Melina Fatsiou-Cowan. Originally from Greece, Melina lived in Alabama with her husband. She had spinal muscular atrophy accompanied, as it commonly is, by pronounced scoliosis. We'd uploaded images of her paintings—mostly fluid, flowing female bodies curved with scoliosis, some in brilliant shades, others in muted tones, all exquisitely sensual.

Melina told us she had been taught in her native Greece that art should depict only the perfect body. Painting disabled bodies was an act of rebellion and extremely liberating for her.

The discussion about the disabled body could get quite personal and emotional for the students and for me, as well—forcing me to relive the shame Audrey and I had felt as girls, the estrangement from my body after so many surgeries, my vulnerability to sexual abuse, the torturous decision to have my polio legs amputated.

"It took me a long time before I could look at my naked body in the mirror, accept and embrace it," I told my students.

I saw Melina had posted in response to Leslie's announcement. After the congratulatory words, she wrote, "I love kids ever so much, but I never dared to have children. I believed it was not my right. Now it is too late."

The pain in her words poured out of the computer monitor like water breaking through a dam. I felt soaked in it.

"You shouldn't play with dolls, because you'll never have children. You're a cripple, *ciunca*." The Sicilian girls' words echoed from that dark place, the so-distant yet ever-present past.

Following Melina's sorrowful comment, I encouraged my students to talk about a disabled woman's right to motherhood and the prejudice that had prevented many of us from having children of our own. "When we hear the word *choice* used in the context of women's reproductive rights, we immediately associate it with the right to end an unwanted pregnancy. But *choice* should also include the right of all women to be mothers if they so desire," I wrote.

I decided to link to an article about the compulsory sterilization laws in the United States in the thirties and forties, which resulted in more than sixty thousand disabled individuals being sterilized. I wrote, "Even today, disabled women, especially women with emotional, cognitive, and intellectual disabilities, judged incapable of taking care of a child, may be coerced by family and health care professionals to abort and to be sterilized. Because the support a disabled woman may need to raise a child is often not available, children may be taken away from disabled mothers." I stopped myself at this point and deleted most of the paragraph I'd just written, reluctant to put such a damper on a joyful circumstance. Feeling drained, I backed away from the computer.

"This is a day for good news. Mr. Cooper is getting out." Danny was smiling.

"Congratulations! Was that him on the phone?"

Danny had been working on getting a sixty-year-old developmentally disabled man out of a nursing home. He had finally managed to procure through various agencies all the services Mr. Cooper needed to live at home, and had convinced the social worker he could safely be discharged.

"I'll miss his calls in the middle of the night," I said. Since NYC ADAPT didn't have an office, our home number was on every resource list. We got calls from people in nursing homes at all hours. Not all got to go home. Some didn't have a home to go to, and finding housing could be an insurmountable problem. We had recently lost a battle, not because we couldn't arrange services but because the woman we were trying to help believed her family would be less burdened if she remained in the nursing home. She died of a pressure sore, caused by staff neglect. Danny took the loss especially hard. The woman had MS.

"*Gemme owtaa heeeere!*" A great impersonator, Danny imitated Mr. Cooper's voice. I wished Danny could do more acting. His friends still called him once in a while to be an extra in films and TV shows, but his limited energy didn't allow for long days on a set. Nor did it allow for grueling ADAPT actions.

As an organizer, though, he remained unsurpassed. In the last few years, he had arranged several times for DIA activists to go to ADAPT rallies in D.C., negotiating with Amtrak to remove seats on trains to make room for fifty or sixty wheelchair users to travel together. He proudly brought the people, while I, in D.C. for the entire action, met the train at the station. Our NYC contingent, with Danny and me leading it, then marched to the rally. Danny's proudest payback was having Justin Dart single him out and thank him for his leadership. After such an active day, Danny's MS also demanded a payback. He might go home with a pressure sore, or, if lucky, just so depleted that he'd be forced to spend a few days in bed.

ADAPT had won some battles. Federal legislation to remove the institutional bias in the Medicaid law had been introduced in Congress a few times, and though it had not yet passed, there was evidence of the tide starting to turn. The year before, the Supreme Court had ruled in a case that unnecessary institutionalization was a violation of the ADA.

At the same time, though, the Court, by ruling in three cases in favor of employers, had narrowed the scope of the ADA. We had been witnessing a backlash in the past years; business was hell-bent on undermining the ADA. Danny and I had been busier than ever writing articles and letters.

In September, Danny had insisted on getting arrested. Not with ADAPT, but with an organization called Not Dead Yet (NDY), founded by my friend Diane Coleman in 1996, at the height of Kevorkian's death-dealing activities. The organization's name came from a Monty Python comedy, but its intent was deadly serious. NDY opposed euthanasia, and legalization of physician-assisted suicide, which Diane called "a lethal form of discrimination," because it created a double standard for who got suicide prevention and who got "assistance." NDY brought the disability perspective to the so-called right-to-die debate, which was always presented as one of "choice vs. sanctity of life," the progressives against the religious right.

Danny and I knew all too well the prejudice and deep-seated fear of disability, which resulted in the common assumption that disabled lives are not worth living and illness and disability are valid reasons for suicide. We knew *terminal* and *incurable* are synonymous for many—the cases that attracted media attention didn't involve people dying of cancer, but quadriplegics and people with chronic diseases like ALS and MS. We were also painfully aware of living in a country where health care was not an equal right, and supportive services were a hit-or-miss game that depended on where you lived, and how hard you could fight. Not getting needed services, and, worse, getting stuck in a nursing home, could drive anyone to despair. As strongly as Danny and I believed in "choice," we fully supported NDY's stand against legislation that could endanger the lives of those with significant disabilities.

Our friends, the progressives, didn't, or didn't want to, understand our concerns. The people whom we didn't consider friends, on the other hand, were eager to declare themselves on NDY's side. At times, I felt extremely uncomfortable finding myself unwittingly rubbing elbows with right-to-lifers, and having as opponents my nondisabled feminist sisters. The relationship between feminism and disability rights had never been free of conflict. I didn't expect us to come to a mutual understanding on the "the right to die," just as we never had on the selective abortion of disabled fetuses. NDY was careful to keep the two issues separate and address only the first. But feminists saw it all as a matter of choice. No matter how strongly I declared myself for true choice free of coercion, and affirmed my readiness to fight for any woman's right to end a pregnancy, my wish that no decisions concerning birth or death be based on disability prejudice was seen as a threat to women's rights. That made me very sad.

Danny didn't have the same allegiances and therefore didn't share my sadness. He wanted to prove his commitment by getting arrested. As worried as I was about his health, I didn't try to dissuade him. We traveled to Boston by train and got arrested, together with Diane and other NDY members, in front of the hotel where a conference on end-of-life issues was taking place. The organizers had refused NDY a seat at the table. The arrest, though relatively quick and easy, was extremely taxing for Danny. He was sick when we got back home, although happy and proud of his accomplishment.

"When I was first diagnosed, I thought of my condition as terminal. So did my doctors, and certainly my family," Danny told me. "If the option of assisted suicide had been offered me, I would have bowed out gracefully and made my ex-wife happy. I would not have met you, and I would never have known how sweet a cripple's life can be."

Danny's attendant, Nathan, a Jamaican man who spoke in monosyllables, was taking packages of underpads, catheters, and colostomy pouches out of a big box sitting in the middle of the living room. I'd been so engrossed in my course and my thoughts, I hadn't noticed that Danny's monthly supplies had been delivered.

I looked at the clock above the kitchen door. It was after six-thirty.

"Should I make some pasta? Are you hungry?"

"I'm always hungry." Danny laughed.

"*Pasta al pomodoro* coming up."

I asked Nathan if he'd mind taking care of the supplies later and helping me in the kitchen.

"Yes," he said, following me.

"Could you please get a pot out, fill it with water three-quarters of the way up, and place it on the front burner?"

"All right."

I added salt to the water and turned the burner on, then asked Nathan to get the frying pan while I rummaged in the refrigerator.

"We only have one tomato? Nathan, didn't I ask you to buy tomatoes when you went to the supermarket for us?"

"No."

"I can't make tomato sauce, Danny. How about pasta with broccoli? We have frozen broccoli."

Danny rolled toward the kitchen door. "You look too tired to cook. How about you make a salad and we have Nathan go to Patsy's to get a pizza. Would you help us eat it, Nathan, if we get a large?"

"All right."

I maneuvered around the box of supplies, trying not to run over any of the packages Nathan had left on the floor, and went to get the money for the pizza.

"I'm glad we don't have to pay for this stuff. You sure have a lot of high-cost needs," I said to Danny while handing Nathan a twenty.

"I'm doing my best to help the economy. Think of all the money being made by so many off of me."

He had moved over to his music center—the shelves where his old vinyl records, his cassettes, CDs, and his players were. "Wanna listen to Joan Baez?" Somehow he had sensed I was troubled. He knew Joan Baez's voice was a healing salve for me.

While we waited for the pizza, I sat close to Danny, the wheels of our chairs touching. I leaned against him and closed my eyes, listening to the music.

Though we had been living together since 1993, we weren't legally married. My income and resources would have been counted as his if we married, making him ineligible for Medicaid. He had Medicare, and also excellent secondary private insurance through the Motion Picture Union. But neither Medicare nor insurance, only the means-tested Medicaid, would pay for Nathan and the other attendants he needed, and whom he hired, trained, and, when necessary, fired, through a program developed by NYC disability advocates. Being in such a program meant more work but also more control. In lieu of a marriage certificate, Danny and I had a domestic partnership, the existence of which was the result of LGBT advocacy. We had gone to get it at the County Clerk's Office on Valentine's Day a few years before.

Joan Baez was singing about a "grey quiet horse." I recognized the song, "Gabriel and Me." It was a lullaby she wrote for her son, Gabriel, when he was a baby. Tears came to my eyes. In the guitar strums between verses, I heard Melina's words, "now it is too late."

"Are you okay?" Danny asked.

"Sure, just tired."

I wondered what a child of ours would have looked like.

As if on cue, our crip cat, Pico, jumped onto my lap. Am I not enough for you? he seemed to ask as he licked my arm with his scratchy tongue. Yes, even our cat was disabled. We had adopted him as a tiny kitten. I bottle-fed him, since he had apparently been abandoned by the mother cat. The vet told us he had spina bifida. He had no tail and a front leg much shorter than the other, as well as many internal problems, which were fixed by costly surgeries. The lack of a tail and the short leg didn't bother him at all. He wobbled around happily and made sure we never forgot that our main purpose in life was to spoil him rotten.

Danny's children didn't play much of a role in their father's life—and even less in mine. The eldest called and visited occasionally, but the younger ones from the second marriage didn't seem at all interested.

When Nathan came back with the pizza, he pushed the supplies box to a corner and opened the butterfly table, which we kept folded when not in use so that we'd have more space. I positioned myself at a right angle to Danny in order to feed him, since his hands no longer worked well enough. I fed myself at the same time. I took a bite of pizza, then held the slice to his mouth, trying not to let any sauce fall off. He took bigger bites than I did, jerking his head back as the stringy mozzarella refused to break. Both of us laughing, I separated the stubborn cheese and let him lick my fingers. Nathan sat at the other end of the table, eating in silence. Joan Baez was still singing—in Spanish now: "Gracias a la vida que me ha dado tanto..." "Thank you, life, for giving me so much."

After our sumptuous dinner, Nathan started getting Danny ready for bed. Though NYS Medicaid would have paid for twenty-four hours,

Danny still used only twelve, mainly out of concern for my need for privacy. He had male attendants; that had always been his preference. For me, their presence was an intrusion. When I felt too beleaguered, I retreated to my studio apartment on Fifteenth Street.

I went back to the computer. Some good discussions were going on, and more expressions of regret, including one from my only male student, a wonderful gay man living with AIDS in Texas.

"Not having children of my own causes me sadness, too. I love kids!"

Leslie, after thanking everyone, wrote, "My decision to become pregnant and the resulting pregnancy have brought out more disability prejudice than I have ever experienced."

And it'll probably get worse, I thought, but didn't say it. I remembered that my friend Susie had told me that when she was pregnant, she could be riding in her chair, proudly patting her big belly, and a complete stranger would take one look and be horrified.

"Yes, Melina," Leslie went on, "many of us who grew up with disabilities were given a message very early in life that motherhood/parenthood was not an option for us."

I found myself responding, without taking the time to think about how best to say what I wanted to say.

"I certainly was made to believe motherhood was out of the question for me, back when I was a 'little crippled girl' in Sicily. I tried to get pregnant in my mid-thirties, but it didn't work out. Who knows, I might have tried harder had I had the support of those I loved. Today my life is so full, I have no regrets. I satisfy my maternal instincts by mentoring/mothering every disabled girl who'll let me."

Indeed, after Leslie, many other "daughters" had come—disabled girls who needed guidance, counsel, affection. I was sure more would come. My being a role model and a mentor gave me enormous fulfillment.

One student wrote, "Although I'm not contemplating pregnancy, I admire your decision to live your life to the fullest, Leslie. You are a role model for me!"

Is it called the "passing of the torch"? I was a role model for Leslie. Now she would be a role model for younger women.

Then the conversation shifted to the lack of information and support for disabled mothers. Leslie wrote, "I've initiated a search for a class or program that teaches adaptive parenting techniques for people with disabilities. I am disheartened and angry to find out there are no such programs in NYC."

"Leslie," I replied, "I can see you starting such a program. What do you say?"

Leslie Heller's beautiful daughter, Zoe, was born on July 30, 2001. I'm proud to be her godmother.

24

I PROMISE WE'LL HAVE FUN

❋

The waiting room clock at NYU Medical Center said it was 12:10 A.M. A man lay stretched out on one of the gray couches. He seemed to be asleep. I spoke softly into my cell phone.

"They've finally taken Danny to the OR," I told my friend Hope. I hated keeping her up so late, knowing she had to work the next day.

"I'm confident things will go smoothly." Her voice was soothing, but her words failed to reassure me.

"I'm scared, Hope."

"I'm praying for Danny."

I thanked her. "I'll speak to you in the morning, unless something goes wrong."

Hope was the one I called in a medical crisis if I needed the advice of a nurse as well as the comfort of a friend. She'd have been at my side if she could have, but the years and her CP had taken their toll. She needed every ounce of her energy to keep working full-time.

I was grateful Hope was praying for Danny. A minister's daughter, she knew about prayer. I wouldn't have been sure what to say or even whom to pray to. The sweet baby Jesus of my childhood that the nuns kept in a beautiful basket?

"He's not a toy!" my mother had said, reproaching me when I confessed my longing to cradle the ceramic doll in my arms.

I never wanted to trouble the tortured Christ, bleeding moribund on the cross in the middle of the altar. Or the dead son lying on the grieving mother's lap, slender limbs draped in lifeless abandonment.

Perhaps I should have prayed to the powerful God of Moses, who parted the Red Sea for his people. After all, Danny was Jewish, and though his parents had lived as avowed atheists, when they died—shortly after mine, first his mother, then his father—a rabbi read the Kaddish at their funerals.

I'd been sitting in my wheelchair for about forty hours. I wished I hadn't worn my prostheses, but I needed them to keep me balanced in my chair when rolling any distance. I couldn't bring myself to take them off and lie down on a couch. Besides, my muscles were so contracted, stretching out would have made me hurt more. On a big flat screen, a slide show of nature scenes was flashing. I wheeled over to where the computer tables were lined up. But looking at a monitor made my head spin. My eyes couldn't focus. I leaned my elbows on the table, rested my head on my hands.

I had called 911, following Hope's advice, because Danny was vomiting and his abdomen was distended. He had refused to eat dinner, itself cause for alarm, since he was such a good eater.

"I don't think the colostomy is working," he repeated.

He'd had colostomy surgery in 1998. That night, I'd sat in this waiting room—same clock but no tables with computers, no big flat screen then. Too many enemas administered by various attendants had caused Danny's colon to become perforated. They had to operate to save his life, and that surgery lasted most of the night. I'd waited alone and afraid then, too.

I had no relatives who were close enough to rush to be by my side. Neither did Danny. Though we had many friends, those I wanted with me at this moment—my disabled sisters or other members of my extended crip family—would have found it difficult to be here in the middle of the night.

So many times I'd waited in this room. My mind went back to 1995. We had been together for only two years when a urinary tract infection spread and Danny's kidney had to be removed to save his life. Even when the situation wasn't as dramatic, sitting in this room always filled me with anxiety. Through the years, he'd had surgeries for pressure sores, a device implanted to control his spasticity, and his right tibia and right femur put back together after bad breaks. And there had been other times also, when he was hospitalized with pneumonia or some other illness, that I'd waited here to speak to a doctor.

I didn't recall ever having been as afraid as I was now. Now Danny was much more vulnerable. In the fifteen years we'd been together, I'd watched him lose more function. His breathing was now compromised and he used a ventilator. Was he strong enough to withstand major surgery?

The question was irrelevant. Once again, the situation was dire. The X-ray and contrast scan had revealed an intestinal blockage. The surgery was necessary to save his life.

Danny had been placed on a stretcher and brought to the emergency room by ambulance. Since ambulances were not wheelchair-accessible, I'd had to make my way to the hospital alone.

I didn't often miss having a car, but that night I did. After my parents died, I no longer had reason to go outside of Manhattan regularly; a car became an unnecessary worry and expense. And getting the chair in and out had become too much of an effort.

Yellow cabs had zoomed by me. But in spite of the good work of the "Taxis for All Campaign," cabs were still not wheelchair-accessible. I avoided the subway, since not all stations were accessible and the gap between platform and train could be dangerous. Buses, my usual means of transportation, ran infrequently at night, and I was too agitated to sit and wait at a stop. Access-A-Ride was not for emergencies; reservations had to be made in advance. Wheeling myself to the hospital seemed the only option. Thankful for June's mildness, I wheeled as fast as I could, supercrip by necessity, in spite of my age and the effects of post-polio syndrome. I got to the hospital not long after the ambulance.

In the ER, they inserted a nasogastric tube through Danny's nose to decompress his stomach, which gave him relief while they ran tests. Dr. Crest, one of Danny's doctors, stopped in after 1:00 A.M.

"Why aren't you home in bed with your wife?" Danny joked.

Dr. Crest told us he would make sure to get the best surgeon. That's how we learned they needed to operate.

But Danny didn't get admitted until after 7:00 A.M. The delay was due to the ventilator. They wouldn't take him on the gastrointestinal floor with a ventilator. Nor could he go on the pulmonary floor if he was having intestinal surgery.

When the woman in the white coat came, I thought she was the respiratory therapist we'd been expecting. She was carrying a thick folder. She smiled a lot, unlike the others, who were too busy for pleasantries. The smiles made me guess she was a social worker. I'd brought Danny's wallet and immediately took out his Medicare and insurance cards.

"Oh, I found him in our database. Unless his coverage has changed, I don't need those. But I do need to ask a question."

I looked up at her, but she was smiling directly at Danny.

"I didn't see a DNR in your chart." At the sound of those three letters, I jumped. "Does that mean you would want to be resuscitated should your heart stop?"

Danny was pretty out of it, yet his answer came quickly. "You bet I would!" Then he gave her one of his own fake smiles, a sinister imitation of hers.

"Wouldn't you if your heart stopped?" I asked, but she wasn't paying attention to me.

"Even if an attempted resuscitation would be disruptive and futile?"

Futile—another scary word. Some hospitals refused care that was judged "futile."

I watched Danny's fake smile growing wider and more sinister. "You better believe it!"

"And are you comfortable being on the breathing machine? Was it your choice to go on it?"

"No, she forced me." Danny indicated me with his eyes. I was glad that, no matter how sick he was, he still had his sense of humor. But this was no time to kid around.

Finally, the woman turned toward me. "You're his wife and you have his proxy." It was a statement, not a question. Her straight hair was platinum-colored and expertly cut, with tapered ends that looked like arrows.

"Yes, I'm Nadina." No matter how I tried, I couldn't produce a smile. "Danny has used the ventilator successfully for three years. He's able to do much more, be more productive, since he can breathe well. We're very happy." Why did I have to stress that Danny was productive? Don't mistake my guy for a useless eater, lady! Why did I feel compelled to say we were happy? I didn't need to justify our lives to this stranger with arrow-straight platinum hair. "We're very happy," I repeated, pushing my own dark, wavy, and unruly hair away from my face.

Should I have told her what a brilliant organizer Danny was? How hard we worked to make this a better world for our people? Should I have mentioned how proud Danny was when friends said that, with the vent and the beard, and the few pounds my Sicilian cooking put on him, he resembled Ed Roberts? The "father of independent living" had died of a heart attack in 1995 but lived on as an icon of our movement. Of course, this classy lady wouldn't have known who Ed Roberts was.

Did she think Danny would have been better off dead? Would she rather have died than be like Danny, or like me?

She nodded, said, "I had to ask," and walked away.

Greater than the fear they wouldn't be able to save Danny's life was the fear they might judge his life not worth saving. A man who couldn't move, couldn't control his bodily functions, couldn't even breathe on his own, did he want to live no matter what?

The doctors who'd treated him for years knew our wishes. But what if they weren't around when needed? I had to be there in case Danny was too sick to tell an eager resident or a smiling lady, "You bet I want to live," and tell them how he loved me and I loved him and how much we loved our crippled lives.

"Don't worry, I'm still worth more alive. I'm too good a cash cow; too many would lose too much money if they killed me," Danny always said.

Indeed, disability had become big business. Huge industries thrived off of us. But at what point did the scale tip too far; when did the high cost to society—and health insurance—outweigh the income-generating benefit? And no matter what profitable cash cows we were, if the disability was as "severe" as Danny's, we had to fear that old lethal prejudice. That's why we all cringed when we heard talk of "death with dignity."

"No extreme measures," most people put in their living wills. Danny's ventilator was considered an extreme measure.

"Oh, I would never want to live hooked up to a machine," some nondisabled friends said right to our faces. When they noticed our reaction, that chilling smile appeared.

"But you're so brave, so exceptional. How I admire you! You're such an inspiration!"

Danny and I continued to be active with Not Dead Yet. Our concerns were still not understood.

Some NDY members had living wills that said "Do whatever it takes to keep me alive." Danny and I couldn't be so inflexible. There would come a time—we hoped not too soon—when death was inevitable and impending, and we didn't wish to prolong the dying process unnecessarily. I remembered my father's choice to stop treatment and his gentle death. My mother's death, too, had been peaceful.

We had each other's health-care proxies. As an alternate, we both named Hope. Our lawyer had added a few lines to the original format, at Danny's insistence, that said I was to be consulted about any decisions regarding his care, even if he was conscious and able to decide on his own.

I'd made sure the health-care proxy was in his chart. I'd also made sure to bring proof of our domestic partnership. They treated it as a marriage at the hospital, referring to me as Danny's wife. Recognized only in NYC, the partnership didn't affect Danny's eligibility for Medicaid.

Thinking of Medicaid made my head ache. Sitting in the waiting room now, I massaged my temples. The man on the couch stirred in his sleep, as if my thoughts were disturbing him. The clock said 1:25.

"The hell with Medicaid; let's just get married," Danny would say at times. But if we did, my savings would have to go for his personal care. There might be no money left by the time I started needing help transferring from wheelchair to bed or to toilet, and getting myself in and out of the tub or shower—"activities of daily living," to use rehab lingo, that with each passing year were becoming harder for me. I'd tried to buy private long-term-care insurance, but, being already disabled, I was rejected.

I tried to slow down my racing mind by looking at the slide show of nature scenes. A beautiful photo of the ocean appeared and I wished there was a way to pause the monitor, but I didn't see a remote control.

Our situation was not unique. We knew many other couples who lived together, considered themselves married, and had domestic partnerships. We also knew couples, some elderly, who, rather than impoverishing themselves when one spouse became disabled and needed long-term care, had opted for divorce.

For those on such government programs as Supplemental Security Income or Social Security for Adult Children, a marriage certificate could mean not only loss of health care but reduction or total loss of monthly payments.

"I decided, in my early days as a feminist, that marriage was not for me," I would joke with Danny.

He responded in kind: "And I guess I don't have a very good track record, with two divorces under my belt."

But humor only helped so much.

Federal and state governments made allowances to help "medically needy" people qualify for Medicaid by letting them place money in "special needs trusts." Control of that money was relinquished and a trustee had to manage it according to stringent rules. That provision had proven helpful when Danny's income increased, after he stopped paying child support. Legislation passed after a long fight allowed disabled people who worked to buy into Medicaid. However, earnings had to remain within a set limit. It infuriated me to see capable young people not living up to their full potential for fear of losing the services they needed to survive—as if discrimination and barriers didn't make employment difficult enough. Had I been so disabled that I needed help with my personal care, I might never have been a teacher.

The whole system was based on old disability stereotypes: "Disabled people don't work; they don't marry; they're poor," et cetera.

"Let's be happy we live in New York," Danny always said when I got worked up about Medicaid. I knew exactly what he meant. In many other states, people as disabled as Danny, such as those on ventilators, didn't live at home; they were in nursing homes.

ADAPT's fight to remove the institutional bias from the Medicaid law—by making the small change that, on my first action sixteen years before, I'd naïvely considered "no big deal"—turned out to be grueling and endless. The nursing home industry was too powerful. But though the federal law that would give people the choice to live in their homes had not passed yet, ADAPT had succeeded in shifting the conversation nationally. People heard and agreed with ADAPT's demand, "Our homes, not nursing homes!" And the home-care industry in many states had jumped at the opportunity to cash in. "Money talks louder than arrests in capitalist America," Danny said.

But without a federal mandate, there was great discrepancy in the availability of services, with some states being a lot worse than others. New York was a good state. Lately, Danny and I had helped disabled people move here from other states, where they would have ended up in nursing homes. Even in our good state, many fell through the cracks. Our home number was still listed for NYC ADAPT; we got calls from people in nursing homes at all hours. "Please, get me out of here!"

According to the waiting room clock, another hour had gone by.

Since Danny's health didn't allow it, I was the one who went to actions and got arrested. I was on probation at present, with an order to stay away from congressional buildings. I'd been arrested so many times, I'd lost count. Memories of arrests flashed now in my mind, the same way the nature scenes were flashing on the screen.

Columbus, Ohio. Sitting in my chair outside the Human Services building—mean wind and wet snow, though it was still fall. My joints and muscles ached because of my post-polio symptoms. I saw the accessible school buses the police brought to transport us, and all I could think was, Those buses are well heated. I repeated "Thank you, thank you" to the policewoman who arrested me.

Washington, D.C., at the White House fence, where we'd been arrested countless times. While "escalating," some of us headed toward the well-guarded gates. To stop me, a policeman hit me on the chest with the back of his arm, making my chair fly backward. Luckily, it was a cold day and I was wearing a wool cap and a hood, or my head, as hard as friends claim it is, might have split open.

San Francisco, California, on a balmy fall day. While blocking the doors to a government building, we were served ADAPT's typical lunch—a McDonald's hamburger. A policeman watched me refusing it, smiled, and walked away. Ten minutes later, he was back, handing me a falafel sandwich. Forty-five minutes later, he arrested me.

And was it in Nashville? The policewoman had such a kind face. She told me how much she admired me, while watching me pee.

I was glad these thoughts were keeping me from focusing on the reason I was in that waiting room, from picturing Danny on the OR table, his insides being probed by a surgeon's hands.

At home in NYC, Danny and I were constantly advocating: visiting and writing letters to legislators, organizing call-in campaigns, coalescing with other groups, such as senior citizens and single payer advocates. After the 1993 march that brought us together, in spite of the Clinton health-care fiasco, we had remained firm in our belief that a single payer national health-care system was the real solution. A system that covered long-term care without forcing people into poverty would have allowed us to get married.

We were now in an election year. Danny and I had been watching in the last few months the debates between the two frontrunners for the Democratic nomination, Hillary Clinton and Barak Obama. Excitement had been spreading at the possibility of the first woman or the first African-American president. Both were committed to health-care reform. At this point, Obama had won in the primaries the number of delegates needed for the nomination, as well as the hearts of many Americans, with his promise of "change you can believe in." In the past, Obama had been a strong single payer supporter. Would he still be if he succeeded in winning the presidency? Danny's answer was simple: "Not if private health insurances pour enough millions into his campaign."

No matter how the political scene unfolded, we could be sure of one thing: Our people's struggle would continue. Danny and I had vowed to keep on fighting for the rest of our lives to bring about desperately needed change. I renewed those vows now in that hospital waiting room. We had to get over this hurdle. I needed Danny to be okay.

When he was admitted, the decision had been made to put Danny in a "step-down" unit—meaning a step down from the ICU. All the other patients there had already had surgery. We expected Danny to be taken to the OR shortly. Instead, we waited all morning, all afternoon, and all evening. We waited for the surgeon to be ready. Emergency surgery, said one of the residents. Exploratory surgery, said another. What for? To find out the nature of the blockage. To remove the blockage if removable.

The more we heard, the more I feared. The anesthesiologist came by, then the pulmonologist. They explained that Danny would have to be intubated.

"Yes, but he must be extubated as soon as possible after the surgery; the longer he's kept intubated, the harder it will be to get him back on the ventilator," I told the pulmonologist. I got a card out of my wallet. "Please speak with Dr. Bach."

Dr. Bach was Danny's ventilator doctor. Not a pulmonologist, but a physiatrist, he treated people with neurological conditions, whose lungs were healthy but who had trouble breathing because their diaphragm muscles had atrophied. Unlike Danny's other doctors, who were all at NYU, Dr. Bach was in Newark, New Jersey, at the College of Medicine and Dentistry. We had gone to his office three years before, when Danny was discharged from NYU Medical Center after yet another bout with pneumonia.

The first time he had pneumonia was in the winter of 2001. We attributed his getting sick to the horror of the events of 9/11, to the unwholesome air we breathed, living not far from Ground Zero, and to Danny's insistence that we not miss a single demonstration—in our wheelchairs, with our signs, OUR GRIEF IS NOT A CRY FOR WAR.

He recovered, but in 2002 he was hospitalized twice, and again in February 2003, after attending a huge antiwar rally on an extremely cold day. The hospitalizations became more frequent in 2004, and even more so in 2005. The doctors kept giving him stronger antibiotics and oxygen. Chronic pneumonia was the diagnosis. And the prognosis? The pulmonologist who was treating Danny shrugged.

No mention of ventilators. But luckily, we knew about them. I called Marilyn, still going strong after forty years on a ventilator, and she told me to make an appointment with her doctor immediately.

I remembered too well the day we first went to see Dr. Bach. It was

June 16, 2005. A phone call, early that morning, brought the saddest news. Dear Frieda had passed away during the night. Her partner, Michael, had awakened and found her lying lifeless beside him. It was a shock, though we knew Frieda had been ill. She had gone through breast cancer surgery and a few rounds of chemo. Then a sudden attack of appendicitis had landed her in the hospital for emergency surgery.

But we'd thought she was recovering, since she had resumed her routine of going from meeting to press conference to demonstration. "Are you sure you feel up to doing all this?" I asked. "I have to" was always her answer.

Frieda always did what she had to do. She had to change the world, one righted wrong at a time. A never-ending job. No life could ever be long enough. But she righted a lot of wrongs in hers.

We decided to keep the appointment with Dr. Bach that afternoon. Danny's breathing was failing. His voice had become a whisper.

"Frieda would want us to go," I said. "Now that she no longer can, we have to fight so much harder. How can you fight if you can't breathe?"

"He won't be intubated longer than necessary," said the pulmonologist. Not the same one who had shrugged three years before. This doctor was a kind woman with a reassuring manner.

Still, I was wary of pulmonologists. I was convinced Danny's first pulmonologist had written him off. Whenever I heard of people with ALS and with MS dying because they could no longer breathe, I asked why they weren't on ventilators. Was it their choice to die? Did their doctors bother telling them they didn't have to? Did a smiling lady make them think that being hooked up to a breathing machine was no way to live?

Doctors stopped in to check on Danny.

"Why are we waiting? Isn't emergency surgery supposed to be performed immediately?" I asked. "Isn't there another surgeon who can do it?"

"I want Dr. Liang to do it," Dr. Crest told us when he stopped in toward evening.

It wasn't until 11:00 P.M. that Dr. Liang came to talk to us. As soon as I saw him, I decided he'd been worth waiting for. The man exuded confidence in a quiet, unassuming way. He suspected adhesions from the old colostomy surgery were causing the problem. If that were the case, he would remove the scar tissue and clear the passage.

I wanted to know more. "Will you be able to remove all the scar tissue?"

"I can't be sure of anything until I go in."

I shouldn't have asked.

Danny's question was simpler. "Aren't you tired?"

"I am, but I'll drink a cup of coffee, don't worry."

But I was worried. The clock told me it was already 3:40. What was happening in the OR? What if it wasn't scar tissue causing the blockage? What if Dr. Liang found a tumor? What if they couldn't keep Danny breathing through the surgery? What if he was too weak to tolerate the anesthesia?

Please let him get through this, I found myself praying to an unidentified god. If he makes it, I promise we'll have more fun. My prayer made me laugh. I was supposed make a sacrifice, offer my suffering in exchange for a favor from this god. But Danny and I loved life and believed it was our duty to enjoy it. I hoped whatever god was listening knew what I meant.

Our life together had changed a lot in fifteen years. Danny needed so much more care now. There wasn't much I could do physically to help him. The attendants continued to be an intrusion for me. My need for privacy had increased as my physical condition had declined. Thankfully, we no longer lived in Danny's one-bedroom apartment. I had sold my studio and we now lived in a big apartment, where I had a room of my own and, even more important, my own bathroom.

Still, it wasn't easy. I'd just turned sixty. I'd decided to stop teaching.

Managing and supervising attendants, making sure they didn't hurt Danny while attending to his care, dealing with doctors, battling with governmental bureaucracy in order to maintain services, keeping our finances straight... and both of us both fighting to make change happen, to make life better for ourselves and our people—it was hard work.

I could hear Danny, imitating George W. Bush, saying with a Texas accent, "It's hard work..." Bush had said those words when talking about the presidency. Now Danny, whenever I mentioned hard work, went into his Bush imitation. No matter how serious the situation, Danny could always make me laugh.

I wanted us to laugh more.

I wanted us to go more often to concerts, plays, museums—how we loved to sit entranced in front of the Temple of Dendur, at the Metropolitan, then wheel to the opposite side to look up in awe at the totem poles in the Michael C. Rockefeller Wing. Maybe we'd splurge and hire an accessible van, ride in style and avoid Stress-A-Ride—that's what many of us called Access-A-Ride because of its unreliability.

Having fun for us could mean simply a quiet stroll in our wheelchairs over to the Hudson River, to the piers where fifteen years ago we had gone to make out, and which had been turned into popular parklands. Having fun certainly didn't mean flying to Paris or cruising to the Bahamas.

At this point, traveling was out of the question for Danny. Aside from the trouble and the expense of transporting delicate equipment, renting other equipment at our destination, and having one or more attendants go with us, traveling would have been too risky. Even the trips by train to D.C. had to stop. The last time he'd been there was in June 2002. The occasion was a sad one: a memorial service for Justin Dart. He'd died of heart failure at age seventy-one. Sincerely dramatic till the end, he wrote a final farewell to disability activists, urging us all to "lead on."

We'd hoped while in D.C. to visit the FDR Memorial. After much advocacy by our community, the year before, a statue had been added of the president with polio sitting in his wheelchair. Unfortunately, we had to skip the visit. The service for Justin Dart left Danny too emotionally drained and physically tired.

I traveled, but usually only to actions or conferences. Traveling by plane was more difficult for me now. Since I no longer walked, I had to transfer from my own wheelchair to an isle chair, at the gate, and be taken to my seat. When I did travel, I was never away more than a week. Arrangements had to be made to make sure Danny got the care he needed. A few times, he'd gotten sick or hurt while I was on a trip.

I hadn't seen my Italian relatives and the disabled friends I made while traveling in Italy with Maurizio in sixteen years. I spoke to relatives on holidays. Maurizio e-mailed impersonal good wishes at Christmas. I called Gabriella when I felt nostalgic; I told her I missed her, she said, "*Anch'io*," assuring me she missed me, too, and we compared notes on the state of the disability movement on our respective continents. "*Quando vieni*? When are you coming?" she never tired of asking.

But a trip to Italy would have been a taxing venture—visiting relatives and friends scattered in various cities, in inaccessible homes, without a faithful traveling companion ready to offer all the help I'd once resented. More important, such a trip would have meant leaving Danny for much longer than a week, which I could not do. Sometimes I dreamed of Sicily, of Riposto. How my father had wanted me to go back. Then I wasn't ready to face my childhood memories. Now the desire to return to my hometown was stronger than any anxiety caused by long-faded ghosts.

So much had changed for Danny and me in fifteen years. Long gone were the days when I held on to the bar in the back of his power chair and let him pull me to unexplored territories. Back then, we could stay out late and manage without an attendant when we got back home— Danny letting himself fall from his chair onto the bed, I playfully helping him get undressed. We couldn't go out by ourselves anymore. An attendant accompanied us wherever we went. An attendant had to place a sling under Danny, attach the straps to a ceiling lift, then operate the lift, so his body was raised out of the wheelchair and lowered onto the bed.

When, in order to have a few hours alone, we gave an attendant some time off, we got overwhelmed trying to make good use of our freedom. Gone were the days when I could do acrobatics, holding onto the trapeze over the bed, teasing Danny, who could still lift himself and use his hands to grab my stumps. Now a few hours of privacy sometimes came with a price, like my having to figure out why the ventilator alarm was going off, or having to empty his colostomy bag, certainly not the most romantic activity.

Years ago, *CBS Sunday Morning* did a segment where they pitted those of us searching for the cure against those of us fighting for rights. Paraplegics and quadriplegics pedaling on electrical muscular-simulation machines versus us rebels blocking doors, occupying politicians' offices. Danny and I were prominently featured. "We want to change our society, which denies us services, denies us access, treats us as second-class citizens because of our disabilities. We're not waiting around for cures."

At times, when we heard of some new treatment for MS, I joked with Danny. "I'm glad I don't have to worry about them coming up with a pill that'll make my legs grow back."

"I, too, consider myself lucky that nothing works on my kind of MS."

We laughed together. Yet, what wouldn't I have given to slow down the progression of Danny's MS? What wouldn't I have given to feel his arms around me again, holding me tight?

But even though so much was harder now, so much was easier. All we'd lost was outweighed by all we'd gained. After fifteen years together, we had no need for words; we knew each other's thoughts; we felt identical emotions. Without effort, we could simply bask in the silent warmth of intimacy, the closeness of our crippled bodies both soothing and exciting. Danny's tongue on my skin brought me to new heights each time. Our lovemaking, no matter what creative form our disabilities required it to take, was still heaven on earth. We relished now more than ever every precious moment of pleasure.

I was the luckiest woman in the world. After fifteen years, my man was still passionately in love with me and I with him.

I heard a woman crying now. I noticed there were quite a few people in the waiting room. I didn't know when they'd all come in. The crying woman was surrounded by relatives or friends who were trying to comfort her. Maybe someone she loved had died.

Oh my god, by the clock, another hour had passed. Danny had been in the OR for over four hours. The woman's sobs were loud, desperate; they tore through me, made me start shaking. I was terrified.

What would I do if I didn't have Danny to surprise me with my favorite Italian delicacies and Moscato wine on special occasions? And who but Danny knew how to make any ordinary evening into a special occasion?

How could I withstand the ordeal of an arrest if I didn't have Danny to give me strength, if I couldn't call him, when the third warning was issued and the handcuffs were ready, to hear him tell me, "I love you. Free our people!"

How could I sleep if I didn't have Danny to sing to me at night? When I was away from home, he sang to me on the phone. From the hospital, when he was stable enough, he'd have a nurse hold the phone for him so that he could sing. If he couldn't, because he was too sick, or if a silly argument had him pissed at me, which hardly ever happened, I had to resign myself to a sleepless night.

And would I look in the mirror and mourn my lost youth if I didn't have Danny to make me feel that, no matter what new lines were on my face or how my breasts were sagging, I was still the most beautiful woman who ever lived?

It was now quarter to five, and suddenly, there was Dr. Liang, standing in front of me in his OR greens, his mask hanging around his neck. Too drained of energy to ask any questions, I stared at his face, waiting for him to speak. His face offered no clue about the outcome of the surgery. He looked very tired. But he was nodding, a good sign.

"I removed the blockage. There was a lot of scar tissue. But everything should be back to normal in a week or two."

I wanted to hug this wonderful man who had saved my man's life. Tell him how grateful I was that never for a moment had I had to worry that he might not think Danny's life worth saving. I wanted to tell him how happy I was that we'd waited all day for him to perform the surgery. I wished I could joke like Danny, say, "I guess that cup of coffee worked wonders." I wanted to tell him about all the struggles Danny and I had ahead of us, how we had to be strong in order to fight and make this a better world for ourselves and our people. I wanted to tell him how crazy in love Danny and I still were after fifteen years. And tell him about my vow to enjoy our life together, have more fun now that, thanks to him, Danny was okay.

But I was too exhausted. I could hardly gather enough strength to whisper "Thank you."

25

RIPOSTO

❋

Almost fifty years had passed and nothing had changed. The rough pavement of the narrow street, the cracks on the stone walls, the wooden doors with glass panels, the plate with the name of the street, Via Libertà, all were the same.

The double doors of the house where I was born had a design of raised rectangles below the glass panels, just as I'd remembered them. But the brown paint on the door was cracked and peeling. When we lived here, my father made sure the paint looked clean and shiny. This house was in perfect shape then, never a crack on a wall, never a broken or loose tile, never any peeling paint. I wondered who lived here now, who had allowed the paint on the door to crack and peel.

As a child, I sat behind those glass panels, watching people go by and neighborhood children chase each other, always waiting for strong arms to carry me outside on *Via Libertà*.

Of course, as a child, I didn't appreciate the irony in the name of the street on which I lived.

All I remembered about the last time I'd been here was how I'd wanted to get away. Get away and never come back. So afraid I'd been of being swallowed inside the memories still fresh and raw of a childhood I wished to forget.

The present for me then had been painful as well. I had lost my blood sister, Audrey. It took years for me to learn how to fight against the violence done to us. And many more years for the wounds to begin to heal.

I was in Riposto for only eight days. I flew to Rome but couldn't stop to see the city I loved. I took a connecting flight to Catania. I was picked up at the airport in a wheelchair-accessible van and driven to the only wheelchair-accessible hotel right near the impressive seaport, which had been built recently. Those arrangements were made with the help of a wonderful man who lived in Catania, a wheelchair user named Roberto DiSimone, a strong fighter and, like me, a polio survivor. He was president of Aldebaran, the only disability rights organization in Sicily I could find when I searched online.

My Italian relatives and friends didn't know I was there. They lived in various cities scattered throughout Italy. With my time so limited, there was no way I could travel around to visit them.

I felt guilty not going to Florence to see Gabriella, *sorella d'oltre oceano,* especially since she had not been well in recent years.

But I had to keep this trip brief. It was the only way I could do it, since I couldn't leave Danny for a longer time.

Perhaps it was best this way. Alone, without the distraction of relatives and friends. Just me and my memories on a journey to the past.

I was so glad I had power-assisted wheels on my chair. I'd bought them after I tore a rotator cuff, when wheeling my manual chair became increasingly difficult and painful. I pushed on the rims as I always had, but the battery-run motor made turning the wheels practically effortless.

Even with the cobblestones slowing me down, I was amazed at how quickly I could roll around the whole town. It was so small, Riposto, which as a child I'd thought immense. Corso Italia, *u stratuni,* the big street, was only a little over a block away from the house on Via Libertà, and not a long block at that. Nor was *u stratuni* a big street.

"*Signora, ha bisogno d'aiuto?* Lady, do you need help?"

I was asked that question wherever I went. I was a novelty, an oddity, rolling around these narrow cobblestone streets in my wheelchair. These streets where there were no sidewalks, or if there were sidewalks, there were no curb cuts, no doors without steps, no banks, no stores, no restaurants with a level entrance. Where, if a car approached, to get out of its way I had to squeeze my chair between parked cars or back away into an alley. From their cars, the townspeople honked their horns, and they came out of their inaccessible stores and houses.

"Are you alone? Have you no one to help you? Where did you come from all alone?" Their voices were full of concern.

I saw no other disabled people on these streets, no wheelchair users like me bumping and rattling over cobblestones, trying to stay out of the way of moving cars. Were there no disabled people in this town? Or were they hidden in their houses, sitting behind glass-paneled doors, prisoners of loving families?

If I answered these good people truthfully, "I came from America," they saw in my answer a confirmation of their fears. I must not be in my right mind, they thought. I heard them murmuring, "*Pazza!*" Who but a crazy woman would go wheeling around in her wheelchair, saying she came from America? Had I come from the local hospital, broken loose from the custody of busy nurses? Or maybe I had gotten away from the stranglehold of a momentarily distracted loving family. I suspected they called the police out of concern for me, these good people. For wherever I went, I was sure to meet up with the carabinieri. "*Signora, ha bisogno d'aiuto?*"

"No, *grazie*, I'm just taking pictures," I now replied politely, holding up my digital camera. "I'm taking pictures of the house where I was born."

Even in broad daylight, the ghosts were out on Via Libertà. I saw my mother standing on our doorstep, her back so straight, her body so strong and supple, her head held high. There were no women around to offer her their pity. She was happy, because she was waiting for my father to come home to eat his *pranzo*. He would put his arm around my mother's shoulders when he got here, and they would walk together into the house. My grandmother must have been in the kitchen. And was my grandfather sitting at the table, still handsome with his well-groomed white hair and mustache? Was he waiting patiently for my grandmother to finish cooking? What was she cooking? Something sure smelled good. It was tomato sauce. I wanted to go inside this house and see the old kitchen and my grandmother in front of the stove, a black straight dress draping her slight body, her hair pulled tightly back in a knot.

"What are you cooking, *Nanna*?"

I asked a passerby to ring the doorbell, but there was no doorbell. "Knock on the door, then, please," I said, but no one answered. "Who lives here now?" Why did I want to know and who was I, a crazy woman in a wheelchair?

The balconies of the roof terrace looked rusted. I wondered if I would still be able to see the sea from there. With so much new construction near the new seaport, I doubted it.

If only my father would get home, he could carry me up those steep stairs. I was too heavy for my mother. If only my father could carry me in his work clothes smeared with cement and I could cling to him, feel his powerful muscles, nestle my head on his shoulder and smell his dusty sweat.

"I've come back, *Papà*. Are you happy I'm here?"

I wheeled up the cobblestoned Corso Italia, and before I knew it, I was on the other side of the train tracks, in Giarre. This was the way my father went, carrying me in his arms, to visit his mother and sister, my little chubby grandmother and my aunt, who was always baking cookies. They were both long gone, and any cousins lived far from here. I didn't recognize the house, so different did it look. But I thought I smelled cinnamon, a faint smell of baked spices, probably coming from a nearby bakery.

I followed the scent and found the bakery a block away. Of course, there was a step. But a woman came to the door. I told her I wanted 250 grams of *piparelle* and I handed her a five- euro note. She came out with the *piparelle* and gave me two euro coins as change.

With great gusto, I chewed the crunchy, spicy almond biscotti as I wheeled down Corso Italia. They tasted good, but not as good as my aunt's.

Heading back toward the hotel, I noticed a group of five older men sitting on chairs they must have brought out of their houses, just chatting. I'd seen a few groups of women and of men sitting outside in the shade—the women not knitting and sewing as I remembered them doing, but leafing through magazines. I'd even seen women and men sitting together in a group.

I'd seen these men already on this same corner in the few days of my stay here. They'd smiled at me, waved, or yelled, "*Attenta*, careful crossing the street!"

They were speaking Sicilian now, and probably thought I didn't understand.

"*Na bedda femmina è, chi piccatu averu?* She's a beautiful woman, what a shame, isn't it?"

I thought, at my age, what beauty I had left no longer could be seen as being spoiled by my disability. But these old men, who obviously found me attractive enough to want to comment on my beauty, also found it necessary to refer to my disability as a shame, a pity. I found them comical, and laughed.

Then I thought of all the disabled people, especially the youngest and most vulnerable, who were deeply wounded by people's pity.

"*Pietismo*." Roberto DiSimone spewed the word with disgust when we met—joined by a few other members of his organization—in a restaurant in Catania. "*Pietismo* is encouraged by the Catholic Church and is impossible to eradicate."

Roberto told me that the *Legge Quadro* and other laws passed later had not helped as much as they should have, especially down in Sicily.

"Other than the hotel where I'm staying, nothing in the town of Riposto is accessible," I said. "It's better here in the city."

The law offered only guidelines, they explained to me. Many small businesses couldn't afford modifications. Those that could but didn't comply weren't penalized.

"We sue," I told them, "to force them into compliance."

"Not here. They get away with it," Roberto said. "But they'll go to hell when they die." We all had a good laugh.

But Italy was way ahead of the United States when it came to benefits and services—all based on level of disability, never means-tested. Everything deemed medically necessary, be it treatment, durable equipment, or home care, was theirs by right, through the national single payer system. That in America one had to prove poverty to receive services was a notion they couldn't comprehend. I was too embarrassed to tell them Danny and I weren't married because of his need for Medicaid. Embarrassed for my adoptive country.

The accessible and comfortable hotel where I was staying was right on the *lungomare,* the road running along the sea. Unlike the town streets, that road was smooth and wide. It was lined with palm trees, the restaurants had outdoor tables, and there were vendors along the side, many selling fresh fruit. Just like my grandfather had sold fruit so long ago.

"*Pessica, cirasi…* peaches, cherries," my grandfather had yelled out.

They didn't yell to hawk their goods, these vendors, but I heard them speaking the dialect with one another. I wheeled over to one of them.

"*Menzu chilu di cirasi,*" I said in Sicilian, asking for half a kilo of cherries. The vendor looked surprised; he probably had thought I was a foreigner.

The Sicilian words tasted as sweet in my mouth as the cherries.

The cube refrigerator in my hotel room was stuffed with cherries and peaches and grapes and figs I bought from street vendors, while the mini bottles of liquor and beer the hotel provided for tourists sat on the dresser.

I wheeled along the *lungomare* with ease, admiring the pristine beaches—the children kicking pebbles and white sand and chasing each other into the blue-green water, the families picnicking, the women in their bikinis, unconcerned with extra pounds and aging flabbiness, and the teenage girls offering their newly developed sexiness to the scorching sun and the appreciation of young men.

They were all in love, the young Sicilians, evidenced by the graffiti on the walls: *Ti amo… Sei la mia vita… Non vivo senza te…* I love you… You're my life… I can't live without you. And they got married, judging by the abundance of bridal gowns in store windows and the many shops that sold *bamboniere,* wedding favors. I wondered if girls still grew up believing marriage and motherhood were a woman's destiny.

In my efficient power-assisted wheelchair, I could go pretty far on the smooth road. If I pushed hard, my chair took flight. People stared—not in pity, but in awe. They'd never seen a wheelchair fly. I felt like I was really flying, with my long hair trailing behind me.

I laughed, remembering my mother's admonition that older women shouldn't have long hair, or they'd look like witches. I was a witch flying on wheels, rather than on a broom.

I wheeled up to Fondachello, another town along the coast, known for its beaches and seafood restaurants. In one of the restaurants on the beach, I ate roasted swordfish, shrimp, and calamari, caught by fishermen in this Ionian Sea, and drank white wine. The other patrons eyed me with curiosity and suspicion. A woman enjoying a meal, alone, and *ciunca*, crippled, to boot, in a wheelchair.

Then I wheeled down to Torre Archirafi, where the coastline is rocky and wild. I ate nougat ice cream in a café practically hanging over the water.

It was amazing how the shortest distance could bring about totally different scenery. As I rolled along the *lungomare,* the coast kept changing—from the peace of pristine beaches to the drama of fierce rocks to the heart-stopping excitement of high cliffs. And no matter where I was, all I had to do was look up to see mountains covered with luscious vegetation or showing bare, savage rock. And scattered here and there were clusters of red-roofed houses, little towns magically suspended on mountainsides. And in the midst of it all, tall and majestic, stood Etna, the volcano.

Such breathtaking, extraordinary beauty! But, while bringing me happiness, the beauty of my homeland also filled me with anger. Amid this beauty, I'd spent my early years; it should have belonged to me, but it never had. My childhood memories did not include this beauty. My childhood memories were filled with the pain of isolation, of loneliness, of oppressive bigotry. I felt I'd been robbed of this beauty. Must I admire it as a tourist, a foreigner, trying to capture it in snapshots, pretty as postcards, to show friends back home in New York? Or could I claim it now as my own?

Could I be proud of my homeland, as my father would have wanted me to be? Could I be proud that I was born in this town? This town that I remembered only with resentment, that for so many years I'd feared coming back to? Could I forgive whatever hurt was done to me so long ago and acknowledge my kinship with these good people? If ever again I traveled in northern Italy, would I let my Sicilian accent sweeten my speech? If anyone said to me, "You don't seem Sicilian," would I declare with angry pride *"Sugnu siciliana?"*

Yes, *Papà,* you win. No matter how bitter the memories, no matter how difficult the journey, I am proud that I come from here. It is real pride that's born of pain and struggle. I understand now, *Papà.* How I wish I could have made you understand this pride is the same as disability pride.

Across the street, on Via Libertà, stood the church of the Addolorata.

I had not pointed my camera toward it at all. I'd been avoiding taking
a close look. This church, this convent with its school and its nuns
had through the years acquired mythical proportions in my memory.
Finally brave enough, I parked my chair in front of the building. It
looked exactly as it had when I was a child: the same four steps leading
to the big double doors of the church, the same plain, unadorned white
walls, the same bell tower, the same cross at the very top. And yet it
was so different, so much smaller than in my memory, so modest,
austere-looking, totally harmless. Nothing like the mighty place of
my nightmares.

On the side of the building was the door with the plate: SCUOLA
PRIMARIA ELEMENTARE. That was the door to the elementary school run
by the nuns of the convent. With me in her arms, my mad mother walked
out of our house, crossed the street, come around to this side door, and
handed me over to the nuns, who'd carried me into the classroom. On
Sundays, she'd carried me up those four steps into the church.

The big double doors were now shut. So was the side door. It was
June and school was over, of course.

"Does this church open only on Sunday?" I asked a young woman
pushing a baby in a carriage. And I remembered how my mother had
pushed me in my baby carriage to the beach that had now been
replaced by the impressive seaport. The young woman shook her head
and shrugged.

Suddenly, another woman came out of a nearby store.

"Do you want me to go ask the nuns to open the church?"

"Oh, no! I was just curious."

But she was walking toward the side of the building, where the door
to the school was, and I followed her. She had dark, rebellious hair, like
my mother's when she was young, and large, dark, expressive eyes.
Judging by her features, she could have been a member of my family.
She told me her name was Fina. I followed her. I felt I could trust this
woman, so I told her I was born here, in the house with the glass-paneled doors, I went to school with the nuns, and I'd come from New

York after so many years to visit this town, to see this street again and this church.

She went into the building through the side door; I wasn't sure how. Had she rung a bell? Had someone unlocked the door? I waited for her to come back out, and when she did, there was a nun with her. The nun's habit was not black, but white. Her face was lined and benign.

"Do you want to go into the church?"

"How can I? There are steps."

"Wait," Fina said, and a man with lots of curly hair and a wide smile appeared next to her. "This is my husband, Melo." Two younger men were there also. "They'll carry you."

Would I allow myself to be carried—I who now entered only places that were wheelchair-accessible, where I could roll in as an equal, not as the unfortunate one who needed help? Would I be carried by these men into this church, where my mother had carried me so long ago, where the nuns had carried me in what now seemed another life?

"This chair is heavy," I said, trying to find an excuse.

But as I said that, I removed the battery and handed it to Fina. I asked her to help me remove the heavy bag hanging on the back of my chair. In the bag was the spare battery, which I carried so that if one got depleted during my wanderings, I could switch to the other. I also had the bottles of San Pellegrino I'd bought at the only semiaccessible market.

"Light as a feather," the men said as they lifted me in my chair. And suddenly I was inside the church. The men stayed outside. The nun and Fina were with me.

What do I do now? I picked up my camera and put it back down on my lap. Taking pictures was not the proper thing to do here. I wheeled forward. Did they expect me to start praying, since they'd gone through all this trouble to get me inside? The church could have been any church. Beautiful stained glass. The main altar with a tall crucifix in the middle. The smell of flowers. The faint smell of incense. Was this really the church of my memories, of my nightmares?

I realized I was trying to hold back, not letting myself feel any emotions. But then I saw her—the *Addolorata*. The statue, sculpted who knows how many years ago by an unknown local artist, was the same. In the same niche, surrounded by flowers and candles, the *Addolorata* in her purple gown and blue mantle with gold embroidery. But where was her son, her dead son?

"We only place the Christ on her lap around Easter. The statue is delicate, you know, starting to chip."

Was the nun speaking? Had I asked the question out loud?

I looked at the *Addolorata*'s sorrowful face and I was the little crippled girl in my mother's arms, my mother kneeling in front of this niche. My mother's face and the *Addolorata*'s face always one and the same. The church always full of people. All of them softly murmuring, "*Maria Addolorata*. Pity the suffering woman, Pity her suffering child."

I stared at the *Addolorata*'s face, symbol of eternal sorrow. In her face, I'd been taught to see my own future of sorrow. I stared at the *Addolorata*'s face, but I could see something else now. I saw strength. My mother's strength. My own strength. My sisters' strength. The strength of womanhood.

Suddenly, I felt a hand on my shoulder. I came back to the present and saw Fina. Was I crying? What was I doing that caused this woman I'd only just met to be alarmed? I smiled at her to reassure her, and told her I was remembering how my mother had knelt with me in her arms in front of this statue.

I moved toward the middle of the church, where the nun was standing. Where were the other nuns? I wondered. Were any of the nuns who'd carried me in their arms when I was a child still alive? I doubted it. Did this nun know any of them?

She said that Sister Prisca, the eldest, had died a long time ago, in the early eighties. Sister Teresina had died only a few years ago, of heart failure.

What about Sister Angelica?

Sister Angelica, the nun told me, had died some fifteen years ago, after a long illness.

Sister Angelica—who had told me I could never in my life be happy. Whose chest I'd hit with my small fists, almost six decades before, as I struggled to get away from her ominous embrace. In how many nightmares had she appeared? How many times had I fought to get away from messages of doom? How many more times would I need to fight?

Sister Angelica was long dead. I would never have the satisfaction of confronting her. But there was no need for confrontation. What was it I'd wanted to say to her anyway? Yes, of course. Thank you, Sister, for awakening a little girl's fighting spirit.

As the men carried me down the steps of the church, I heard the sparrows singing. They sounded as cheerful as they had when, as a child in my bed, I'd listened to them announcing the dawn of each new day.

I thanked the men.

Fina hugged me, and I hugged her back.

"*Come sono contenta!*" I exclaimed. "How happy I am!"

Protest against the telethon, with Frieda Zames and
Michael Imperiale, NYC, 1992.

Danny and I in our Piss On Pity shirts, NYC, 1993.

Disability Independence Day March, NYC, July 25, 1993.

I'm handcuffed to the White House fence waiting
to be arrested, February, 2005.
(Photo and permission by Tom Olin.)

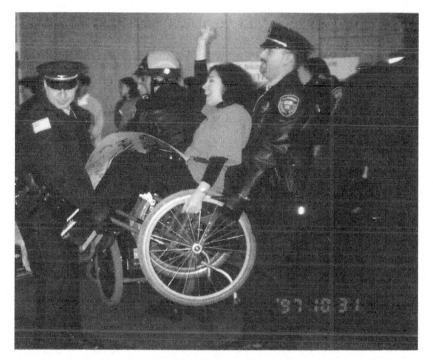

I'm under arrest, being carried away by the police
from Not Dead Yet (NDY) demonstration, Boston, 1997.

EPILOGUE

✼

When the young people put up their tents in a park near Wall Street, the name of which no one had known but which was about to become a household word, old hippies' hearts exploded with happiness. The revolution is here. The long-awaited revolution. Come one and all. Don't let the risk of a little myocardial infarction hold you back. Come on down to Zuccotti Park.

Danny and I heeded the call. Down Broadway we went in our wheel chairs. It didn't matter that Danny could no longer drive his power chair and had to be pushed—in a custom-made manual chair with the ventilator and its own heavy eight-hour battery mounted to the back—by a strong personal-care attendant who didn't always share our unbridled enthusiasm. We could not let the revolution happen without us. Disability issues had to be included in the agenda.

We took part in their general assemblies. Mike check. Mike check. How smart these kids are, how beautiful! I had absolute faith in their youth and their energy. I hugged each one, and we chanted along with them: "We are unstoppable! A better world is possible!" We believed in those words as one does in doctrinal truths and love promises.

We roused the troops at Disabled In Action. We lined up near the tall abstract red metal structure, carrying signs that read: CRIPS AGAINST GREED; DON'T CUT SOCIAL PROGRAMS TO BAIL OUT THE BANKS; and WE WILL NOT SUFFER FOR THE SINS OF WALL STREET.

A young woman named Michele, who only recently had started using a power chair, after a cyst in her brain screwed up her central nervous system, always carried the same sign—one she had made out of a cardboard box. In black Magic Marker it screamed THE REVOLUTION IS WHEELCHAIR-ACCESSIBLE.

A few bright young disabled people—what I called the budding "second wave" of disability activism—announced their presence with DISABILITY JUSTICE signs. I knew that *disability justice* was to become the preferred terminology and that those of us who identified as disability rights activists were dating ourselves.

But we all happily stood behind the big multihued banner, made by our artistic friends, proclaiming DISABILITY PRIDE.

We decided to make our presence there official. We founded the Disability Caucus of Occupy Wall Street. I got arrested. The first time, on November 17, 2011, I was the only one using a wheelchair. Photos of me surrounded by cops got tweeted and retweeted—Michael Moore got a hold of one and launched it to his millions of followers. And what were people saying? "Woman in wheelchair arrested! Have police no shame arresting a disabled woman?" The few who realized I had planned to be arrested admired my courage, or questioned my sanity. I was furious. Didn't anybody freaking hear me when, as the cops grabbed my wheelchair, I yelled that I was being arrested for all the disabled people locked up in institutions, and for those being denied health care, services, entitlements, education, employment, accommodations, while one percenters thrived?

I got arrested again on August 8, 2012, in front of Gracie Mansion, at a demonstration organized by our caucus. Mayor Bloomberg—called "the 1 percent mayor" by occupiers—had appealed a court ruling mandating that the city provide wheelchair-accessible taxis. And he had won. There were eight arrests that day. An occupier Danny and I had grown to love, Justin, who had come out to us as autistic, was the first to get arrested. He and three other nondisabled-looking demonstrators were separated from the four of us using wheelchairs—a fact that infuriated me. Along with accessible cabs, New York City also lacked wheelchair-accessible paddy wagons. So wheelchair users usually get taken to jail in Access-A-Ride vehicles.

Just before he left office, in December 2013, Bloomberg would sign an agreement that would result in 50 percent of the city's yellow cabs being wheelchair-accessible by 2020. At the time of this writing, getting a cab has finally become a real option for wheelchair users.

Shortly after the Gracie Mansion action, on September 17, 2012, at the OWS anniversary action, I and three others were arrested for blocking Broadway. Four of us in manual chairs, strategically spaced across the avenue, that's all it took to stop all traffic, with the crowds cheering and the cops so dumbfounded they had to scratch their heads for a good half hour before proceeding to arrest us. It was an impromptu action. ADAPT sure trained us well.

Three arrests within a year; yet I got away with fines and ACDs (acquittals in contemplation of dismissal), thanks to the excellent and free representation from the National Lawyers Guild. "I don't advise anyone to follow my example," I say whenever I conduct civil disobedience training sessions.

The next year, 2013, although the tents had long since been ripped out of Zuccotti Park, that "unstoppable" feeling still permeated the air. We breathed it in deeply, Danny through his ventilator hose, and we made a bold decision: to get married. Actually, we had been planning it for quite a while. What helped, ironically, was that Danny's MS, also "unstoppable," had progressed to the extent that he now satisfied two conditions that made him eligible for the Medicare home-care program. He was "in need of skilled services" and he was considered "home-bound." How we laughed at the notion of Danny being "home-bound." The term had been redefined, thanks to the advocacy of a man with ALS, to mean "impossibility to exit one's home unaided." In addition, thanks to the resolution of a lawsuit (*Jimmo v. Sebelius*), "improvement of one's condition" was no longer a requirement. That removed a stumbling block that had made Medicare home care strictly short-term. Now, as long as a doctor periodically restates the need for care, it can continue indefinitely.

Medicare is not nearly as generous as Medicaid with the number of hours of care allowed; but after much research, we were lucky to find an agency that awarded Danny forty-two hours a week. We needed more hours—a lot more. After countless calculations, we concluded that if we tightened our belts, we could afford to pay out of pocket for the additional hours. We were—and are—very conscious of being privileged, compared to other couples.

Medicare also required a certified home health aide, not just a personal-care attendant. Our luck did not abandon us. We found the ideal guy. An Occupy activist, Gabriel, had recently earned his certification.

Danny officially went off of Medicaid—I wanted to be sure I wouldn't be held accountable for any money he supposedly owed the state—and, on a sweltering Friday afternoon, July 26, the ADA anniversary, we went to the County Clerk's Office, Gabriel pushing Danny's wheelchair. A couple of weeks before—on July 8— we had celebrated twenty years of living together and loving each other. We said our "I do's" in front of a rushed officiant. Two close friends acting as witnesses and two former attendants we'd grown especially fond of comprised the whole wedding party. Access-A-Ride, which several times had taken me to jail, took us there and then back home. The return-trip vehicle—a total surprise!—displayed a banner that read JUST MARRIED.

Together with our marriage vows, we vowed to fight harder than ever to end the injustice of enforced poverty, and of work and marriage penalties. We had always had trouble getting members of our disability community mobilized around this issue. Busy fighting against cuts to vital services and afraid to lose allowances such as special needs trusts, most do not dare rock the boat. We worked with senior citizens, whose ranks we had joined. We joined single payer advocacy groups, demanding the inclusion of long-term care in existing and future bills. Our advocacy has, at the time of this writing, paid off. The proposed New York Health Act, our state single payer bill, now fully includes long-term care. All we need is for the bill to pass.

The fourth time I got arrested at an Occupy Wall Street-related demonstration, my "new" husband got arrested with me. I could tell he was itching for action; he had not been arrested in many years, and I felt it was safe enough. We were at the Flood Wall Street Action, on September 22, 2014, the day after the People's Climate March. Bloomberg was out and de Blasio in, and NYPD had adopted a kinder MO, at least for the moment. New Yorkers had experienced firsthand—with Hurricane Sandy—the evidence of climate change. We had learned about the great difficulty of evacuating significantly disabled people, as well as the dangers of long power outages for those relying on machines like ventilators. A dear old friend who had come from California and a new young one, both wheelchair users, got arrested with us. "We'd be the first to perish because of climate change," we told those members of the media who were around to listen while we were processed on-site— no need for Access-A-Ride.

Gabriel stayed at Danny's side, adjusting the ventilator hose, giving him water, and risking his own arrest. But the police listened when Danny asked that his home health aide not be arrested.

The Disability Caucus, we decided, would now have the purpose of presenting the disability perspective when working within different movements—single payer, climate justice, Black Lives Matter, Me Too...

And then... the results of the 2016 presidential election left us dismayed and appalled. Together with the majority—yes, the majority!—of Americans. Immediately, Danny and I did what good old activists do: We took to the streets. We will not allow our hard-earned rights—or anyone else's rights—to be stripped away. We will quickly put an end to the political nightmare. But the nightmare continued.

At times, the air feels poisoned by intolerance and hatred. We find comfort in the reawakened passion that has resulted in a stronger than ever and a more united than ever progressive movement. But the past few years have taken their toll on us, and our advancing disabilities have slowed us down. Danny has lost what little function he had left, and is now having trouble swallowing. The term *home-bound* has become more fitting, less humorous.

In 2017, throughout what became known as "the summer of ADAPT," we could only watch on national media as our comrades time and again were dragged by Capitol police out of congressional buildings and arrested. We could only cheer from our bedroom, as we realized it was mainly thanks to ADAPT that, at least for the time being, everyone's current health care was saved.

More and more, now, Danny and I find we need so much energy just to get through the day. We have little left for organizing and protesting—and even less for getting arrested! But our old hippie hearts— proud of all that our generation of disability rights activists has accomplished—persist in the hope of a better world and the promise of the next generation.

Danny and I in Zuccotti Park, September, 2011.

Wedding Day, July 26, 2013.

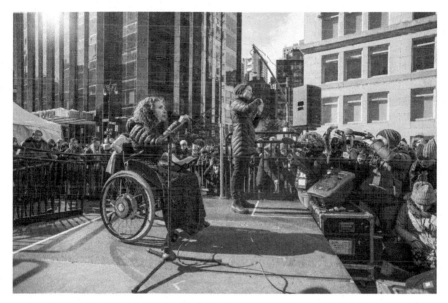

Speaking at Women's March rally, NYC, January, 2018.
(Photo and permission by Steve Ferdman.)

ACKNOWLEDGMENTS

❖

I thank Lynne Elizabeth, the publisher of my dreams. I am so grateful not only for her expertise and her insight, but for her kindness and for her understanding. I also thank the publishing team at New Village Press, especially Ignacio Choi, as well as the marketing and distribution team at NYU Press.

I would have given up on this book were it not for my dearest friend and mentor, Alix Kates Shulman. I thank her for her unwavering confidence in the book's merits, the perseverance of her efforts to see it published, and the heart-sustaining talks over tea at the Rubin Museum.

My thanks also go to Frances Goldin, activist and literary agent extraordinaire, who made me so happy by telling me I was a great writer, and to her agency for trying hard to sell this book.

I'm lucky to have had the help of the following teachers and editors at various stages of writing: Bea Gates who encouraged me by telling me I had a unique narrative voice; the incredibly skillful and justifiably celebrated Alan Rinzler, whose criticism was always mitigated by his humor ("There are more characters in your book than in *War and Peace*"); and, finally, the detail-loving Cecelia Cancellaro.

Author, publisher, and friend Robert Roth was an early reader. I thank him for his initial praise, which gave me the self-confidence I desperately needed at that point, and for his continued interest.

Fusun Ateser, a dear disabled sister who has sadly passed on and is greatly missed, read the first version of this memoir and provided valuable feedback and much loving support. Leslie Heller read the latest version. I don't know how I can adequately thank Leslie. She has repaid me for being her mentor and guide into the disability movement, not only by letting me share in the joy of watching her daughter, Zoe, grow into a beautiful young woman, but by becoming my reader, my editor, my consultant, my sounding board, my greatest supporter.

I thank all my disabled sisters, from the older ones who mentored me and embraced me, to the young ones who allowed me to mentor and to mother them. Of all disabled sisters, I must single out Harilyn Rousso for always being there for me, and for her valued advice—on writing and on all aspects of life—often lovingly-given over an afternoon glass of wine. I do wish I could thank you all by name, my sisters, and all my comrades in the disability movement and in other social justice movements, but the list would be much too long.

Finally, my infinite gratitude and endless love to Danny, my husband, my partner of 27 years, the great love of my life, who patiently listened while I read every word of this book, over and over again, and who tried, but just couldn't hang in there long enough to see it in print—he took the last breath from his ventilator on March 13, 2019. Even as my heart is breaking, I still consider myself the luckiest woman in the world.